Up Close & Personal

Zondervan/Youth Specialties Books

Adventure Games
Amazing Tension Getters
ArtSource™ Volume 1—Fantastic Activities
ArtSource™ Volume 2—Borders, Symbols, Holidays, and Attention Getters
ArtSource™ Volume 3—Sports
ArtSource™ Volume 4—Phrases and Verses
Attention Grabbers for 4th–6th Graders (Get 'Em Growing)
Called to Care
The Complete Student Missions Handbook
Creative Socials and Special Events
Divorce Recovery for Teenagers
Feeding Your Forgotten Soul (Spiritual Growth for Youth Workers)
Get 'Em Talking
Good Clean Fun
Good Clean Fun, Volume 2
Great Games for City Kids
Great Games for 4th–6th Graders (Get 'Em Growing)
Great Ideas for Small Youth Groups
Greatest Skits on Earth
Greatest Skits on Earth, Volume 2
Growing Up in America
High School Ministry
High School TalkSheets
Holiday Ideas for Youth Groups (Revised Edition)
Hot Talks
How to Survive Middle School (Get 'Em Growing)
Ideas for Social Action
Incredible Stories (Get 'Em Growing)
Intensive Care: Helping Teenagers in Crisis
Junior High Game Nights
Junior High Ministry
Junior High TalkSheets
The Ministry of Nurture
More Attention Grabbers for 4th–6th Graders (Get 'Em Growing)
More Great Games for 4th–6th Graders (Get 'Em Growing)
More Quick and Easy Activities for 4th–6th Graders (Get 'Em Growing)
On-Site: 40 On-Location Programs for Youth Groups
Option Plays
Organizing Your Youth Ministry
Play It! Great Games for Groups
Quick and Easy Activities for 4th–6th Graders (Get 'Em Growing)
Super Sketches for Youth Ministry
Teaching the Bible Creatively
Teaching the Truth about Sex
Tension Getters
Tension Getters Two
Unsung Heroes: How to Recruit and Train Volunteer Youth Workers
Up Close and Personal: How to Build Community in Your Youth Group
Youth Ministry Nuts and Bolts
The Youth Specialties Handbook for Great Camps & Retreats
Youth Specialties Clip Art Book
Youth Specialties Clip Art Book, Volume 2

Up Close & Personal

How to build community in your youth group

Includes a 13-Week TalkSheet Curriculum

Wayne Rice

Up Close and Personal

Copyright © 1989 by Youth Specialties, Inc.

Youth Specialties Books, 1224 Greenfield Drive, El Cajon, California 92021, are published by Zondervan Publishing House, Grand Rapids, Michigan 49530

Library of Congress Cataloging in Publication Data

Rice, Wayne.
    Up close and personal: how to build community in your youth group / by
      Wayne Rice.
    1. Church work with teenagers—Problems, exercises, etc. 2. Teenagers—
Religious life—Problems, exercises, etc. I. Title.
BV4447.R445   1989   89-16416
259'.23—dc20   CIP
ISBN 0-310-52491-1

Edited by J. Cheri McLaughlin
Designed by Jack Rogers
Illustrated by Dan Pegoda

Printed in the United States of America

96 97 98 99 / CH / 10 9 8 7 6

Acknowledgements

Many of the ideas in Section Two appeared originally in the Ideas library, published by Youth Specialties, and are reprinted here with permission. I want to thank the many creative youth workers who developed these ideas, used them with their youth groups, and shared them with us. Among them —

Bill Abell, John Adams, Dave Aldridge, Corey Amaro, Phillip Beaudoin, Robert Bell, Cecilia Bevan, John Boller, Tom Bougher, Jim Bourne, James Braddy, Brad Braley, Doug Bretschneider, Bruce Burkholder, Mark Christian, Keith Clark, Dan Craig, Dick Davis, Glenn Davis, Karen Dockrey, Marty Edwards, Glenn Embree, J. Allen Eubanks, Hal Evans, Greg Fiebig, Denny Finnegan, Eric Finsand, Mary Kay Fitzpatrick, Greg Foley, James Gilbert, Jr., Bobby Guffey, Carter Hiestand, Don Highlander, Brad Hirsch, Milton Hom, Linda Hudson, Anne Hughes, Tom Jackson, Shane Jent, Joy Jones, Marti Lambert, Ed Laremore, Philip Lopez, Paul Mason, Dennis McDonnough, Donna McElrath, Michael McKay, Scott McLain, Mark Melhorn, Al Michael, Bill Moore, Jim Munson, Craig Naylor, Phil Nelson, Doug Newhouse, Scott Oas, Robin Petura, Timothy Quill, Sr. Audrey Quinn, Rod Rummel, Suzanne Rushworth, Laura Russell, Gary Salyer, Syd Schnaars, Mark Skorheim, James Taylor, Julia Thompson, Nick Tomeo, Paul Tonna, Randy Trotter, Jim Walton, David Washburn, Steve Waters, Peter Wilkinson, Bill Williamson, Andrew Winters, Lew Worthington, David C. Wright, and Bobbie Yagel.

Thanks also to Rod McKean and Dave Sheffel for their contributions to the material in Section Three of this book.

Wayne Rice

Contents

Section One

Community Building as Youth Ministry

> How good and pleasant it is
> when brothers [and sisters] live
> together in unity!
>
> Psalm 133:1

The youth group at Old First Church:
• Donnie, Shane, and Steve are ninth graders who are close friends, but not with Jeremy, so they tease him about being short.
• Janine and Amber are upset because several other girls in the group have been spreading rumors about them.
• Alicia has stopped coming because some of the boys call her "Tubbs."
• None of the kids from Roosevelt High will sit next to anyone from Central.
• Everyone ignores the three kids from Montgomery Junior High School who are always showing off.
• Brent and Suzanne think they are in love, so they constantly sneak off by themselves.
• Jason started dating Kim, which means that he and his former girlfriend, Chris, aren't talking to each other.
• There's also a problem between some of the kids who were at last month's lock-in because nobody's really sure who broke the window.
• Of course, nobody in the youth group likes the four kids who go to Christian High because they act like they know everything.
• Jessica is the new girl who has been coming to the youth group now for three weeks but still hasn't made any friends.
• The Thompsons are leaving the church because Tammy, their 15-year-old, "just isn't enjoying the youth group any more."
• Steve, the youth pastor at Old First, is seriously thinking about going into some other line of work.

Does any of this sound familiar to you? If you are involved with a normal group of teenagers, chances are it does. It's not unusual to find this kind of disharmony in a typical group of adolescents.

Notice that I used words like *normal* and *typical*. Don't be alarmed if your youth group experiences problems like those at Old First Church. All adolescents are at a special time of identity formation in their lives when relationships become very important. But they are not experienced or sophisticated in the fine art of developing relationships. They believe, for example, that the way for two or three to become good friends is for them to *not* be friends with everyone else—a problem of cliques. Or many adolescents believe that the best way to make themselves look good is to make others look bad—a problem of put-downs and negative language.

Other dynamics are at work as well. Whenever you bring a group of people together—whether they are young or old—there is likely to be tremendous diversity. People have different interests, different likes and dislikes, different abilities, different reasons for being there. While adolescents are alike in many ways (they share many things in common because of their age), they are different from each other as well. Each adolescent has his own unique set of problems and needs, her own wants and desires. For this reason, adolescents won't be naturally inclined to get along with each other or to "live together in unity."

But that's the beauty of the church. The people of God come together in spite of their diversity and become the forever family of God. We become one in Christ. And our unity comes not because we are all alike or because everyone is instantly compatible, but because of what God has done and is doing in our community of faith.

But unity and oneness also have a practical, visible side, and that's what this book is about. **Up Close and Personal** helps you build upon the unity that is already present because of the work of the Holy Spirit so that you may overcome the division that diversity can create in the group. The objective of this book is to give you practical ideas and tools to enable individuals to live together in unity.

Although community building is not an easy task, it is perhaps the most important task in youth ministry. Why? One reason is that youth ministry by nature is relational—which is another way of saying that young people need to feel accepted, liked, affirmed, involved, and included. Forming relationships, in other words, is more important than programs. You can have the most gifted leaders and the best programs, activities, and resources, yet fail in youth ministry because the relational needs of the kids aren't met.

When we think of relational youth ministry, we usually think of adults relating to youth. But it is also *youth* relating to youth. We give much attention to the former but ignore the latter. This book is designed to teach youth workers how to encourage positive relationships among all the members of the youth group, youth and adults alike. This is a book about building community.

Community Building Defined

The church uses the term *community building* to describe a variety of ideas. For some community building is synonymous with playing games or participating in mixers. For others it conjures up images of small group discussions and weekend retreats. Some picture gathering around the refresh-ment table for light conversation, while others think of it strictly in theological terms.

A dictionary defines *community* as "a social group of any size whose members reside in a specific locality, share government, and have a common cultural and historical heritage." A community is a neighborhood, in other words. But that's not what we mean by *community* in this book. We are not interested in building neighborhoods.

Still, *community* is a good word. It contains or suggests other words that help us to understand the ingredients of oneness in Christ. One of the most obvious is the word *unity*, another word for *oneness*. A community is a group of people who are one with each other. Another word is *commune*—"to talk or dialogue intimately"—from which comes the word *communication*. *Community* also suggests the word *communion*, which not only describes the sacrament of the Lord's Supper, but also means "the act of sharing or having something in common."

In the Christian community, what we have in common is faith in Jesus Christ. Christians are one in Christ. It is not membership in a particular church or adherence to a set of beliefs and doctrines that make us one in Christ, however. Lots of groups share common belief systems. The Flat Earth Society, for example, believes that the earth is flat. The members of this group are one in their belief. What makes the Christian community one in Christ is not common beliefs, but God's power. When a person becomes a Christian, he or she mystically becomes one with other Christians by the power of the Holy Spirit (2 Corinthians 13:14).

But it is not enough for Christians to sing "We are one in the Spirit, we are one in the Lord." Christian community must go beyond the mystical or spiritual reality to be a practical, functional reality. It must be lived out and put into practice among Christians who come together in groups.

In youth ministry community building takes on a special meaning and importance.

Perhaps the best way to describe community building in youth ministry is to describe it in terms of friendship. A youth group that builds community is a youth group whose members develop significant and lasting friendships. Group members grow to like each other and enjoy spending time together. The group is inclusive—each person feels accepted as a part of the group regardless of background, status, economic situation, physical appearance, school, or ability. Cliques and cruel put-downs are out of place. A youth group that encourages and demonstrates community welcomes new friends and strengthens old friendships. It's a group that grows together spiritually and celebrates together the joy of knowing and serving Jesus Christ. But does such a group exist? *Can* such a group exist?

Although perfect community may never be attainable, any youth group can become *more* of a community than it is now—more one, more accepting, more loving, more Christlike. The purpose of **Up Close and Personal** is to give you proven strategies for building community and developing positive relationships among teenagers in a youth group setting.

The Biblical Mandate for Community Building

Community building is important because the Bible teaches that it is important. The Scriptures encourage God's people, the community of faith, to love each other, to care for each other, and to live together in harmony and peace.

In John 17 Jesus prays for the future church. In his prayer Jesus expresses his deepest desire for "all those who will believe in me." What does he pray for? He could have prayed that the church would grow in numbers. He could have prayed that the church would be politically powerful. He could have prayed that the church be spared persecution. Instead he prayed

> that all of them may be one, Father, just as you are in me and I am in you. May they also be in us so that the world

may believe that you have sent me . . . May they be brought to complete unity to let the world know that you sent me and have loved them even as you have loved me. (John 17:21,23)

Clearly Jesus cared deeply about Christian community. When we work to build unity and oneness in the church, we help to achieve Christ's desire for his people.

Many Christians would say that evangelism is the church's number one priority. After all, Jesus gave us a direct mandate for evangelism and missionary work in the Great Commission (Matthew 28:19). It is indisputable that Jesus wants the church to take the Good News to all nations and to share the gospel with everyone. This is the mission of the church. But perhaps we have overlooked the even greater priority for the church that Jesus himself prayed for—unity.

Unity and evangelism, however, are not unrelated. Perhaps John 17 describes our best *strategy* for evangelism. After all, Jesus indicates in this prayer that unity attracts others to the gospel and convinces them of its truth (verse 23). The early church successfully practiced this strategy according to Acts 2:44-47: "All the believers were together and had everything in common [community] . . . And the Lord added to their number daily those who were being saved [evangelism]."

I have seen this strategy work in youth ministry. For seven years I was youth director at a small California church that gave high priority to community building. As a result, the youth group grew from a small group of six to a not-so-small group of 35—simply because young people who visited us wanted to be a part of our caring community of friendship and faith. The Bible gives a high priority to community building for many reasons, but certainly an important one is that true Christian community witnesses to the radically transforming nature of the gospel.

I once knew a teenage girl named Dolores. A sophomore in high school, she was short, overweight, and wore clothes that weren't in style. For these reasons she had few friends. She endured life at school as a loner. Dolores also attended a church youth group for a short time but decided that it just wasn't for her. Why? The youth group rejected her for the same reasons she was rejected at school. For her there was no difference between the school environment and the church environment.

The church must be a place that's radically different from the world. If a youth group cannot offer young people like Dolores an alternative to what they find in the world, there's no reason for its existence. Dolores should look forward to attending the youth group at church each week because it's the one place in the world where physical appearance doesn't matter. It is the place where she is accepted, loved, included, and made to feel an important part of the group. That is what Christian community is about, and that is what Jesus prayed for in John 17. He wanted then—and he wants today—that his people demonstrate a supernatural love and unity to the world.

Many other Scriptures mandate community building in the church. Among them are the following verses.
• "Make every effort to keep the unity of the Spirit through the bond of peace." (Ephesians 4:3)
• "I appeal to you, brothers, in the name of our Lord Jesus Christ, that all of you agree with one another so that there may be no divisions among you and that you may be perfectly united in mind and thought." (1 Corinthians 1:10)
• "Finally, all of you, live in harmony with one another; be sympathetic, love as brothers, be compassionate and humble." (1 Peter 3:8)
Community building is important because God's Word considers it to be important.

The Cultural Mandate
for Community Building

"Community is currently rare," states psychiatrist M. Scott Peck in his book *A Different Drum* (Simon & Schuster, 1987). Modern life has robbed people of the ability or desire to live in community with others. There was once a time in history (I am told) when people did live together in close-knit communities, knew who their neighbors were, and experienced some form of community. But in today's world the kind of natural community that our ancestors enjoyed is rare indeed. As Robert Bellah has written in *Habits of the Heart* (University of California Press, 1986), "Isolation and fragmentation have become the order of the day."

In today's individualistic world, the average person feels alone and lonely, even in the midst of the crowd. Peck writes,

Our hometowns may well be geographical collections of human beings with tax and political structures in common, but precious little else relates them to each other. Towns are not, in any meaningful sense of the word, communities. And sight unseen, on the basis of my experience with Christian churches in this country, I can be fairly confident that each of the churches in your hometown is not likely to be much of a community either.

It is unfortunate that churches more often reflect or mimic changes in society than offer viable alternatives to them. But as Dr. Peck has rightly pointed out, community is rare even in our churches. People talk a great deal about the loss of community in modern society, but few know how to recapture it or to experience it in any meaningful sense.

Cheers, a popular television series, features a theme song with these words:

Sometimes you want to go where
    everybody knows your name.
And they're always glad you came.
You want to be where you can see
    troubles are all the same;
You want to go where everybody
    knows your name.

These lyrics could describe a church, but instead describe the local pub, a bar. The tragedy is that bars often do a better job of making people feel wanted and accepted than do many churches. People need to be part of a group where "everybody knows your name."

The Christian church is in a strategic position to offer the world that kind of place, where true community can become a reality.

Community building in youth ministry is especially important at the end of the 20th century because today's young people are unlikely to find community anywhere else. Traditional family structures, where community was almost always found, are gone. A 1940 census reports that more than 70 percent of all American households included grandparents living in the home. By 1980 that figure had dropped to 2 percent. Psychologist Stephen Glenn says that ours is the first civilization in history to reverse its lifestyle in a single generation. In the past children came home to living rooms filled with dialogue and interaction with parents. Now they come home to empty houses and family rooms filled with TV sets.

This Lonely Generation of modern teenagers is forced to fill the emptiness of their hearts with videos, movies, music, drugs, alcohol, and—sometimes, when these fail—suicide. David Breskin, in a *Rolling Stone* article about teenage suicide, pictures the typical suicidal adolescent:

> There's no extended family around for him, not with the geographic mobility for which Americans are famous. The moving is hard on him. He must keep readapting to new environments. One teen suicide in Houston treed himself and left a note: "This is the only thing around here that has any roots." (*Rolling Stone*, November 8, 1984)

Youth workers who want to meet the psychological, emotional, and spiritual needs of today's lonely and abused adolescents are well advised to design a strong program encouraging Christian community. Especially teenagers want a place where everybody knows their name.

I am reminded of a now-famous story once told by the former president of Young Life International, Bob Mitchell. At a local high school, he started a Young Life club that attracted a large number of teenagers to every meeting. Along with the fun and singing, Mitch shared the gospel at every meeting. One evening, a teenage boy who had come faithfully for several weeks approached Mitch and announced, "I just wanted you to know that this week I decided to give my life to Christ." Mitch was overjoyed and asked the boy, "What brought about your decision? What led to it?" The boy responded, "It was when you remembered my name."

The Developmental Mandate for Community Building

Community building is especially important for youth ministry because it is "developmentally appropriate," as educators and researchers like to say. In other words, adolescents have reached a point in their development as human beings when they have a special need for the kinds of relationships that community building provides.

When children reach adolescence, they begin what psychologist Erik Erikson calls a "search for identity." The most important questions during early adolescence are questions like "Who am I?" and "Am I okay?" and "Do you like me?" Young people leaving their childhood behind seek out others who will validate them and give them positive feedback about themselves. The questions they are asking can only be answered in community with others. Having friends is the very lifeblood of adolescence.

I have asked students if they liked going to school. Not surprisingly, many say yes. When I ask them why they like school, most tell me it's because they get to be with their friends. Rarely do junior-high and high-school students say they like school because of the education they are receiving. And students who say they do not like school either have no friends at school, or they have enemies there.

This should tell us something about how we need to approach youth ministry in the church. If we want our youth groups to be places where kids enjoy coming, then we need to make them places where kids have good friends and no enemies. That is what community building is all about.

David Stone tells the story of a dog-food company that called a meeting of all its employees. At the meeting, the president of the company shouted out a series of questions to the employees: "Which dog-food company makes the most nutritious dog-food in the world?" With one voice the employees shouted back the name of their company. "And which dog-food company has the best marketing program in the world?" Again the employees responded with the name of their company. "And which dog-food company has the best employee incentive program in the world?" Again the employees proudly identified their company. After several questions like this, the president asked, "Why, then, aren't we *selling* more of our dog-food than any other dog-food company in the world?" The room grew silent. Finally one man stood up and said, "It's because the dogs don't like it."

Sometimes the church is a lot like that dog-food company. Most churches have excellent resources, great programs, and the Good News of the gospel to proclaim, but young people are staying away by the millions because they simply don't like it. Their felt needs are not being met. They need a place where they will feel accepted and validated and where they will find true friendship.

Community Building: How It's Done

A certain man wanted to learn how to figure skate, so he went to an ice-skating rink and signed up for lessons. The instructor began by showing the man intricate diagrams and charts and explaining to him the terminology used in figure skating. "Before you take the ice," said the instructor, "you've got to learn the basics." The man became frustrated by all this and found the instructions and the language to be extremely complicated and confusing. "I'll never get this," he muttered to himself.

Leaving the rink, he noticed a brassy young teenage boy be-bopping all over the ice, performing effortlessly all the steps that the man wanted so badly to learn. Intrigued, he asked the boy how he did it. "Easy," said the boy. "You just get out on the ice, skate real fast, and move your feet around a lot. That's all there is to it."

Somewhere between studying the charts and getting out on the ice lies the best method for teaching things like figure skating and community building. Though there are some basics to learn, in actuality the best way to do it is to just do it. Community building cannot be learned from formulas, charts, and diagrams. No program or curriculum guarantees community as a result. Community building is a commitment over time that people make to each other to move toward relational wholeness. To make community building happen, you simply have to keep a few basics in mind, then take to the ice and move your feet around a lot.

Prerequisites for Community Building

Several presuppositions about community building are important to understand before considering any methods or strategies.

• *Community building must be intentional.* In other words, community doesn't happen automatically. Christians tend to view community as a theological reality, a job for the Holy Spirit, so they are not compelled to help it along by design and hard work. That's why community is rare for the Christian church. But a theological concept must make a difference in how we live, or it might as well not exist at all. Building Christian community must be intentional—we must *do* it.

Community building resembles marriage. In order for a couple to enjoy a happy marriage, they must work at it. A neglected marriage atrophies and dies. Good marriages happen by design; they are not the result of luck or mysterious forces. Couples who want to stay married must *do* the things that keep marriages strong. So it is with Christian community—community building must be intentional.

• *Community building requires commitment over time.* There are two important truths here: commitment and time. Commitment is closely related to intention. In order for community to happen, there must be a commitment to making it happen. At first only the adult leaders may be wholeheartedly committed to community building. But as kids experience community, they may begin to understand the significance of what is happening and why it is happening and to share in the commitment to making it happen.

The second truth—that community building requires time—means community doesn't happen overnight. Although this book includes a 13-week course in community building, Christian community cannot be built in 13 weeks or even 13 months. My experience has been that it takes three to four years before a youth group begins to reflect true Christian community. That doesn't mean that good things don't happen along the way, but in order for authentic Christian community to become a reality, the relationships must survive the test of time. A youth group that is characterized by a genuine sense of community is one that has been at it for an extended time. Further, it is a group that has failed at community more times than it has succeeded.

Bottom line: don't expect instant success. Teenagers will disappoint you and each other often. It will seem like your best efforts have been in vain much of the time. But don't give up. Community building takes commitment over the long haul. Positive changes in the group will be so gradual as to go unnoticed at first, but they *will* happen.

• *Community building is limited by size.* If your youth group is larger than 15 people, you will probably need to divide it into smaller units to enhance community building. A group of 25, for instance, can be divided into two smaller groups. A group of 100 may need seven, eight, or even more groups. These groups can be divided according to age, grade in school, geographical location, or by some random method. Although the large group can come together for many activities and programs, it is the smaller groups that nurture true community. And when community building is taking place in the small groups, the large group is affected. There will be a warm and friendly spirit in the large group, even though many of the young people don't know each other well. Community always moves from the small group to the large.

And there is a biblical model. Jesus had a ministry to multitudes of people at various times, but he surrounded himself with a select few who made up his community. These were the people who stuck with him even through the difficult times, and eventually took the gospel to the world.

We need to be at least as reasonable—when it comes to numbers—as Jesus was. Too many overly ambitious youth workers believe that they can disciple or build close relationships with groups 10 times larger than the group Jesus led. This doesn't mean that our groups can't grow or that they must become exclusive. On the contrary, growth is a natural result of community building, and exclusivity is to be avoided at all costs. What it does mean is that we need to recognize our limitations and plan accordingly.

• *Community building must respect individual needs.* By its very nature, community building involves groups of people. Yet today much emphasis—maybe *too* much emphasis—is given to what happens in groups. For groups are composed of individuals who have individual needs, personalities, backgrounds, and agendas, and these things must be considered and respected.

A good starting place for community building in a youth group is to discover the individual needs of the group members, one at a time. You will discover that some kids are quite confident in group situations while others fear them; some make friends easily, but others are relationally handicapped; some of your youths may have a maturing relationship with Christ while others have little or no faith. All of these young people will make up your community, and they will impact the unique flavor of that community.

Never force community building on anyone. Go slow if your group requires it. On the other hand, if your group is *ready* for a deeper level of Christian community, you may be able to move deliberately, even swiftly, toward it. The important point here is to *know your kids*. Make sure you respond appropriately to their needs as individuals as well as their group needs.

• *Community building requires an environment which invites community.* Certainly one reason that most churches have a difficult time developing a sense of community is that they most often meet in rooms that don't lend themselves to community building. It's not easy for a person to feel part of a community while sitting in a pew staring at the back of someone's head. Understandably, most church buildings are designed for worship, preaching, and other programs presented concert-hall fashion. They were never intended for community building. Even the room designated "fellowship hall" in many churches is a cold and lifeless room with a tile floor, a few folding chairs, institutional tables, and a kitchen. Not a particularly inviting place.

If you want to encourage community building, then you must create an atmosphere where everyone feels comfortable and accepted almost from the moment they arrive. When you enter a meeting room, how does it feel? Does it feel like a warm and friendly place? Or does it feel cold and sterile? What is being communicated by the way the room is set up—that lectures are presented here? That dialogue and interaction take place here? That large impersonal groups gather here for meetings? That small groups of friends gather here for fellowship? Interaction seems out of place in a room with rows of chairs and a lectern up front. But if the chairs are positioned in a circle, without a lectern or stage area, then discussion is more likely to happen. Things like room size, seating arrangement, room temperature—even the color of paint on the walls—are not neutral. They make a difference.

This is one reason I enjoy meeting with youth groups in homes. Homes almost automatically communicate warmth and friendliness. Teenagers feel more comfortable when they can flop down on a sofa, sit on the floor, sprawl in a chair.

It's possible, of course, to design a warm and friendly meeting space at the church. One youth group converted an old shack behind their church into a meeting place and called their meetings "Pack the Shack." They carpeted the room with a patchwork of brightly colored carpet samples, scattered pillow-cushions on the floor for seating, covered the walls with attractive posters, and installed a stereo system. The youth group considered this room to be their place, thus creating an atmosphere of acceptance that enhanced community building.

• *Community building includes everyone.* Does the organization of your youth group result in a pecking order that makes some people appear more important to the group than others? There is nothing wrong with having officers or youth-group leaders who have specific responsibilities. In order for community to happen, however, every group member needs to feel valued for some significant contribution to the life of the group. Avoid a hierarchical structure that gives all the leadership or responsibility to a privileged few. Everyone needs to be included.

• *Community building is Christ-centered.* Christian community exists only because of Christ. Christian theologian and martyr Dietrich Bonhoeffer put it this way:

> Christianity means community through Jesus Christ and in Jesus Christ. No Christian community is more or less than this. Whether it be a brief, single encounter or the daily fellowship of years, Christian community is only this. We belong to one another only through and in Jesus Christ.
> What does this mean? It means, first, that a Christian needs others because of Jesus Christ. It means, second, that a Christian comes to others only through Jesus Christ. It means, third, that in Jesus Christ we have been chosen from eternity, accepted in time, and united for eternity. (*Life Together*, Harper & Row, 1954)

This is what makes Christian community different from other communities. Christian community is a gift from God. It is not something that we create, for it is created by God. Although this book contains many practical programs and strategies beneficial for community building, true Christian community cannot be programmed. "Christian brotherhood," says Bonhoeffer, "is not an ideal which we must realize; it is rather a reality created by God in Christ in which we may participate."

The more genuine Christian community becomes, the more Christ-centered it becomes. The purpose of Christian community is to glorify and honor Christ. The true test of Christian community is how devoted it is to obeying Jesus Christ.

Qualities of a Healthy Community

What does a healthy community look like? Is it a group in which no one ever gets angry? Where there are no cliques? Is it a group that meets together more than once a week? A group that has no leaders?

Below are eight qualities that define a healthy community and allow you to rate your own community. Score your group from 1 to 5 on each of the eight qualities. (The higher the rating, the healthier the community *and* the individuals participating in it.) If your group is doing great, give yourselves a 5; if you're not doing so great, give yourselves a 2 or a 3.

1. *Interaction.* At its heart, interaction is communication or dialogue. A healthy group creates opportunities to talk with and listen to each other. Many churches are not healthy communities because their congregations come to services only as audiences. In meetings that encourage little personal interaction with the leaders or other participants, it's possible for new people to attend unnoticed for weeks. The members never get to know their names or to find out who they are on any kind of level—all because they never have the opportunity to interact as a group. A healthy community stimulates discussion, dialogue, and a sharing of ideas.

Marriage Encounter—a weekend retreat for couples that uses dialogue and open communication to strengthen marriages—doesn't lecture on how to have a happy marriage. Instead the leaders facilitate dialogue between the husbands and wives who come. Each couple spends the entire weekend sharing their thoughts and feelings with each other in healthy dialogue. Couples who attend these retreats report that the experience caused them to fall in love with their mates all over again. The intense interaction brought them closer together.

Community building also requires significant communication. Every time you get together, ask questions of each other, exchange views, weigh decisions together, air feelings. This frankness invigorates community by drawing the group members closer together.

2. *Intensity*. Intensity measures the depth of a group's interaction. A healthy community frees people to get beyond small talk and to share deeply with each other, without fear of ridicule or shame. It does not mean that everyone must bare their souls, but rather that people are honest and open with each other and that masks are unnecessary. People let their hair down a little bit, revealing their faults and shortcomings as well as their strengths and talents.

It's always exciting to watch a youth group on a mission trip or work camp. They get dirty, yet have no access to showers, hair-dryers, or even mirrors. They cluster around the campfire and talk late into the evening, sharing experiences rather than watching TV and goofing off. The young people soon find themselves becoming a close and caring community because the level of involvement with each other is intense. Unfortunately, many groups return to former patterns of individualism and mask-wearing when they get home, and the sense of community is lost.

3. *Affirmation*. In a healthy community every member feels included and appreciated by others in the group. Unfortunately, most groups have people on the fringes who rarely receive this kind of affirmation. They don't feel that they can contribute or that the group values them. These people may be new or different or shy or less talented and outgoing than the leaders. Still, they need to be accepted and made to feel part of the group. Community is inclusive, not exclusive or cliquish.

4. *Corporeality*. The word means *practical*, *material*, or *tangible*. What it means to community building is that community must be more than a concept or creed—it must translate into real life.

The New Testament church demonstrated corporeal community. Acts 2:44-46 says they went so far as to have "everything in common. Selling their possessions and goods, they gave to anyone as he had need. Every day they continued to meet together

in the temple courts. They broke bread in their homes and ate together with glad and sincere hearts." The church translated the ideal of community into a lifestyle.

A youth group that is growing into community may not have everything in common, but they will begin to care about each other, want to spend time with each other (apart from youth-group activities), and help each other out when they can. They may go places together, help each other with homework, pool their money for things they can share, and counsel each other in difficult situations. Corporeality means that community is working and making a difference—away from the meetings.

I am part of a small group which meets weekly for Bible study and prayer. We have developed close relationships with each other. But what makes our friendship and closeness genuine is that it goes beyond those weekly meetings. We get together at other times, as often as we can, for social activities and special occasions. We play together, take trips together, and work together. We borrow tools from each other, share meals with each other, and take care of each others' children. A corporeality of that kind enriches and adds substance to our sense of community.

5. *Reciprocity*. The responsibilities and benefits of community must be equally shared among all who participate in that community. Interaction, intensity, affirmation, and corporeality flow from one member to another and back again among all the members of a healthy community. Many groups are dominated by a few people who do all the giving, all the interacting, all the affirming, without getting much of anything in return. Though these people are well-intentioned and unselfish, they are opening themselves up to frustration and burn-out.

Rick was in a small group that I belonged to at one time, and right from the beginning he was surprisingly candid about things that were going on in his life. Week after week he would share intimate failures and struggles—almost to the point of embarrassing some of the group. No one else felt comfortable enough to share on such a personal level as Rick, so Rick dominated the sharing. But he eventually left the group. In an angry outburst at one meeting, he complained that he was tired of being the only one who was willing to open up and accused the other group members of not trusting him.

When some people do all the giving and others do all the receiving, community suffers. The Apostle Paul, in 1 Corinthians 12 teaches mutual sharing of responsibility so that everyone is ministering and being ministered to. Everyone has a spiritual gift. Everyone is an important part of the body of Christ. Everyone can have a ministry. The old saying "You scratch my back and I'll scratch yours" sounds crass, but in one sense describes how community works. We don't say, "I'll give to you if you give to me," but we do say, "I'll give to you *as* you give to me." This affirms each person's value to the community. Community is reciprocal.

6. *Commitment.* Just as a couple commit themselves to staying married to each other "till death do us part," and just as that commitment to marriage holds them together through conflict and changeable affection, so group members who want to build community must commit themselves to the *idea* of community, not depending on comfortable relationships to hold the group together.

Groups typically go through four stages when attempting to become a genuine community, says M. Scott Peck in *A Different Drum*. The first stage he calls *pseudocommunity*. In their enthusiasm for community, a group tries to be instantly vulnerable, to force community into existence, or even to fake it. But they can't keep it up. Stage two follows—*chaos*. Angry, disappointed, group members attack not only each other, but their leader as well. After chaos comes what Peck calls *emptiness*, a kind of group death. Weary from the fighting, group members lay aside their differences, their

prejudices, their need for control, their need to heal, convert, fix, and solve and die to themselves.

When a group is finally willing to experience that death, they open up the possibility of encountering *genuine community*—the final stage. In other words, things get worse before they get better. But the result of sticking together through the chaos is a healthy and enduring community. Commitment means being willing to tough it out through stage two for the sake of the community.

The curriculum in Section Three of this book can help build community because it provides young people a biblical basis for understanding why community is important. Youths who grasp the meaning of community are more likely to remain committed to it, even when things are not going smoothly.

7. *Continuity.* There is no substitute for time in the community-building process. Community happens slowly and deliberately over a period of weeks, months, even years. A healthy community has established *continuity* over an extended period of time.

How much time is required? The answer to that question varies from group to group, of course. If the group meets once or twice a week, however, and if the group and its leaders are committed to community building, the *process* will begin almost immediately. Each time the group gets together, they take another small step toward genuine community. A year or two later, when the group looks back at where they began, they'll see how far they've come.

8. *Openness.* A final characteristic of a healthy community is its openness to those who are not already part of the community. Community avoids the exclusivity of a clique or a private club. In fact, a healthy community goes beyond passive openness and reaches out to others, inviting them to be a part. As a result of the early church's faithfulness to open community, God "added to their number daily those who

were being saved" (Acts 2:47). The church grew rapidly because the community was alive and healthy and open to anyone who wanted to become a part of it.

A Strategy for Community Building

We now come to the more practical part of this section, the how-to's that can help you program more effectively for community building. Keep in mind that there really is no step-by-step process for building community in a youth group. While there is a logical order in which things should be done, there are no guarantees and no formulas that work for every youth group.

My strategy for community building is simple: *Program with community building in mind*. For example, leading a group discussion that gets everybody talking naturally enhances community. Lecturing before a passive group seated in rows, however, diminishes community. As obvious as this strategy appears, many youth workers who want community continually shoot themselves in the foot with their poor programming.

Several years ago, I served as volunteer youth director at the small church my family and I attended. From the outset I emphasized community building with those six kids. And they needed it. Some of our young people came from broken homes. Some of them were loners or rejects at school and had trouble making friends. Our church drew from a large geographic area, so the youth rarely saw each other, except at church. There was no sense of community when we started.

We usually met once a week in someone's home. At first not everyone came. Many times only two or three youths showed up, but at every meeting we intentionally did things that strengthened community. We talked, we played, we shared, we studied together, we did crazy stunts together, we ate together. Gradually more youths came. Some of the regulars even asked if they could bring their friends. I was shocked. I was used to begging kids to bring their friends. Now they brought them on their own. Over a period of several years, the group grew into a strong community of 35 Christian friends, many of whom remained friends long after they graduated from the youth group.

What kinds of programs and activities build community? Below are nine general categories listed in order from those things requiring less commitment to those requiring more. A group should walk before it runs, so it's a good idea to start with simple, non-threatening ice-breakers before moving to the deeper levels of sharing characteristic of a more mature community. But no formula for community building works for everyone. Let the needs and personalities of your kids shape your strategy.

Let's look at the nine categories of activities that can build community with a youth group.

1. *Discovering each other*. This is a general heading for activities that help young people to get acquainted with each other in a non-threatening way. Mixers, ice-breakers, and guessing games fit here—anything that encourages mingling with each other, laughing together, touching, and learning names. If your group includes newcomers or young people who don't know everyone else well, games like "Autograph Hunt," "Eye Chart," "Group Up," and "Human Bingo," break down barriers between kids. (See Section Two for game instructions.) Even if your group is well acquainted, kids can always discover something new about each other. I regularly begin a meeting with a few ice-breakers just to get us comfortable with each other.

2. *Playing together*. One of the best ways to build community is to play games together. I believe that every church that is serious about community building needs a good recreation program. Games bring people into contact with each other in a positive way. When you are playing a game, you are usually being yourself—the masks are off, the barriers are down, and you genuinely communicate with others. Cooperating

with teammates, laughing, touching—just having a great time—builds community. Too many of us have lost our sense of play. Friends and neighbors no longer play games together just for fun. Today the emphasis is on either fitness or spectator sports, seldom on fun. Even children (some still in diapers) join leagues to play tee-ball and soccer and are robbed of their sense of play by intense competition.

Playing games with your youth group builds community *if* you choose the right kinds of games. Intensely competitive games divide the group. Within your group are some youths who are very competitive and athletically skilled, and some youths who are not. Playing a game that requires a great deal of skill drives a wedge between the two groups. The jocks dominate the game and shun the less-skilled ones, who become resentful and uninterested. On the other hand, if you play games in which competition is minimal or secondary to enjoying the game, community thrives. Hundreds of great games do *not* require athletic skills but are still fun and exciting.

Competition, by the way, is not inherently wrong or evil. Competition as a motivator is good—it makes a game fun. Participants play hard and concentrate in order to win. There is nothing wrong with trying to accumulate points or out-perform another team, so long as *winning* is secondary to the enjoyment of *playing*. Winning should be almost anti-climactic.

(For hundreds of great games, read *Play It!* by Wayne Rice and Mike Yaconelli [Zondervan/Youth Specialties, 1986]. For some excellent non-competitive games, see *New Games* and *More New Games* by Andrew Fluegelman [Dolphin/Doubleday, 1981] and *Playfair* by Matt Weinstein and Joel Goodman [Impact Books, 1980.])

3. *Communicating with each other*. People in community need to share their feelings, thoughts, and ideas with each other in healthy dialogue and discussion. The best kind of communication is spontaneous conversation among group members during the week. But young people also need to interact in group settings. If you want community to develop in your youth group, then allow time *in every meeting* for kids to talk and listen to each other. Never plan meetings in which your students are passive spectators. Find ways to get them talking.

Large groups do not lend themselves to a discussion format. Not only is it impossible for everyone to take part, but the intimidation factor is hard to overcome. Not many kids want to talk in front of a large group of people. If your group is larger than 8 or 10 people, divide it into groups of four or five (separating friends if possible). Give each group a well-defined question to discuss among themselves. You might say, for instance, "I want everyone to answer this question: What is one thing you'd like to change about this youth group? You will have one minute to share your answer. Let's begin with the person in your group who had a birthday most recently, okay? Ready, begin!"

Section Three includes a number of excellent discussion starters and other strategies that encourage dialogue in the group. But the main strategy to remember is *get them talking*. If you are showing a movie, allow time for discussion afterward. Debrief everything. Draw your young people out. Listen to them and encourage them to express themselves to you and to others. Not only will this stimulate the growth of community in your group, but it will help your kids to become better overall communicators. Today's young people have trouble communicating because they are rarely given the opportunity to be open and honest without being ridiculed or put down. Studies show that the most successful professionals are the people who communicate well. If you teach good communication skills to your young people, you equip them for life.

4. *Affirming each other*. Mark Twain once said "I can live three months on one good compliment." Teenagers would say the

same thing, only they can't live quite as long on one compliment. Three days—or even three hours—is more like it. Everybody needs to be affirmed, to feel appreciated and valued. People are drawn to those who affirm them like moths to a lamp, and so it follows that the gift of affirmation is at the heart of community building.

Affirmation does not come naturally. Especially teenagers tend to look for the worst in each other to make themselves look good by comparison. Putting others down makes them feel superior. That's why most youth groups are flawed by cliques, put-downs, and fighting among group members. *Intentionally* creating times for those in the group to affirm one another gives kids needed practice in building each other up. Although affirming one another is not a natural behavior for most people, they discover that it's not so hard after all once they get used to saying nice things to each other. And they also enjoy receiving affirmation rather than derision from their peers. It feels good.

Section Two in this book includes numerous ideas for encouraging affirmation. Try "Compliment Contest" or "What Others Think of Me." Play a game like "Positive People Bingo." Your kids will appreciate opportunities to reverse the tide of negativism in their world. And you'll find that they will enjoy being together more and will depend upon each other more for the strokes they need. Affirmation builds community.

5. *Spending time together.* Quality time means nothing unless it is accompanied by an adequate quantity of time. People need to spend time together in order to become a community. There really is no substitute for it. A youth group that meets only once a week for an hour-long meeting probably won't experience community simply because there is not enough time for relationships to develop. A group consisting of youths who attend different schools and have different circles of friends the rest of the week will also struggle with community

building. Teenagers will spend their between-meetings time with the friends they can see most frequently.

Plan with your youth group ways to get everyone together during the week, even on a casual, unstructured basis. Experiment with a before-school breakfast, or organize an after-school recreation program. Some youth groups offer volunteer tutoring and study halls at church once or twice a week.

Social activities on the weekends encourage your group to be together. You can attend high-school football and basketball games together, and then do fifth quarter events or go out to eat after the game. Most teens today want to party on weekends, and this often leads to trouble. Your youth group can offer an alternative party—a well-organized and supervised gathering for watching TV, eating food, dancing and listening to music, or just hanging out. Or with some extra planning, the group can create special events like scavenger hunts, car rallies, and game nights. (For hundreds of ideas, pick up a copy of the book *Creative Socials and Special Events* by Wayne Rice and Mike Yaconelli [Youth Specialties/Zondervan, 1986].)

Camps and retreats provide an opportunity for kids to be together over an extended period of time. There is perhaps no better way to build community in a youth group than to take kids away from their normal environment for a week or weekend of living together, eating together, and traveling together. Lasting relationships grow during a week of camp.

A few years ago I took 16 teenagers from my youth group on a 10-day backpacking trip into the high Sierras near Yosemite National Park. We organized into four tent groups of four persons each who shared tents, cooking equipment, and other supplies. Each afternoon, after a day on the trails, these tent groups pitched their tents and cooked their evening meal together. I deliberately put kids into tent groups with kids other than their best friends.

I'll never forget two boys who were in the same tent group. Arnie was a star football player, a tall, good-looking, popular guy. Alvin was a non-athletic reject. The first day on the trails, Alvin wore blisters on his feet and struggled to carry his backpack. Arnie, mostly out of frustration with Alvin, volunteered to carry some of Alvin's gear the rest of the trip. Alvin was relieved and grateful, of course, and went out of his way to make it up to Arnie by doing most of the household chores. Over the course of the week, I watched those two boys become friends. And when they returned home from that trip, they remained friends—which I have always considered a miracle. When kids spend time together unexpected relationships develop. That backpacking trip completely changed the personality and character of my youth group. From that point on, they were a community.

I especially enjoy primitive camping with teenagers because of its community-building potential. By primitive camping I mean taking kids backpacking or pitching tents in a campground for a few days. Costs are lower for primitive camping since you can usually borrow the equipment and supplies you need. And you don't need to plan a huge program of games, seminars, meetings, or special speakers like you do with normal camps. All you really need is a Bible study in the morning and a time of singing and sharing around the campfire at night. A primitive camp like this can be done beside a lake or stream, at the beach, in the mountains or desert—the possibilities are endless.

Travel camps, ski retreats, trips to amusement parks, motel retreats, or "lock-in's" at the church also get kids together for longer than a meeting. Investigate church camps and non-denominational youth gatherings, which are wonderful experiences for your youth group as well. Community building, however, progresses best when you think small most of the time, planning events that only include the members of your youth group.

6. *Serving together.* A group that *gives* to others is a group that receives many bene-fits in return, not the least of which is a stronger, closer community.

I love the story about the man who was caught in an Alaskan blizzard. Hopelessly lost in the wilderness, he desperately struggled to find his way home through the wind and falling snow. Exhausted, cold, and hungry, he finally gave up, resigning himself to the fact that he was going to die. But as he lay down in the snow, he heard the faint whimpering of a puppy. He crawled through the snow until he found the small dog who was shivering and near death. Immediately he wrapped the dog in his coat and began rubbing the dog's fur, hoping to keep the dog's blood circulating. He continued rubbing the pup all through the night, trying to keep it warm and alive. Sadly, the little dog did not survive the night. But the man did. By giving of himself to save the life of the little puppy, he had saved his own life.

So it is with service. Jesus wasn't stretching the truth when he said that it is more blessed to give than to receive. A youth group that gives of itself to serve others receives a great blessing in return, and many times that blessing comes in the form of Christian community. Relationships are formed, healed, and deepened.

Humility is an important ingredient in community building. In Philippians 2:2-3 Paul writes, "Make my joy complete by being like-minded, having the same love, being one in spirit and purpose. Do nothing out of selfish ambition or vain conceit, but in humility consider others better than yourselves." When young people are serving others, they are experiencing and practicing humility. I am always amazed at what happens to kids when they are on a work camp. Giving up hot showers, nice clothes, cosmetics, hair-dryers, and all the other things they think they need to survive is a humbling experience—a life-changing experience. As kids serve others in humility, they discover each other and are drawn closer together as a group.

Kids can serve both at home and away. Arrange for them to help out in a hospital, a home for the elderly, a retarded children's home, a soup kitchen, a shelter for the homeless, or an urban mission. Or take your youth group on an extended mission trip or work-camp experience during Easter break or summer vacation. (There are many project ideas in *Ideas for Social Action* by Anthony Campolo [Youth Specialties/Zondervan, 1983].)

7. *Learning together*. Sunday school classes, small-group Bible studies, discipleship groups, and confirmation classes can do more than teach the Christian faith—they can be places where community is developed.

For many years I have been part of a Bible-study group that meets one night a week. The purpose of the Bible study is to deepen our knowledge of the Bible and to help us grow in the Christian faith. And we achieve those goals. But probably our more important achievement is that we have become a community—a feat that is ultimately more significant than the learning that takes place. When people come together for a common purpose and commit themselves to that purpose over a period of time, community often results.

Unfortunately, learning environments for teenagers are not often conducive to community building. A cold, sterile, and academic approach to learning kills community. Warm up your your group's learning environment so that everyone feels comfortable and involved. Spend some class time sharing with your kids what's going on in your life and listening to what's going on in theirs. Play a quick game, tell a few jokes. These things that seem unimportant and time-consuming pay off in the long run. The kids will enjoy being there, and they will have a chance to get to know one another a little better. And when you teach, involve your young people in the subject matter through discussion and experiential learning strategies like role playing. Don't just lecture or read the lesson to them.

Learning *about* community with the group can also strengthen community. Just as young couples receive premarital counseling about what they are getting into, so people in Christian community need instruction about genuine community. The 13-week curriculum in Section Three of this book provides that instruction. If your young people work through these studies, they will have a better understanding of what the Bible says about community, why community is important to Christians, and what role they can play in their Christian community.

8. *Worshipping God together*. People who worship God together are drawn into community. I believe that their oneness comes not only because of the mystical, supernatural work of the Holy Spirit among the worshipping community, but also as the inevitable result of the worshipping posture: humility. Worshippers humble themselves before God. And, as I said earlier, humility paves the way for love and fellowship within the body of Christ. When people altogether humble themselves before the Lord, they are ready for community.

I am not a hugger by nature. I'm not inclined to go up to someone and give them a hug unless I know them fairly well. Some huggers I know hug anyone and everyone who crosses their path. But that's not me. I shake hands or wave. In a few worship services, however, where we all felt God's presence and the working of Holy Spirit, for some crazy reason I felt like I wanted to go hug somebody. My defenses were down, the mask of stoic reserve came off, and I suddenly felt intimate with my fellow worshippers. And that closeness remained. We sensed that we had shared a common gift of grace.

Someone once used a cone to illustrate how worship builds community. God is at the top of the cone, and the worshipping community is at the bottom.

As the people draw close to God during worship (moving up the sides of the cone), they come closer to each other, until finally all are one at the top. In the worship of God, the worshipping community is drawn together into his presence and made one.

Young people need to experience meaningful worship with their peers. Most teen-

agers consider worship boring and irrelevant; they don't understand it. For this reason, it's a good idea to teach kids about worship and to give them opportunities to worship God in settings other than the regular worship services of the church. A few ideas in Section Two describe different settings for worship in the youth group.

Teenagers can worship. In fact, they can probably worship better than adults. If you have ever attended a rock concert, you know that this is true. Hero-worship comes easily for them. The challenge for the church is to direct teenagers to worship the infinite, personal God who loves them very much. And one important result will be a deepening and strengthening of Christian community.

9. *Ministering to each other.* Your youth group can mature into a community to which teenagers come for support and help not from the adult leaders, but from their peers. Youth ministry is too often ministry *to* youths rather than ministry *with* them. Yet teenagers are uniquely qualified to minister to each other. They have the right credentials: similar experiences, closeness in age, sincere empathy, and availability. All they lack is the training and experience in using their spiritual gifts, natural talents, and abilities to serve Christ and the church.

In her book about peer ministry, *Real Friends* (Harper & Row, 1983), Barbara Varenhorst encourages teenagers to help and counsel each other. "Each of you is a living *potential* resource of caring, which most of you your age crave, especially some who are on their way to feeling like zeros," she writes. "Even those of you who feel like zeros can be a source of help to others, and if you try, you may find it helps you, too. Also, by learning what to do for others, you will be learning how to improve your own relationships. You'll find you like yourself much more."

As teenagers learn basic helping skills and learn to use their spiritual gifts, they will also learn what it means to be the church, the body of Christ. Involve your young people in ministry. Teach them how to listen to each other, to support each other, and to pray for each other. Create a climate favorable to community building. Intimate caring and sharing doesn't grow overnight, but that kind of community is worth striving for.

Section Two
Ideas for Community Building

The small-group exercises, discussion-starters, initiative games, get-acquainted activities, Bible studies, and leadership ideas in this section are designed to build your youth group into a strong, caring community. Many other categories of ideas, however, do not appear in this book. Camping, socials and special events, mission and service projects, and games all build community. Let your own group's needs stimulate other creative ideas.

The ideas in this section are organized alphabetically so that you may easily browse through them, choosing the most appropriate ones for your group. The categorical index of this section groups the ideas according to a theme for easy reference. Use the ideas sparingly, as a supplement to other activities and programs. If you try to use them all, you could blow a fuse.

Categorical Index to Ideas

ACCEPTANCE
  Big Brothers and Sisters
  Identity Masks
  Surprise Package
  Unwanted Guest
  Welcome Coupon Book
  Welcome Questionnaire

AFFIRMATION
  Affirmation Booklets
  Affirmation Stickers
  Compliment Contest
  Complimentary Tickets
  Encourage One Another
  Encouragement Beans
  Forgivers and Judgers
  How Many F's?
  Love Target
  Name Affirmation
  Passing Out Compliments
  Positive-People Bingo
  The Sky's the Limit
  Spin the Compliment

  Strength Voting
  Teen of the Week
  Thanksgiving Exchange
  Uppers and Downers
  Valentine Candy
  What Others Think of Me

AWARENESS OF OTHERS
  Awareness Game
  Eye Chart

BIBLE STUDY
  Four Pictures of Unity
  Lights of the Round Table
  Reciprocal Commands

BODY OF CHRIST (I Corinthians 12)
  Body Balloon Burst
  Body-Life Skit
  Body Poster
  Body Puzzle
  Brother Hood Hour
  Football Stadium

Match Mixer
Meet the Press
Positive-People Bingo
Psychiatrist
Sharing Cubes
Shirt Sharing
Shuffle the Deck
Whopper

NAMES, LEARNING
Bob! Bob! Bob!
Human Bingo
Human Crossword
Identity
License-Plate Name Tags
Name Affirmation
Zip Zap

PEER MINISTRY
Big Brothers and Sisters
Care Company
Christian Responsibility
Dear Abby
Fragile Friends
Giving Spirit
Guardian Angels
Homework Night
How Can I Help?
Prayer Calendar
Prayer Candles
Servant Certificates

PUT-DOWNS, NEGATIVISM
Negative Board
Put-Down Covenant
Put-Down Potty
Uppers and Downers

RESPONSIBILITY
Christian Responsibility
Reciprocal Commands

SELF-IMAGE
Identity Masks
Putting Myself in a Box

SOCIALS AND SPECIAL EVENTS
Church Tailgate Party

TRUST
Trust Test
Trust Walk

UNITY (see also BODY OF CHRIST)
Common Ground
Four Pictures of Unity
Group Photo
Group Story
Make a Melody
Nine-Legged Race
Spy Game
Tinker-Toy Unity
Unity Soup
Yarn Sharing
Youth-Group Letterhead

WORSHIP
Candle Wish
Lights of the Round Table
Prayer Candles
Progressive Worship Service

YOUTH GROUP
Great Moments in History
Group Baseball Cards
Group Photo
Inclusive Elections
Jobs for Everyone
Live-In Lock-In
Mailboxes
Observers
T-Shirt Solidarity
"Us" Quiz
Youth-Group Covenant
Youth-Group Letterhead

Affirmation Booklets

Before your next retreat assemble the following materials: colored paper, pens, pencils, markers, crayons, magazines, scissors, staplers and staples, glue, tape, and yarn. Then write the names of all the retreat participants (including the advisors) on slips of paper. On the first day of the event, have each person draw a name. The name he draws becomes his secret friend for the weekend.

Using the materials you've assembled,

campers and advisors make an "Affirmation Booklet" during the retreat, filling it with pictures, drawings, poems, Bible verses, and comments that will tell their secret friends what they've learned about them. This can include what they like or admire about them—what talents they recognize, what they think their secret friends contribute to the group, what they miss most about their secret friends when they aren't around—anything that will affirm the secret friends. Everyone must get to know his secret friend

without getting caught (so he must get to know several other people as well in the process).

At the end of the retreat, gather everyone together for a prayer service, with time set aside to share the booklets. One at a time, the one who made the booklet presents it to her secret friend. The last person to receive his booklet is the next to present the one he made. Close the prayer service with a group hug and a familiar song.

Affirmation Stickers

Here's another way to help young people look for positive qualities in each other. It takes a little extra preparation, but the results are worth the effort.

Preparation: In big letters, write the name of each person in the group at the top of a sheet of paper before the statement, "We are thankful you are you . . . because we see these qualities in you."

Make a sheet for each person in the group, even if he won't be at this meeting. Next, write positive qualities like "Friendly" or "Cares about others" on heart-shaped slips of paper. (They don't have to be heart-shaped, but the

hearts help convey the positive message.) Make more hearts than you have young people. In other words, if you have 20 kids, make at least 20 slips of paper *for each quality*. Label hearts with a variety of qualities, and leave some hearts blank so that kids can write additional positive qualities.

Hang up all the sheets of paper with the names of students on the wall around the room, and place all the heart-shaped slips of paper on a table in the center of the room. Provide some tape or stick-on dots. Then allow the kids to go around the room and attach to the right sheets of paper qualities that describe the person named on each sheet of paper hanging on the wall. Encourage each person to attach at least one quality to each sheet of paper. He may attach a quality that someone else has already attached if he wants to—in other words, one person might have 10 "Friendly" hearts stuck to her sheet. When the exercise is over, let each person take his sheet home as an encouragement. For those kids who aren't there, mail them their sheets to let them know that the group is thinking about them.

Autograph Hunt

This mixer for medium- and large-sized groups has many variations. Print up a game sheet similar to the one below. Beside each category leave a place for people to sign their names. Be creative and come up with some fun

categories of your own. The object of the game is for people to mingle around the room getting others to autograph the category that describes themselves. No one is allowed to autograph more than one category per sheet.

Autograph Hunt

1. Find someone who uses Listerine. _____

2. Find someone who has three bathrooms in his house. _____

3. Find someone who has gotten more than two traffic tickets. _____

4. Find someone who has red hair. _____

5. Find someone who gets hollered at for spending too much time in the bathroom. _____

6. Find someone who has been inside the cockpit of an airplane. _____

7. Find someone who plays a guitar. _____

8. Find someone who likes frog legs. _____

9. Find someone who has been to Hawaii. _____

10. Find someone who uses your brand of toothpaste. _____

11. Find someone who has used an outhouse. _____

12. Find a girl with false eyelashes on. _____

13. Find a guy who has gone water skiing and got up the first time. _____

14. Find someone who knows what *charisma* means. _____

15. Find someone who is on a diet. _____

16. Find a girl who uses a Lady Remington Shaver. _____

17. Find a guy who has a match with him. _____

18. Find someone who has his own private bath at home. _____

19. Find someone who didn't know your last name. _____

20. Find someone who has a funny sounding last name. _____

Awareness Game

Have everyone pair off with someone else. Give them a minute to introduce themselves and to talk about anything they want. Then tell them to stand back to back, about a foot apart. Partners should not be able to see each other.

Now ask each person to change three things about her appearance. She can change anything at all. She can take his glasses off, unbutton his shirt, put a pen in his shirt pocket, take off a piece of jewelry, part her hair differently, or whatever. After all have done this, ask them to face their partners and to try to identify the three things that are now different about their partners. Most will be unsuccessful.

This demonstrates how much we miss in ordinary day-to-day living. Make the point that in order to really understand each other and care for each other, we have to pay closer attention to what is going on in each others' lives. Discuss how that can be done with the group.

Back to Back

Cooperation, coordination, and teamwork make this a fun crowd breaker or an effective object lesson that stimulates discussion.

Have everyone pair off and sit on the floor, back to back. Next tell them to lock arms and try to stand up together at the same time. It takes commitment and good timing.

Now have each pair join with another pair and try it again with all four people sitting back to back. When these groups have been successful at standing up, combine larger and larger groups until the entire group is all in one big circle trying to stand up together in the locked-arm, back-to-back position.

Best Friends

Print up or read aloud the accompanying case study—or "tension getter"—dealing with friendship, forgiveness, cheating, priorities, and more (page 33). Ask students to respond to the questions that follow the case study.

After the group discussion, lead a Bible study and discussion about the verses listed below.

- Colossians 3:12-14
  What is to be the measure of our forgiveness? How much are we to forgive?
- Matthew 6:14-15
  What will be the measure of God's forgiveness? How much will he forgive?
- Matthew 18:21-35
  What are the disciples learning?

Big Brothers and Sisters

This idea is designed to involve your more mature young people in ministry and to make it easier for the younger kids to feel accepted and appreciated. Select several of your high-school seniors or college students to become "big brothers" or "big sisters" to the incoming freshmen in the group. They can meet with them, make sure they are doing okay, call them up, and help disciple them during the first year that they are part of the group. The main thing is that they try to be sincere friends with the younger kids. Something like this helps build community and gives kids a chance to participate in peer ministry.

BEST FRIENDS

Jack, a Christian, hadn't had time to do his homework the night before. There was a special speaker at his church, and Jack was attending and learning a lot. His best friend, Bill, also a Christian, was enjoying the speaker, too; but he had done his homework in the afternoon. He didn't have a job, as Jack did.

So Jack asked Bill if he could copy his homework this morning. Just this once. Bill agreed. After all, he and Jack were best friends.

The next day as they picked up their homework papers at the end of the period, each had a note attached—"See me at the end of class." When they came up afterward, the teacher said, "It looks like you two copied off each other."

Wanting to be honest, Bill confessed—yes, they had copied off each other. The teacher then told them that they'd both receive F's for the assignment and that notes would be mailed home to inform their parents.

Jack was furious. Out in the hallway he let Bill know how angry he was—and that their friendship was over. To this day neither has tried to renew the friendship.

DISCUSSION QUESTIONS

Where did Jack go wrong? What did he do that he shouldn't have done?

     1. Went to church to hear the speaker

     2. Got a job

     3. Asked to copy Bill's homework

     4. Remained silent in front of the teacher

     5. Became angry

     6. Broke off the friendship

     7. Never forgave Bill

     8. Other: _____

Where did Bill go wrong? What did he do that he shouldn't have done?

     1. Went to church to hear the speaker

     2. Did his homework

     3. Let Jack copy his homework

     4. Wanted to be honest

     5. Confessed

     6. Never forgave Jack

     7. Other: _____

Birthday Guess

Have all your students write their birthdays on a sheet of paper. Collect that sheet, then read the birthdays aloud one at a time while your kids try to match birthdays with people. Kids can guess aloud as you read the dates, or else they can do the matching individually on paper. This crowd breaker works best with groups of less than 20 people.

Bob! Bob! Bob!

Here's a fun way to learn everyone's first name quickly. Everyone should be seated in a circle (or casually around the room), and the leader should stand up in the middle. The leader moves around the group randomly pointing at different people. When the leader points at a particular person, the rest of the group should chant that person's name loudly and in rhythm, i.e. "Bob! Bob! Bob!" The leader keeps the momentum going by pointing rapidly from one person to another until everyone has been pointed to at least once. The group chants as loudly as possible and claps their hands in time. It's a simple idea—really wild and great for learning names.

Body Balloon Burst

Kick off a discussion on the body of Christ or spiritual gifts by secretly and randomly assigning each person in your group one of the parts of the body listed below. One way to do this with larger groups is to use birthday months or last-name initials to regroup the kids, and then assign a body part to each group. For instance, those whose last names begin with A through E are a right hand.

There's also a corresponding motion or gesture for each part of the body.
- "Right hands" raise and wave their right hands.
- "Left hands" raise and wave their left hands.
- "Right feet" hop on their right feet.
- "Left feet" hop on their left feet.
- "Mouths" yell.
- "Rear ends" (or "torsos," if you prefer) do the Twist.

When the signal to go is given, each person performs the motion for his part of the body in an attempt to attract other body parts and form a complete, six-person "body." No other talking is allowed during this part of the game. Each body must include a right and left hand, a right and left foot, a mouth, and a rear end.

After the group of six is together, the two feet carry one of the hands to the leader where the hand is given a balloon. The hand (still being carried by the feet) takes the balloon back to the group where the mouth must blow it up. But the mouth cannot touch it—the hands must hold it for the mouth. After the mouth blows it up, the hands tie it and place it on a chair—at which time the rear end sits on it and pops it. The first team to successfully pop its balloon is the winner.

This active and exciting game is a simple yet effective way to show how the various parts of the body must work together in order to accomplish a common goal.

Body-Life Skit

This skit for six characters is based on I Corinthians 12. Each person who portrays a part of the body should wear a sign or T-shirt that identifies the part she is playing. The reader should hold a Bible.

THE BODY-LIFE SKIT

Cast: Reader
       Nose (shy, sneezes a lot)
       Foot (wearing big shoes)
       Ear (wearing earphones)
       Eye (wearing big glasses)
       Head (acting conceited)

The skit begins with the body parts in a huddle.

Reader: I'll be reading selections from 1 Corinthians, chapter 12. "The body is a unit, though it is made up of many parts. (*the body parts spread apart and begin showing off their individual talents as the* Reader *continues*) And although all its parts are many, they form one body. So it is with Christ. For we were all baptized by one Spirit into one body—whether Jews or Greeks, slave or free—and we were all given the one Spirit to drink. Now the body is not made up of one part, but of many parts. If the foot should say—"

Foot: Because I'm not a hand, I don't belong to the body.

Reader: "—it would not for that reason cease to be a part of the body."

Foot: Oh, yes, it would. I mean, I can go places, give senior citizens rides to church, and drive for Meals on Wheels. But I can't give a lot of money like a hand could or cook the best dish at the covered dish supper like a hand could. Maybe I'm just not needed around here!

Reader: "And if the ear should say—"

Ear: Because I'm not an eye, I don't belong to the body!

Reader: "—it would not for that reason cease to be a part of the body."

Ear: Oh, yea? I mean, I can hear and understand a sermon pretty well, but I can't see places where someone needs help like an eye could. What good is it to be able to hear and understand if you can't see to do anything? Maybe I'm just not needed around here!

Reader: "If the whole body were an eye, where would the sense of hearing be? If the whole body were an ear, where would the sense of smell be? The eye cannot say to the hand—"

Eye: I don't need you, Hand! I mean, I'm the most important part around here. That's pretty obvious. Anyone can see that without me this body's just stumbling around in the dark. What good are you, Hand?

Reader: "Nor can the head say to the feet—"

Head: Well, I don't need any of you. I can think and reason and make all the important decisions without any help at all from you guys. I'm the brains of this outfit.

Reader: (*At this point, all the parts of the body begin arguing with each other so that the Reader must plead with them to stop. The nose moves off to the side and begins to cry.*) "On the contrary, those parts of the body that seem to be weaker are indispensable, and the parts that we think are less honorable we treat with special honor. God has combined the members of the body so that there should be no division in the body (*the arguing gets progressively worse*) but that its parts should have equal concern for each other." (*exasperated*) Oh, I give up! (Reader *walks away*)

Ear: Hey, wait a minute. Listen! I hear someone crying. (*everyone finally gets quiet*)

Eye: Look, it's [the name of the person playing the nose]. Poor guy, I wonder what's wrong?

Head:	I've got an idea! We could go over there and find out.
Ear:	Hey, I like the sound of that idea!
Head:	(*acting proud*) Of course! It's a good idea!
Eye:	But how could we get there?
Foot:	I could take you, I suppose. (*General agreement. Everyone lines up behind Foot, forms a train, and goes over to Nose.*)
Ear:	(*to Nose*) We heard you crying and we're kind of worried about you. Can we help somehow?
Nose:	I don't know. I get so lonely sometimes. I wish I had some friends. But who wants to be friends with someone whose greatest talent is sniffing out trouble!
Eye:	Well, I don't know about the rest of this crew, but it seems to me that we've got some trouble that needs sniffing out. (*everyone looks at Head*)
Head:	(*looking sheepish*) Well, maybe you're right.
Foot:	You just come with us. We're not perfect, but when we all work together, we can do a lot of good after all. (*body parts form a line with arms around each others' shoulders*)
Reader:	(*stepping in front to read*) "If one part suffers, every part suffers with it; if one part is honored, every part rejoices with it. Now you are the body of Christ."
All:	And each one of you is a part of it!

Body Poster

To help young people visualize the meaning of the church as the body of Christ, read 1 Corinthians 12 and then lay a large cardboard cut in the shape of the human body—minus the head—on the floor. Equip the kids with colored marking pens, and tell them to choose a part of the body that they feel represents them. Have them write their name on that part of the body—or let them mark it with a symbol or a phrase that relates to their choice. Afterward each person can share why he chose the part of the body he did and explain the meaning of the symbol or phrase he used. Post the finished "Body Poster" on the wall with a cutout head of Christ.

Body Puzzle

This idea will encourage kids to see themselves as important parts of the body of Christ. Enlarge a picture of your church or of the youth group to poster size. Mount it on a piece of stiff paper or cardboard, and cut it into a jigsaw puzzle. Or mount the photo onto a completed, already cut, wooden jigsaw puzzle. After the glue dries, use an Exacto knife to cut the photo to match the puzzle pieces.

After the group puts the puzzle together, talk about what it means to be a part of the body of Christ. Then give each person in the group a piece of the puzzle to take home as a reminder.

Brother Hood Hour

Here is a humorous skit to start a discussion on the body of Christ. Read 1 Corinthians 12:12-31 to conclude the discussion.

BROTHER HOOD HOUR

Set up the stage like a typical television talk show. The actors should know their lines well enough to perform without scripts.

Cast: Announcer
       Brother Hood
       Mr. Foot
       Señor Hand
       Rev. Ear
       Mr. Eye

Announcer: And now, from Hollywood, it's (*music*) the Brother Hood Hour, featuring the inimitable Brother Johnny Hood himself! Here's Johnny!

Bro. Hood: Thank you, thank you. (*applause*) Thank you, thank you. (*applause*) THANK YOU! Have we got a show lined up for you! We have guests from around the world to discuss tonight's topic: Who or what is the body of Christ? So let's get started and bring on our first guest. And here he is, from Ringworm, Georgia, Mr. Foot!

Mr. Foot: Well, hello, Brother Hood!

Bro. Hood: Mr. Foot, I can't tell you what a pleasure it is to have you on our program.

Mr. Foot: I'm glad to be here, Brother. I bring you greetings from the N.A.E.F.

Bro. Hood: I'm sorry, but I'm not familiar with the N.A.E.F.

Mr. Foot: A man of your caliber? I find that hard to believe! Well, anyway, the N.A.E.F. is the National Association of Evangelical Feet, of which I am a charter member.

Bro. Hood: Oh, yes! As I recall, your group has recently come out with a new paraphrase of the Bible.

Mr. Foot: Paraphrase, my foot! This is a superior translation of the Bible!

Bro. Hood: And what is it called?

Mr. Foot: Dr. Scholl's Authorized Version. It is truly a remarkable work. This man has studied widely. He speaks eleven foreign languages, including Greek and Hebrew.

Bro. Hood: Is this in any way related to the Odor Eaters' Translation?

Mr. Foot: No, no! The N.A.E.F. looks with disdain upon the Odor Eaters' Translation. In fact, we just think it stinks!

Bro. Hood: Well, getting down to our topic, how do you, as a Foot, feel about the rest of the body of Christ?

Mr. Foot: Well, as a group of Feet, we feel that we have been trampled on by the rest of the body of Christ.

Bro. Hood: And what makes you feel that way?

Mr. Foot: Let me answer that by telling you a little story. The other day at my country club—

Bro. Hood: You belong to a country club?

Mr. Foot: Oh, yes. Club Foot. Anyway, I ran into a woman that is in my Sunday school class. Do you know what she said to me? "Mr. Foot, you are a big heel!" Can you imagine that? I whipped around in holy anger and said, "Woman, you ain't got no soul!" It's just terrible the way we're treated as Feet.

Bro. Hood: I agree, that is bad! But who would you say makes up the body of Christ?

Mr. Foot: Primarily Feet.

Bro. Hood: Would you go so far as to say that to be a member of Christ's body you must be a Foot?

Mr. Foot: Are you trying to buttonhole me?

Bro. Hood: Oh, no, Mr. Foot! But surely you must have some thoughts on the matter?

Mr. Foot: Well, I do. I do believe you must be a Foot to be a member of the body of Christ.

Bro. Hood: Thank you, Mr. Foot. I'd like to chat with you a bit more, but I must bring on our next guest. Won't you welcome with a big hand, from La Salada, Guatemala, Señor Hand! *(applause)*

Señor Hand: Buenas noches, Hermano Hood.

Bro. Hood: Welcome, Señor Hand. Could you tell our audience what your occupation is?

Señor Hand: I am professor of religion at La Salada Universidad de los Manos.

Bro. Hood: I understand that La Salada University of the Hands is a private school that grips the more traditional, fundamentalist position. Is that true?

Señor Hand: Sí.

Bro. Hood: How do the Hands feel about the body of Christ?

Señor Hand: I'm so glad that you asked the question, Señor. We feel that, as Hands, we aren't getting a fair shake in the body of Christ. For some reason, we're always in hot water!

Bro. Hood: Do you feel, as a result of this, that the Hands become callous to the other members of the body?

Señor Hand: Sí, Señor. In fact, there are some Hands that say if things don't improve, they're going to get rough!

Bro. Hood: That would be disastrous! Who do you think is the most important part in the body of Christ?

Señor Hand: Oh, most definitely the Hands! We feel that we have a great deal of common sense—we grasp things easily.

Mr. Foot: How can you say something like that?

Bro. Hood: Mr. Foot! Control yourself! This man is my guest and you have had your turn to speak! Señor Hand, I am so sorry!

Señor Hand: It is all right, Hermano Hood.

Bro. Hood: Thank you for your enlightening remarks, Señor Hand. And now, may I introduce our next guest? From Canterbury-on-Avon, Worchestershire, England, Rector of the Q-tip Anglican Church, bring him on with a big hand, Reverend Ear! *(applause)* Good evening, Reverend, and welcome to the Brother Hood Hour.

Rev. Ear: What did you say? I didn't hear you.

Bro. Hood: I said welcome to the Brother Hood Hour!

Rev. Ear: Oh. I'm sorry. Yes, it is good to be here.

Bro. Hood: Rev. Ear, you have just written a book entitled *A History of Ears Within the Body of Christ*, published by Earwax Press. In the book you mention, and I quote, "As a result of spiritual and social forces, Ears have become the greatest contributors to the body of Christ." Why do you say that?

Rev. Ear: Well, I feel that Ears, as a group, have gained superiority because they are good listeners. We are indispensable to the body.

Mr. Foot: And you call yourself a minister? That's a laugh!

Rev. Ear:	What did he say?
Bro. Hood:	Please sit down, Mr. Foot. Rev. Ear, what other contributions have the Ears made?
Rev. Ear:	We have been experimenting with musical instruments and have developed a new one for worship services. It's called an ear drum.
Bro. Hood:	That sounds very interesting. Do you feel that the rest of the body is deaf to these contributions?
Rev. Ear:	They are deaf only because they want to be. I believe this is because they are jealous.
Bro. Hood:	Thank you, Rev. Ear, for your remarks. I'd like to discuss your book with you further, but I must bring on our next guest. Please welcome Mr. Eye from Bloodshot Hills near Lake Wawanunu, Minnesota. (*applause*) Welcome to our program, Mr. Eye.
Mr. Eye:	Thank you, Brother Hood. I'm so glad to be here. My wife thought that I didn't have the nerve to appear on national television.
Bro. Hood:	I guess you'd call that optic nerve! Seriously though, Mr. Eye, we are discussing this topic: Who or what is the body of Christ? In general, how do the Eyes see the body of Christ?
Mr. Eye:	We believe the Eyes have it.
Bro. Hood:	Why do you say that?
Mr. Eye:	Because of our great scholastic standing. We have many pupils enrolled in our schools, you know. Due to our immense contribution to academia, we feel that we are indeed the most important part of the body of Christ.
Mr. Foot:	That's it! I've had it! I'm not going to listen to any more of this garbage.
Rev. Ear:	I say, calm down old boy.
Mr. Foot:	You wanna take it outside, Parson?
Señor Hand:	You are nothing but a bully, Señor!
Mr. Foot:	Take that! (*hits him*)
Bro. Hood:	Please, Mr. Foot (*Mr. Foot hits him, too. A rumble occurs between all the guests. Brother Hood scrambles to his feet and speaks while the rumble continues.*) Well, that's our show for tonight. We hope you enjoyed it. Tune in next week when we will be discussing the Baptism of the Holy Spirit.

Candle Wish

This experience in sharing can also be used for worship. The whole group sits in a circle with the lights out. Everyone has a candle. A designated person lights his candle, verbally expresses a wish (or prayer), then lights the candle of the person on his right. She then says her wish, turns to the person on her right, and lights that person's candle. That person expresses his wish, and the sequence continues around the circle. When everyone has had a turn and each candle is lit, the candles are blown out simultaneously.

Care Company

Here's a way to get the group involved in small *koinonia* or fellowship groups which function apart from the regular youth meetings and activities.

Assign everyone to a "Care Company," using any method of selection you choose. Each Care Company should have about five people in it. Allow each Care Company to spend some time together getting to know each other, and then ask them to commit to the following:

FOR THE NEXT SIX MONTHS,
I PLEDGE TO:

1. Call or contact the members of my Care Company at least once a week, just to see how things are going.
2. Make a personal effort to get to know members of my Care Company as well as possible.
3. Pray daily for each member of my Care Company.
4. Work with my Care Company to meet new people and to expand to at least seven members by   _(date)_ .

Christian Responsibility

The following is a list of responsibilities that Christians have to each other, according to the Bible. Pass out the list to your group, read the passages, and then try to answer these questions:

1. How many of these responsibilities are being met in your group?
2. Is there one that surprises you or with which you disagree?
3. Is there one you are having difficulty doing?
4. Are these responsibilities optional or are they to be expected of all Christians?
5. Is there one you would like to work on as a group?

The meeting can be concluded by making a covenant with the other members of the group to work toward one or more of the responsibilities. Close with a worship service or prayer of dedication for your new goals. It is helpful to set an evaluation date to check on your growth.

Our Responsibilities to Each Other as Christians:

Love one another
Ephesians 5:1
Romans 12:10
1 Peter 4:8
John 13:34,35
John 15:12,13
Hebrews 13:1
1 John 3:16,17 (Lay down our lives for each other)

Serve one another
Galatians 5:13
Ephesians 5:21
1 Peter 4:9,10

Take material care of each other
Deuteronomy 15:7
Romans 12:13

Discipline each other
Galatians 6:1,2
Matthew 18:15
1 Thessalonians 3:14,15

Pray for each other
Ephesians 6:18,19
James 5:16

Forgive one another
Ephesians 4:31,32
Matthew 18:21,22
Matthew 5:22 (Don't hold grudges)

Confess sins to one another
James 5:16

Carry each others' burdens
Romans 15:1

Be patient with each other
Ephesians 4:2

Worship together
Psalm 133:1

Church Tailgate Party

Tailgate parties are common at sporting events, when friends get together before the game to eat and have a good time together. A tailgate party usually makes going to the game more exciting.

As a community builder, why not have the youth group gather in the church parking lot on Sunday morning for a "Church Tailgate Party?" The kids can eat a breakfast of donuts, cereal and juice, or cold pizza. They are more likely to attend the worship service of the church that Sunday if you kick if off with a tailgate party.

Cliques

Do your kids realize how stifling cliques can be? How difficult it is to meet others when you tie yourself exclusively to a single group? Try this—divide your teenagers into small groups of five to ten, then with ropes tie each group together, everyone facing out. Tell them that they must now meet at least ten people from any of the groups but their own.

When the dust settles and the ropes are untied, talk with your group about why it was so hard, how the activity relates to cliques, how a high schooler feels who's not in a youth-group clique, and how God's work is hurt by this.

Cliques and Loners

Here's an idea that gets kids talking about the effects of cliques on a youth group. Ahead of time arrange the chairs in the room to represent common groupings of youths at a meeting.
1. *A group of chairs in a circle all hooked together* represents the group of teens who regularly attend the youth group.
2. *A chair in the middle of the circle* represents the person who wants to be the center of attention.
3. *A few chairs outside the group* represent newcomers who don't feel part of the group in the circle.
4. *A chair next to the door* represents a person who has never come before.
5. *A chair just outside the door* represents someone who is afraid to come into the meeting.
6. *A chair on top of the table* represents a critical person who looks down on everyone else.
7. *A broken chair or a chair that's different from all the others* represents a person in the group who is a little different from the rest because of a handicap, a foreign accent, etc.
8. *A small cluster of three to four chairs off from the large circle* represents an exclusive clique.

(You can probably think of some other ways to represent various groupings of your youths.) There should be a chair for every student, with no chairs left over. Now tape a number to each chair. As each person arrives give him a number at random corresponding to one of the chairs in the room. Tell him he may not move the chair and he must stay in his assigned seat during the entire meeting.

Being sensitive in your selection, choose certain kids who are part of established cliques as well as one or two of the loners to interview in front of the group. Ask the group to compare the experiences of the kids interviewed by discussing what the problems are and how they can be solved without destroying relationships or coercing friendships. Use the following questions to stimulate their thinking.
1. What is a clique?
2. What are the advantages or disadvantages of being in a clique?
3. What are the advantages or disadvantages of being a loner?
4. What would be the ideal situation in a youth group such as ours?

5. If Christ were in our group, where would he sit? Would he be in a clique? Or would he be a loner?

6. What are some ways we can reach out to loners?
7. How can we develop positive groupings within our youth group?

Common Ground

This small-group experience "breaks the ice" by helping kids discover how much they have in common with each other. Divide the group into discussion groups of five to seven students, and give each group a sheet listing a variety of categories (see list below). Each group must come up with something that they *all* like or *all* dislike in each category and choose a secretary to record their preferences. Ask them to be honest not just to "go for the points."

For each item common to everyone in the group, give the group 10 points. But if, for instance, only five out of a group of seven have a particular thing in common, they receive only five points. Set a time limit of ten minutes for this exercise.

During the next five minutes, each group must list as many other shared experiences as they can. Any experience is acceptable, as long as each person in the group has shared that experience. For example:
1. Got a B on last report card
2. Been sad over the death of a loved one
3. Been stood up by a friend
4. Went on a back-packing trip
Give additional points for each shared experience. At the end of the time limit, the group totals up its points.

Category	Like	Dislike
1. Food		
2. Game		
3. TV show		
4. Gift received		
5. School subject		
6. Chore at home		
7. Song		
8. Hobby		
9. Way to spend Saturday		
10. Sport		

Community Communion

Here's a meaningful way to involve your young people in communion. It's especially effective with junior highers. After a time of prayer and a few songs, move the group into the kitchen to make their own unleavened bread. Give each person a job to do—from cracking the eggs to taking turns rolling out the dough paper thin. Here's the recipe.
Cream together:
  1/4 cup sugar
  3/4 cup shortening
Mix in:

1 teaspoon salt
1 1/2 cups buttermilk
  (milk soured with 1 tablespoon vinegar may be substituted)
1/2 teaspoon soda
Add:
  4-5 cups flour
Divide the dough into four balls.
Roll out on floured surface until wafer thin.
Place on greased cookie sheet.
Prick the dough with a fork to prevent shrinkage.

Bake at 450 degrees until light brown, approximately 15-20 minutes.

While the bread is baking, the kids can make the "wine" (grape juice). Let them crush a large quantity of whole, seedless grapes in a bowl using a crushing stick. Explain how the crushing of the grapes symbolizes that we as sinners all had a part in the crucifixion of Christ.

When the grapes are all crushed, strain the juice into glasses and serve communion as you normally would.

Community Quiz

This mixer works best when you know everyone who attends. Contact each person in advance to find out humorous or interesting little-known facts about him. Then using your inside information, compose a multiple-choice and true-false quiz for everyone to take at the next meeting.

One way to use the quiz is to give everyone a copy to fill in as they mill around the room asking each other for the correct answers. At the end of a time limit, whoever has the most corerect answers wins. Another method is for everyone to take the test first and then take turns giving the correct answer to the group. If you like a combination of ideas, tell everyone to fill in their quiz and *then* mill around the room asking each person listed on the quiz for the correct answer.

Some sample questions:
1. Danny Thompson is saving his money to buy:
   a. a Lear jet
   b. a hair transplant
   c. a moped
2. Lisa Burns hates:
   a. sardines
   b. artichokes
   c. Danny Thompson
3. Bill Florden's dad once appeared on the Johnny Carson show.
   True/False
4. Next Christmas, Paula Lovik's family is going:
   a. to stay home
   b. to Aspen, Colorado
   c. crazy

Compliment Contest

If some of your kids have trouble saying nice things to each other, try this. It makes a contest out of giving compliments.

Seat the group in a circle around one person who is seated in a chair in the middle of the circle. The person in the middle chooses one person that she will compliment and a second person who will try to beat her compliment with a better compliment. After hearing both compliments, the person who is the object of the compliments decides which compliment he likes the best. He may have trouble deciding, of course, but he must choose one over the other. The person whose compliment was not chosen takes the center chair for the next round.

A variation is to place the person who will receive the compliments in the center to choose her two complimenters, and then replace her with the person whose compliment she likes best.

Complimentary Tickets

This is something you can do now and again to encourage affirmation within the group. Distribute to everyone a "complimentary ticket" with someone else's name on it. Ask each person to write on the back of the ticket a compliment—something he appreciates about the person who is named on the ticket. After he writes the compliment, he gives it to the person named on the ticket.

Let the kids know that if they receive a ticket with someone's name on it whom they don't know very well, they can trade with someone else who might know that person better.

Cross 'Em Up

Here's a fun way for your group to get acquainted. On index cards have each kid write one thing about himself that not everyone knows. Collect the cards and use the information for clues to create your own crossword puzzle, with the kids' first names as the answers in the puzzle. (Many computers have a crossword puzzle program that makes this project easier to complete.)

When it's time to play the game, hand out pencils and copies of the puzzle. Then let kids mix freely, asking one another questions. First one to complete the puzzle wins. "Cross 'Em Up" is a great game for quiz nights, retreats, regular youth meetings, or anytime you need a get-acquainted activity.

Across
1. Member of the drill team at Montgomery High
3. Father is a United Airlines pilot
7. Heavyweight wrestling champion
8. Family owns A & B Market
10. Friend of Angi's from Piner High School
11. Plays the drums in a band
12. Tennis star at Piner
15. Duran Duran fan
19. Loves any sport
21. A track star and on Student Council
24. Enjoys good rock 'n' roll and guys
25. Our football hero
26. "The Motorcycle Kid"
28. "The Hick"
29. Just moved here from Texas
31. Has a last name like "Rock"
33. Esoteric (Don't try to figure this one out, just write the word!)

34. Loves to dance
35. Loves horses.

Down
1. Likes board games
2. Just got braces
4. Likes to play tackle football
5. Favorite sport is tennis
6. Loves to run track
7. Loves marine biology
9. Favorite hobbies: swimming, dancing, boys
13. Plays basketball
14. Grew up in Florida
16. Was in the play "Grease" at school
17. Recently injured left hand
18. Wants to be a school teacher
20. Worked the light board at our school's plays
22. Drives a '66 Mustang
23. Drives a '67 Mustang
27. Has a dog names Amos
29. Dad sells life insurance
30. Loves to golf
32. Collects stickers

Dear Abby

This simple exercise not only gives kids the opportunity to minister to each other, but it provides you with insight into the concerns of individuals in your group.

Give each person a piece of paper and a pencil to write a "Dear Abby" letter explaining an unresolved problem that they have. Tell them to sign the letter "Confused," "Frustrated," or any name other than their own.

After everyone has finished writing, collect the papers and redistribute them so that everyone has someone else's letter. Each person now becomes "Abby" and writes a helpful answer to the letter. Allow plenty of time.

When the answers are complete, collect the letters and read them one at a time to the group. Ask the group to discuss whether the advice given was good or bad. Let them suggest other solutions to the problems. Often their answers are sincere, sensible, and practical.

Electric Fence

This group game stressing teamwork and cooperation can be played just for fun or you can debrief the experience with the group afterwards to learn more about how the group works together to solve problems.

Divide into teams of 10 or less, and have each group perform the task separately. Tie a string or rope about five feet off the ground between two poles or objects. The object of the game is for the entire group to get over the string ("the electric fence") without touching it. Other rules: no one can go under the fence or around the fence, and no one is allowed to touch the poles or objects the string is tied to. In most cases, the group will have the most difficulty with the first person and the last person over the fence.

Encourage One Another

Give all the students a piece of paper to pin on their backs. Then ask the group to circulate and write one thing they like about each person on his piece of paper. This may take 5 to 15 minutes, depending upon the size of the group. Allow time for everyone to read his own piece of paper. Follow with a devotional on the need to encourage each other, using such passages as 1 Thessalonians 5:14 and Hebrews 10:24.

Encouragement Beans

During a long bus trip or on a retreat, you can have some fun while teaching your group how to encourage each other and praise another's good deeds. First give each student 20 beans. Explain to them that more beans can be earned in the following ways:
- By giving a sincere and encouraging word to another person.
  (Flattery—that is, giving words of praise for personal gain—is not rewarded.)
- By doing kind or helpful actions.
- By participating in activities with a good attitude.

Beans are awarded by leaders under the following conditions:
- When they observe kids encouraging others

by their actions, words, or attitudes.
- When a young person observes an encouraging action, word, or attitude and tells a leader. In this case not only the encourager but perhaps even the reporter will earn a bean. Beans can be confiscated by leaders under the following conditions:
- When leaders observe discouraging actions, words, or attitudes (e.g., criticizing, complaining, ridiculing, showing disrespect).
- Students who receive a discouraging action, word, or attitude may request a bean from the offender provided they
  1) not reciprocate with an unkind action, word, or attitude,
  2) simply smile politely and hold out their

hand.

- Here's what a student may do who observes discouraging actions, words, or attitudes:

1) If an observer tattles to a leader, the tattletale loses a bean to the leader.

2) Before reporting the offender to a leader, the observing student must ask the offender to turn himself in to the leader or to confess the discouraging action, word, or attitude to the observer himself.

3) If the offender refuses at the first opportunity to admit his wrong to a leader or another student, then the observer may report him to a leader without incurring the tattletale penalty.

4) If an offender admits his wrong, he loses one bean; if he refuses to admit and is consequently reported, he loses two beans.

To remind the kids that being encouraging pays, the ones with the most beans at the end of the trip or retreat receive rewards.

Eye Chart

Here's a good mixer that encourages communication and observation. Make up a chart like the one below, and print enough so that everyone has a copy.

The object of the game is to mingle around the room and, *without talking*, write down on the chart everyone's name and eye color. This game could also be done with other categories, like hair color, shoe styles, etc.

Name	Brown	Blue	Green	Grey	Bloodshot

Face to Face

This game is great for giving people a non-threatening way to communicate what they believe. It is also great for helping people discover how well they know each other.

The game is played by two to four people with a regular deck of playing cards. Each player receives cards of the same suit, except the queens. Queens and jokers are not used. The players sit face to face, and the first player expresses an attitude (not necessarily his own) about something. His statement may describe an *emotion* (I feel fine when I am alone), an *opinion* (I am against capital punishment), a *reaction* (I blush when someone praises me), a *taste* or *preference* (I like working out of doors), a *value* (I feel it's more important to have a good reputation than to be rich), or a *belief* (I believe in reincarnation). Each player indicates his own position on the statement made by choosing a card between one—the ace—and ten. She chooses the card on this basis:

1 indicates:	total disagreement
2 or 3 indicates:	strong disagreement
4 or 5 indicates:	slight disagreement
6 or 7 indicates:	slight agreement
8 or 9 indicates:	strong agreement
10 indicates:	total agreement

The players then place the cards that register their degree of agreement face down to their left on the table. For the same statement, each player chooses a number that he thinks represents the position the player to his right takes on the statement and places this second card face down to his right. The players then turn over their cards, taking care not to reverse the positions of the cards.

Each player counts his points by noting the difference between the value of the right hand card (the one by which he describes the other player's position) and the card the other player has actually chosen, (namely the card at the other player's left hand).

For example, let's say John and Louise are playing "Face to Face." John says, "I never finish assignments till the last minute." He places a 7 card face down to his left, indicating that he slightly agrees with his own statement—that he is something of a procrastinator. He then places a 9 card face down to his right, showing that he pictures Louise as one who leaves things to the last minute. The card on Louise's left, however, is a 5 indicating that she doesn't think of herself as a procrastinator. John's score is the difference between the card on his right (the 9) and the card on Louise's left (the 5), a score of 4.

Meanwhile, Louise has placed an 8 face down on her right to indicate what, in her estimation, is John's position on the statement. Since John rated himself with a 7, Louise's score is 1.

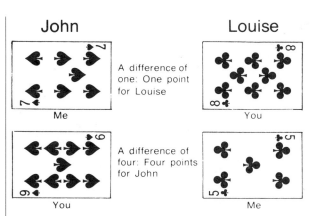

John   Louise

A difference of one: One point for Louise

A difference of four: Four points for John

The players note their scores, take back their cards, and the next player makes a statement. Once again, each player lays down two cards as described above. Points are counted again and the first person to score 50 or 100 points loses the game.

If a player doesn't want to reveal her position on the statement given or doesn't want to guess the position of the player to her right, she puts down a king. She then gives herself a score one number higher than any of the scores at the table for that particular statement. The person to her left receives a zero for that statement. If a player needs a duplicate card of any number or the king, he uses the jack to represent that duplicate.

"Face to Face" can be played with more than four people if you use all or part of a second deck of cards. To have a shot at guessing the positions of more than one of the players, have everybody shift after each one makes a statement once around the table.

Family Matters

Here is a Bible study that can help you build personal relationships within your youth group by focusing upon the "family" responsibilities that are called for in the church. Begin by brainstorming this question: What are some ways a church is like a family?

Allow several responses. Affirm each. Then announce that you're going to examine the concept that a church should have intimacy like a family, and this intimacy should carry over into your youth group. Have them turn to Matthew 18.

Divide students into groups. Assign each group one of the following passages and topics:

Matthew 18:1-4	Family Attitudes
Matthew 18:5-14	Family Concern
Matthew 18:15-20	Family Discipline
Matthew 18:21-35	Family Forgiveness

Instruct the groups to read the passage assigned to them and write down how the church, and specifically their youth group, is to fulfill these responsibilities. They should also make note of how this illustrates the intimacy of a family. Encourage them to pay special attention to key words, concepts, or statements.

After several minutes of study, allow each group to share their findings. These questions may be used to stimulate further discussion.

Family Attitudes
1. What is the key attitude described here? Why is it so essential? If it is present, what will it do?
2. Define the "children" in the kingdom.

Family Concern
1. According to verse five, what is the first concern?
2. Who are the "little ones" in the kingdom?
3. Why is leading others to sin such a serious thing? Do you think most Christians today recognize this? Why or why not?
4. What does verse 10 tell you about angels?
5. How faithfully should a church pursue "lost ones?" Do we do this? Why or why not?

Family Discipline
1. What is the purpose of this passage?
2. What is the role of the witnesses?
3. How would you explain verses 18-20?
4. Do you think this should be practiced today? Why or why not?
5. If this were practiced regularly, what do you think would happen?

Family Forgiveness
1. How does Peter's question in verse 21 relate to Jesus' teaching about discipline?
2. What prevented one servant from giving forgiveness? Does this happen today in the church? Why?
3. How easily do Christians forgive each other? What hinders forgiveness in the church?

Close your study by suggesting that all these responsibilities are given to individual Christians. If you fulfill them in your youth group, an intimacy will develop like the intimacy of a family. Then ask, "What are some ways we can begin to do these things?" Allow the kids to brainstorm some answers, and close the meeting with prayer.

First-Guess Favorite

For this mixer print up copies of the game sheet on the next page (or make up your own) and give one to each person.

The game is played this way. First, each person chooses his own favorite in each category (by marking it on his own game sheet.)

Then the kids circulate around the room trying to guess (on the first guess) the favorites of others in each category. If they successfully guess someone's favorite on the first try, then that person initials to the right of that category on the guesser's sheet.

Football Stadium

There is a saying that goes, "The church is a lot like a football game—22,000 people who are badly in need of exercise watching 22 people who are badly in need of rest, play the game."

In small groups, have the kids imagine the youth group (or the church) as a football stadium. They are to share with others in the group *where they see themselves*. Are they on the field playing the game? If so, which player are

they? Are they a coach, a referee, a cheerleader? Are they a spectator in the stands? An empty seat? The possibilities are many.

This will give kids a chance to think through their present involvement in the youth group, and allow them to think about where they would like to be.

First-Guess Favorite

Directions: First, put a check to the left of your own favorites in each category. Then circulate around the room and guess what the favorites of others in the group are. If you guess correctly on the first try, they initial to the right of the category on your sheet. No more than two initials from the same person.

1. Favorite music _____
   _____ Country-Western
   _____ Classical
   _____ Rock 'n' roll
   _____ Gospel

2. Favorite food _____
   _____ Mexican
   _____ American (meat and potatoes)
   _____ Chinese
   _____ Italian

3. Favorite car _____
   _____ Luxury
   _____ Sports
   _____ Economy
   _____ Truck

4. Favorite movies _____
   _____ Adventure
   _____ Comedy
   _____ Mystery
   _____ Science fiction

5. Favorite vacation _____
   _____ Beach
   _____ Mountains
   _____ World travel (plane, cruise)
   _____ Sight-seeing America (by car)

6. Favorite sweet _____
   _____ Pie
   _____ Cake
   _____ Frozen (ice cream, yogurt)
   _____ Candy

7. Favorite animal _____
   _____ Dog
   _____ Cat
   _____ Bird
   _____ Exotic

8. Favorite TV show _____
   _____ News, or news program
   _____ Comedy
   _____ Drama
   _____ Soap opera

9. Favorite reading material _____
   _____ Magazine
   _____ Fiction books
   _____ Nonfiction books
   _____ Newspapers

10. Favorite spectator sport _____
    _____ Football
    _____ Basketball
    _____ Baseball
    _____ Tennis or golf

11. Favorite color _____
    _____ Dark (black, brown, rust)
    _____ Light (white, tan)
    _____ Pastel (yellow, pink, baby blue)
    _____ Bright (red, blue)

12. Favorite season _____
    _____ Winter
    _____ Spring
    _____ Summer
    _____ Fall

13. Favorite time of day _____
    _____ Early morning
    _____ Afternoon
    _____ Evening
    _____ Late night

Foot-Washing Experience

Begin this meaningful experience in humility and service by reading John 13:1-18. After the reading, discuss questions like these with the group:

1. Why did Jesus wash the disciples' feet?
2. Why was foot-washing a custom in those days?
3. Who usually did the foot-washing in those days?
4. How do you think the disciples felt when Jesus washed their feet?
5. How would you feel if Jesus washed your feet?

After the discussion, divide into groups of four or five. Give each group a water-filled dishpan and towels. Allow each group to take turns washing each others' feet. Encourage them to do it in the same spirit as Christ when he washed his disciples' feet.

Following this experience, ask the group to reflect on what happened: "How did this make you feel?" "Which was most difficult? Washing? Being washed?" "How can we symbolically wash each others' feet in on a regular basis?"

Forgivers and Judgers

To reinforce the values of affirmation and forgiveness, divide your group into two or more teams. Set up some kind of target or dart board for each team (foam targets and balls with velcro strips would be best). Then have a contest to see which team can score the most points.

But before the contest begins, give each kid a slip of paper with an assignment as either a *forgiver* or a *judger*. When players on their own team don't make a perfect hit, the *forgivers* are supposed to say things like "That's okay," "Keep trying your best," and "We still like you." *Judgers* are supposed to say things like "Can't you do better than that?" "That was a bad throw, we'll never win," and "Whose team are you on, anyway?"

After the game is over and the scores are added up, ask the group these questions:

1. On a scale of 1 to 10, how much did you enjoy this game? Why?
2. What difference did the *forgivers* make? Why?
3. What difference did the *judgers* make? Why?
4. Did you enjoy being a *forgiver*? A *judger*?

Four Pictures of Unity

Every youth group struggles to maintain relationships characterized by harmony and mutual concern. It's all too easy for young people to pick at petty differences, and without warning those small problems can become devastating schisms within the group.

This Bible study is intended to help young people identify the aspects of living in God's family that are shared by all. By recognizing the kind of unity God desires for his people, they can take steps to restore that harmony and heal any breaks that may have occurred.

These four pictures identified by the Apostle Peter in 1 Peter 1:22-2:10 are outlined by Warren W. Wiersbe in his book *Be Hopeful* (Victor, 1982). Use the following questions to talk with

your group about the need for unity:

I. **Children of the Same Family** (1:22-2:3)
1. How did we become children in the same family?
2. What brought about our new birth?
3. How is the Word described? What do you think this means? How important is the Word to God's family?
4. According to Peter, how should brothers treat each other?
5. Can we disagree with each other and still have sincere love for each other?
6. How was the Word "preached" to you?
7. Describe how children in God's family are like newborn babies. Do we ever

leave this stage? How? Do some remain spiritual babies? Why? What's the result when babies won't grow up?

II. **Stones in the Same Building** (2:4-8)
1. What is Jesus called in this passage?
2. What are we called? What's the difference between Jesus and us in this building?
3. How was Jesus treated? What was the result? What does that say to us, who are part of the same building?
4. What are some characteristics of a stone? How do these apply to the Christian?
5. Why is it valuable to have different kinds of stone when you're building? How does this principle apply to our group?

III. **Priests in the Same Temple** (2:9)
1. What are the privileges of priests?
2. What are the responsibilities of priests?
3. How do other people view priests? Is this good or bad?
4. How should priests live in relation to other priests?
5. How should priests live in relation to other people?

IV. **Citizens of the Same Nation** (2:9-10)
1. How are these citizens described?
2. What does "a people belonging to God" mean?
3. How does the ownership of something increase its value? Give some examples. Now apply that truth to the Christian who is "owned" by God.
4. Where should Christians find their source of self-worth? Where do we usually try to find it?
5. What "nation" are we a part of? Where is this nation located?
6. Read Philippians 3:20. What insight does this verse add to the words of Peter?
7. What is our responsibility to each other as citizens of God's nation? What happens when citizens fight each other?
8. What is our responsibility to other people?

Conclude your Bible study by reviewing the reasons Peter outlines for maintaining harmony and unity in your group. If time permits or need demands, briefly discuss any problems that have been dividing the group. Ask group members to resolve that they will make an effort to heal wounds and promote harmony. Ask for specific ways they can accomplish these goals. If group members can verbalize their decisions, encourage them to do so. Close your study with prayer.

Fragile Friends

This exercise alerts kids to the fragility of other people and the importance of being gentle with each other. It can be used anytime but is especially appropriate for a camp or retreat.

Give each person a raw egg. Tell them to punch a small hole in each end of the egg with a pin or nail and then blow on one end of the egg. The contents of the egg will be forced out the other end, and they'll have an empty, unbroken eggshell. They can seal the egg up with a small amount of candle wax. The insides of the eggs can be served next morning for breakfast.

Discuss with the kids how the delicate nature of the eggshells reflects the delicate nature of our relationships with each other. Then give the group several thin, colored marking pens that will write on the eggshells. Have the kids write the names of several kids in the group on the eggshell. While doing this they need to be careful not to break the egg.

Now each person must carry her egg with her all day, devising some means of protection and accepting responsibility for its condition. At the end of the day, collect the eggs, whole or smashed, and discuss the feelings of responsibility, the task of caring, and the problems of protecting something so fragile. Tie this in with how we treat each other personally and how we can avoid hurting each other.

Friendship Notes

To open up communication lines among members of your group and strengthen the community-building process, print some note paper like the samples below. Write the beginnings of sentences to start a thought, leaving room to complete each thought. Write in the names of the kids in the group on the salutation part of the letter so that each person in the group will get one, then pass them out. Allow several minutes for the kids to complete the notes, then collect them and "deliver" them to each person they are written to.

After the kids have read their notes, they can read them aloud to the group (optional). Some will be humorous, some will be serious, but they will all lead to better communication among group members.

Dear _____ ,

Today I was thinking about you and _____

_____

I hope we can _____

_____

You have been _____

_____

Whenever we are together _____

_____

Let's plan to _____

_____ sometime soon.

Your friend,

_____

Dear _____ ,

I'm glad you're in our youth group because _____

_____

When we can spend time together, why don't we

_____

I think that you _____

_____

I know that others think you are _____

_____

As we look forward to the future _____

_____

Your friend,

_____

Gift Guessing

This game helps kids focus on the discovery and use of spiritual gifts. Prepare ahead of time adhesive labels with various gifts or qualities on them like teacher, counselor, leader, helper, listener. When the students arrive, place a label on everyone's back without telling them what it is. Everyone then mingles around the room and tries to guess what their gift is. Each person asks someone else "What is my gift?" The person who is asked *may not talk* but communicate only by pantomime or charades.

Once a person has guessed her gift, the sticker may be moved from her back to her front (like a name tag) and she may help others guess. After everyone has guessed his gift, he is allowed to exchange his gift with someone else if he would like, or he may get a new name tag and write any gift on it which he thinks is more apt to be his gift.

Follow up with a time of discussion and affirmation of each other's gifts and abilities.

Gifts of Beauty

The following is a short skit that effectively opens up discussion on the concept of the body of Christ or on spiritual gifts (1 Corinthians 12, Ephesians 4, Romans 12). Each participant in the skit should ham up his role to emphasize the part of the body that he is playing. The eyes, for instance, could wear some of those giant glasses, and the mouth could use a megaphone. You might want to label each actor with a sign telling what part of the body he is.

The script below can be used as it is, or you can add other parts of the body and create your own dialogue.

Gifts of Beauty

Cast: Ear
Eye
Hand
Mouth
Nose
Feet

Ear: Where is Hand when I need him?

Eye: He's over there picking Nose.

Ear: What! He's always goofing off when I need him!

Mouth: What do you need him for anyway?

Ear: I need him to clean out the wax in me.

Hand: I don't know why you guys are yelling at me. Look, Foot's in Mouth!

Ear: You both are a couple of goof-offs.

Eye: To be honest, we've all been goofing off a lot lately.

Nose: Yeah, look how bad we've made this kid we're on look.

Ear: I hear the ugliest girl in town turned him down for a date.

Mouth: Thank goodness! I'd hate to have to kiss *her* goodnight!

Feet: Does anybody know how we can help him look better?

Eye: I was reading the Bible the other day, and it said that everyone has a spiritual gift. Maybe if we all find our spiritual gifts we can make this kid look a lot better.

Everyone: Yeah! Let's go.

Some time later

Eye: Well, did all of you find your gifts?

Everyone: Yeah!

Nose: My gift is to smell all of the wonderful things God has made.

Eye: My gift is to read the Scripture and to see the good in others.

Ear: My gift is to hear the sounds of nature and the voices of people.

Mouth: My gift is to tell others about God.

Hand: My gift is to help other people.

Feet: My gift is to take us places where we can use our gifts.

Eye: I'm sure glad I found my gift.

Nose: Me, too. I was getting tired of running anyway.

Give and Get Game

This simulation game is simple but teaches some profound truths concerning the value of being a *giver*.

Have everyone reach into his pocket or purse and produce a small amount of change. Any amount will do. It works best when people use real money. If they don't have money, give them some or use play money. The game consists of three one-minute rounds.

The first round is a *giving* round. Announce that when the signal is given, the kids should try to give away as much money as they can. The second round is a *getting* round. During this round the kids should try to get as much money as possible. There are no rules for how you give or get money. The third round is optional. It can be either a *giving* or *getting* round. Let them vote with a show of hands and then do whichever they decide.

After this short but active game, discuss some of these questions:
1. How many kids came out ahead? How many lost money?
2. Which round did you enjoy the most? Why?
3. How did you feel during the *getting* round? During the *giving* round?
4. Did greed enter into this game?
5. Did you place a limit on how much you were going to give?
6. Did you have a strategy for getting?
7. What did you learn about giving from this game?

Giving Spirit

An ancient legend tells of a small group of monks who were told in a vision that one of them was the Messiah. Since they didn't know which one of them was actually the Messiah, they all treated each other *as if* each one of them were the Messiah. People were so attracted by the great love they showed to each other that their small monastery tripled in size.

This idea is based on that concept. At the beginning of the year, everyone in the group is assigned a "Giving Spirit," but no one knows who his Giving Spirit is except for the leader who makes the assignments. A Giving Spirit does several things for the person she's assigned to: she prays for her regularly; she remembers her with gifts on her birthday and other special occasions (secretly, of course); and she does other "nice" things for her person whenever the occasion arises. Because this is all done secretly, everyone is encouraged to treat everyone else in the group *as if* he were his Giving Spirit. He wouldn't want to do or say anything bad to the person who is his Giving Spirit!

At the end of year, throw a party at which all the Giving Spirits are revealed. Everyone can share Giving Spirit stories and thank those people who were faithful to the role.

Great Moments in History

One way to strengthen the sense of community in a youth group is to remind members of the great things that have happened in the life of the group over the years. Most teenagers have a short memory.

Why not create a bulletin board in a prominent place to display photos, clippings, and other memorabilia of all the really exciting or meaningful times the youth group has enjoyed together? This will prolong those "mountaintop" experiences and help kids to look forward to the future as well.

Group Baseball Cards

Here's a great idea for large youth groups. Print baseball cards for each member of your group with photos on one side and vital statistics on the other—address, phone, age, grade in school, right- or left-handed, likes and dislikes, batting average, etc. Give each person many copies of his own card, and then encourage everyone to collect a "complete set" by trading with others. It's fun and a great community builder.

Group Juggle

This circle game is something like hot potato, with a dash of Concentration. Throw a ball to one person in a standing circle of kids. That person throws it to another, and so on until everyone has received and thrown the ball once—but exactly once. No one should get the ball a second time, which means each player needs to remember where the ball's been. If your group's frustration threshold is high, increase the speed of the game and add more balls.

Group Photo

At least once a year, have your group pose for a group photo to enlarge and reproduce so that everybody gets a copy. If the budget allows, make poster-sized photos that the kids can hang on their bedroom walls. Also post a photo in the church lobby or wherever adults congregate. For added fun let the kids choose a creative theme for the photo like "It's a jungle out there " (in safari attire) or "A typical church service" (kids looking bored, distracted, or unruly). A group photo helps kids visualize themselves as a unit, a community of faith.

Group Story

Here's a crazy way to illustrate group unity. Give everyone in the group an index card. One card has "Once upon a time . . . " written on it, and all the other cards have "And then . . . " written on them. One card also has "The End" written at the bottom.

Ask the group to write part of a story on their cards. It can be about anything, but made as interesting, exciting, or emotional as possible. Then collect all the cards and read the completed story. It will be disjointed, but all the kids enjoy it anyway because they wrote it.

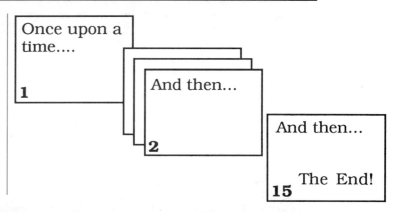

Group Up

This mixer is best when played with groups of 25 or more. As everyone mills around the room, the leader yells out a qualifying characteristic like "Same first initial!" Quickly, the group members try to find others who have the same first initial as they do and stick together. Whoever is in the largest group wins that round of the game.

Possibilities for qualifying characteristics are endless. They can be informative or a little wild and crazy. Some examples:
Same favorite TV show
Same age
Same birth month
Same brand of shoes
Same number of people in your immediate family
Same color eyes

Guardian Angels

At the beginning of your next camp or retreat, assign to each person a same-sex partner that they don't know very well. At the first meeting, after the partners introduce themselves and listen to the guidelines, give them a few minutes to get to know each other a little better. For the rest of the retreat, those two young people are each other's "Guardian Angels."

Guardian Angels must sit together at certain meetings and during certain meals. They agree to pray for each other each day of the retreat. They also perform at least one act of Christian service for the other person during the retreat. At the end of the retreat, let some of the kids tell how being a Guardian Angel changed the retreat for them. Or let them share how their Guardian Angel made the retreat special for them.

A variation is to assign Guardian Angels secretly. The rules still apply, but the caring and acts of kindness are done anonymously. At the end of the camp, reveal identities.

Guess Who

For an easy get-acquainted activity, ask each young person to write down something about themselves that probably no one else knows. If she has trouble coming up with a unique contribution, suggest an unusual pet she might have, or a weird snack or sandwich she likes. If you get really desperate, ask for her mother's middle name. Collect all the responses.

Next, instruct the group to listen to the clues as you read them and try to guess the person they think the clue identifies. Give 1000 points for each correct guess, everyone keeping his own score. For a prize give away a copy of the church directory or an address book.

Handcuffed

For an exercise in problem-solving and communication, pair off the kids giving each pair two pieces of string about three feet long. Each person should tie the ends of the string around both wrists so that the string connects his right and left wrists. But before he does this, he need to make sure that his partner's string passes behind his own string, linking the partners together (see diagram).

Now see how long it takes for each couple to disconnect themselves *without breaking or untying the strings*. It can be done.

Here's how: Pass the center of one partner's string through the wrist loop and over the hand of the other partner.

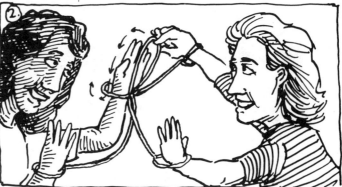

Heartboards

One way to make communication among the group members fun is to hang a bulletin board or "heartboard" up where kids exchange notes, advertise needs, post giveaways, and read announcements. Print up youth group memos to encourage the exchange of personal notes. The kids can save postage by using the board for exchanging birthday cards, Christmas cards, and invitations to group events. See to it that everyone in the group gets a personal note with their name on it regularly. The more the kids receive, the more they will think to give.

Cut one or two large hearts (4' X 8') out of Masonite and paint them bright red. Drill evenly spaced holes around the edge of the hearts and mount metal clips with nuts and bolts to the board. Paint someone's name on each clip. Hang these heartboards in areas that receive the most youth traffic.

Homework Night

Set aside a regular night every week or every other week for kids to meet and do homework together. Any student is invited to participate as long as he abides by three rules: 1) You must have homework to come. 2) You must keep conversation at a quiet level. 3) If you goof off, you go home. These times not only provide academic assistance, but also give kids practice in reaching out and helping one another.

How Can I Help?

Because teenagers naturally spend more time together and talk more to each other than they do to adults, it's a good idea to equip kids to help each other when a crisis or problem occurs. This idea may encourage better peer ministry among your students.

On the next page are several case studies designed to help kids think through some of the issues involved in helping a friend or acquaintance through a crisis. Print them up and distribute them to the kids, use an overhead projector and a transparency of the case studies, or simply read them to the group and let them respond.

Issues that should surface include these:

- Is it best to encourage the person to talk about the problem or to try and get their mind off it?
- Does it help people to tell them that their problems aren't really so bad compared to other people's problems?
- When is it good to bring God's perspective into the conversation? When isn't it good?
- What do you do when someone seems extremely depressed or suicidal?

If you are not trained as a counselor, it'd be advisable to invite a professional counselor to attend this meeting to help deal with issues like these.

How Many F's

Tie this little experiment in with a lesson on awareness. Print up some half-sheets like the one at the right and hand them out face down to each person in the group. Everyone should turn the page over and begin at the same time, working alone. (Try it yourself before you read the answer that follows.)

> Read the following sentence in the enclosed block. After reading the sentence, go back and count the F's. You have *30 seconds*.
>
> FINISHED FILES ARE THE RESULT OF YEARS OF SCIENTIFIC STUDY COMBINED WITH THE EXPERIENCE OF YEARS.
>
> Number of F's in the block _____ .

Case Studies

Read each situation carefully. Consider both what has actually happened as well as how the person is reacting to what has happened. As a group, rank the responses from best to worst based on what you know about the situation. Discuss together the strengths and weaknesses of each response. Be sure that each member of your group shares in making the decisions.

Situation #1

Fourteen-year-old Susan has been your friend for a long time. You notice that she seems very angry and irritable one day. You ask her what the problem is. Susan pauses for a moment, then blurts out, "Mom and Dad told me last night that they're getting divorced."

RESPONSES
1. I'm really sorry to hear that, Susan.
2. Why are they doing that, Susan?
3. You can come and stay with me for a while.
4. I know exactly how you feel. My parents fight a lot, too.
5. [Make up your own response.]

Situation #2

Seventeen-year-old Ben is in your calculus class. You've heard through the grapevine that Ben's application to MIT has been rejected. You and Ben aren't great friends, but he has told you that he's looked forward to attending MIT since he was a little kid. During class you notice that his eyes are kind of puffy and red, like he's been crying. You have a chance to talk to him after class.

RESPONSES
1. Hey, buddy, cheer up! With your grades, there are a dozen other colleges that will be excited to have you!
2. I was sorry to hear that you didn't get into MIT, Ben.
3. Ben, there's going to be a great party tonight. How about going with me?
4. It's too bad about MIT. I guess God must have some other plans for you.
5. You look kind of down today, Ben. What's the matter?
6. [Make up your own response.]

Situation #3

Sixteen-year-old Mary has a locker next to yours. Report cards have come out today. You're feeling a great sense of relief over your geometry grade. Mary, however, appears very upset. She is extremely agitated and is walking back and forth, talking to herself. You ask her what the problem is. "My grades are terrible," she replies. "There is no way I can go home with these grades. I'm really afraid of what my dad might do to me. What am I going to do?"

RESPONSES
1. Maybe you should just come home with me this afternoon.
2. What are you afraid of, Mary?
3. How bad were your grades?
4. Maybe you could just not tell them about the grades, or try to change them on the report card.
5. Come on, Mary. Everyone's parents get upset with grades.
6. [Make up your own response.]

Situation #4

Ted, a junior at your school, has been your best friend for as long as you can remember. He's seemed to be very depressed lately. He's tired all the time. He doesn't want to go out and have fun with you like he used to. You know that things are not going well with his parents, and that his girlfriend broke up with him last week. Until now you've avoided the subject directly, trying instead to encourage him to do fun things and cheer him up. You've just asked him what's been bothering him so much. "I really don't know," he says. "Sometimes things just seem so hopeless. Lately I'm not sure if it's all worth it."

RESPONSES
1. Everyone gets down sometimes, Ted. I'm sure you'll feel better soon.
2. I'll pray for you, Ted. God understands your feelings and wants to help you.
3. Maybe you just need to get out and do some fun stuff. Let's go to the mall together and get your mind off your problems.
4. What seems so hopeless, Ted?
5. What do you mean, "I'm not sure if it's all worth it"?
6. [Make up your own response.]

After the 30 seconds are up, ask the group how many F's they counted. Most people find three or four. Only a few count all six F's. People tend to overlook the word *OF* because they aren't looking at the smaller words. This test is sometimes given in driver training classes to demonstrate how we often fail to see motorcycles because we aren't looking for something so small.

Explain to the youths that we do the same thing with people. We often miss the good qualities in other people because we aren't looking for them. We tend to look instead for the things we want to see—usually the bad things—to make ourselves look good by comparison.

Continue exploring this idea with an exercise like "What Others Think of Me" (page 91) that helps kids look for the good in each other and affirm each other's gifts and abilities.

Human Bingo

Here's a fun way to learn everybody's name. Give each person a Bingo card (like the sample below) with a clue in each square. The object of the game is to get the signature of the person in the group who fits the various descriptions. The first person to complete five blocks in a row gets Bingo.

Someone who owns a dog	Someone who is wearing contact lenses	A foreign student	Someone who owns a motorcycle	Someone with three brothers
Someone who is going bald	Someone with red hair	Someone who got an "A" in English	Someone who just ate at McDonald's	Someone with blond hair at least 12 inches long
An amateur photographer	Sign your own name	Someone who has been to Canada	Someone who weighs less than 100 pounds	Someone who plays football
Someone who likes to jog	Someone wearing blue socks	Someone who drives an imported car	Someone who owns a horse	Someone born out of the U.S.
Someone with a pimple	Someone who can play a guitar	Someone who had a bad date over the weekend	Someone who has a cowboy hat	Someone who weighs over 200 pounds

Human Crossword

Make up a crossword puzzle similar to the one pictured here. Plan your crossword so that several names of your young people will fit into the puzzle, but add extra word-spaces for surprise entries. In the allotted time, fill in as many spaces as possible in your crossword puzzle with the names of people in our youth group. You can use any combination of their first names, middle names, last names, or nicknames. Letters must match up when adjoining names. Use the freebies at the bottom for those names that just don't fit. (Abbreviations are allowed, within reason: Rodney/Rod is okay, but Darren/Dar won't pass.) Award prizes to those who fit the most names into their puzzle.

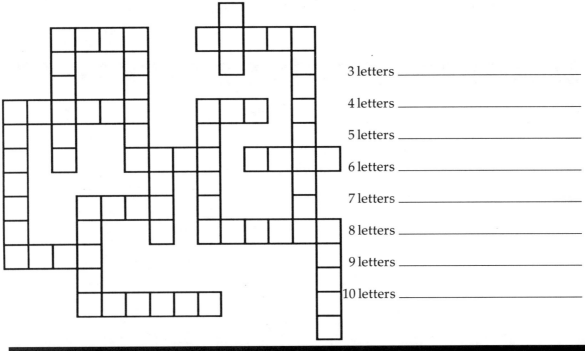

3 letters _____

4 letters _____

5 letters _____

6 letters _____

7 letters _____

8 letters _____

9 letters _____

10 letters _____

I Never

Give each person in this discussion game 10 tokens of some kind— marbles, matches, pennies, buttons. The point of the game is for kids to collect others' tokens by telling them how life has passed them by—"I've *never* ridden a roller coaster," "I've *never* been to Disneyland," "I've *never* eaten at Taco Bell"—taking turns relating life experiences that most have had, but not them. Then everyone who experienced the event must give a token to that player.

Kids should tell the truth and use good taste in choosing what experiences they share. Your students will usually see that everyone has missed out on something in life. And in this game the person who has missed the most takes home the most.

Identity

As your group enters the room, have them fill out a name tag and drop it in a basket. After everyone has arrived, have them stand in a circle. Pass the basket around for each person to take a name tag (not their own) without letting anyone else see the name on the tag.

Then ask everyone to turn and stick the name tags they chose onto the backs of the one on their left. The object of the game now becomes for the players to discover the name printed on their backs by asking only questions answered by a yes or no ("Do I have red hair?" "Am I wearing jeans?"). Players can ask only two questions of the same person.

When a player discovers whose name she's wearing, she must go to that person, place her hands on his shoulders, and follow him around the room. As more and more players discover who they "are," the lines of players with hands on shoulders will lengthen—until the last person learns his identity.

Identity Masks

This exercise generates healthy discussion on self-image, relationships, and the need for affirmation. Cut eye holes in large grocery sacks in order to make head masks. On the front of each mask write in red one name of several that reflect the standard types of personalities on most high-school campuses; below each name, in black, write how that person is to be treated. For example:

- Joe Cool
  —ask me to parties
  —accept me
  —laugh at all I say
  —tell me how cool I am
- Patty Party
  —invite me to any social gathering
  —accept me
  —act wild and uninhibited around me
- Betty Bod
  —ask me out
  —accept me
  —flirt with me
  —tell me how good looking I am
- Jerry Jock
  —tell me how strong I am
  —talk about sports around me
  —flirt with me
  —ask me to be on your sports team
- Ivan Intellect
  —respect me for my "smarts"
  —ask me to sit by you in class
  —tell me how intelligent I am
- Steven Stud
  —ask me out
  —tell me how good looking I am
  —flirt with me
  —accept me; get in good with me
- Bryan Bookworm
  —reject me
  —tell me I'm boring
  —poke fun at me

- Ralph Runt
  —kid me about being small
  —reject me subtly
  —act big around me
- Andy Klutz
  —reject me
  —tell about the dumb things I do
  —tell a joke about me
- Paul Problem
  —feel sorry for me
  —tell me how you understand
  —ask me if it's going better today
  —don't respect me
- Susie Dumblonde
  —treat me as spacy
  —flirt with me
- Nelson Nerd
  —reject me
  —make nasty remarks to me
  —make fun of me
- Wanda Wallflower
  —reject me
  —don't acknowledge me
  —don't speak to me even if I talk
- Ms. Liberation
  —accept me
  —tell me how good I am in sports
  —act free around me
  —don't ask me out or tell me I'm pretty
- Ted Tough Guy
  —act afraid of me
  —ask me if I've heard any off-color jokes lately
  —try to get on my good side
  —ask me to help you get even with somebody

Tell all participants to shut their eyes as they receive their masks and put them on; this way they won't read what's written on them. (Try giving the negative roles to the outgoing, accepted kids and the positive roles to quieter, less-noticed kids.) Then tell them to mill around the room and guess the type of person they are by how others respond to them. Remind them to keep in touch with their feelings—especially with their feelings about themselves.

After they've mingled for a while and begun to absorb their "personalities" from the remarks and attitudes of others, get them together to discuss how who we are comes largely from others' opinions of us; how labels are not our real selves; that God's opinion of us is what should shape our lives.

Inclusive Elections

Youth-group officers are the ones in many groups who run the meetings and plan the events. Often, however, officers are merely a group of close friends or the most popular teenagers. To prevent this and to give everyone an equal opportunity to serve, try some of these ideas:
• List all the offices on separate slips of paper (mixed in with a sufficient number of blank slips, of course), and choose officers by allowing members to draw the slips from a paper bag.
• Let members write secretly who they think would be best for each office. (Youth leaders can sort out and appoint the choices.)

• Before a meeting write on note cards the offices to be filled, one office per card. Then tape the cards at random on the bottom of several of the chairs in the youth room. When the kids enter the room and take their seats to begin the meeting, let them discover who the next slate of officers are.
• Change officers every three months or so, and allow no one to hold an office more than once.
• Only after everyone has served as an officer, hold a genuine election. By this time group members will have observed how different classmates perform—and their votes will be wise ones.

Intergenerational Interviews

Community building in the church-at-large should also include the older adults of the church. Divide your youth group into "interview teams," and send them to the homes of adult church members with tape recorders or note pads and a list of questions like these:
• What are some of your early memories of attending church?
• Will you tell us about your decision to follow Christ—when you decided, the circumstances surrounding your decision, etc.?
• What have the Christian faith and the church meant to you and your family down through the years?
• What is a favorite Bible verse or Bible story? Why?
After the teams return to church, ask each of them to share their answers and the feelings

they had during the interviews.

You'll need to call the adults in advance to arrange the visits, and you may even want to inform them ahead of time of the questions you'll ask, too. You may want to let the adults know that the teams will bring with them some small refreshment so that they'll not feel obligated to serve food themselves. And make sure you have enough drivers and that the homes you visit are near enough to conduct the interviews and still get back to church with time to spare for discussion.

Adults invariably enjoy visits like these, and it gives them a chance to share their faith with the young people. Not to mention the benefit of the teenagers listening for a few moments to the memories and the faith of their elders.

Interrogation

This get-acquainted activity spurs your group to get to know new-comers better. It's especially fun when the subject of the interrogation is a youth sponsor.

First divide into teams and assign to each of them a person to be interrogated. You then tell the teams that you have in your pocket a list of 20 questions that you will later ask each team about their subjects (e.g., "What is his favorite food?," "When is her birthday?"). Meanwhile, they have 10 minutes to drill their subjects and get as much information out of them as possible in order to correctly answer your questions. The team that does the most thorough job of interrogating its subject will tend, of course, to answer correctly most of your questions. The team with the most correct answers to your questions wins.

Interview Mixer

To occasionally encourage good communication and interaction in your group, try this: divide your kids into pairs. Give everyone a few minutes to interview their partners, asking a few selected questions that you chose in advance. For example:
• Who is your greatest hero? Why?
• Is there a day in your life you'd like to live over? Why?
• What do you like best about this youth group?
• If we pray for you, what should we pray about?

After the interviews ask the teens to introduce their partners and share the answers they received during the questioning period. "Interview Mixer" can be played from time to time, with different questions each time.

Jobs for Everyone

Want to exemplify the value of including everyone as an important part of the group? Listed below are jobs for a group bus trip. Either let the kids sign up for the ones they want, or you can assign them. You'll find an otherwise long and boring bus ride become a lot more enthusiastic and positive when everyone has something to do. If you need more jobs, throw in some crazy ones—Chief Tire Thumper, On-Board Photographer, Visual-Perception Technician (who cleans windshield), etc.

• **Secretary**—Keeps track of pertinent information from Odometer Orator, Timekeeper, Personal Secretary, and others in order to compile *The Story of Our Workcamp Experience*. Will keep and collate all information from others upon trip's end.
• **Bus Attendant #1**—Checks oil, adds if necessary. Inspects for underhood leaks or malfunctions. Assists in fueling the bus. Checks front lights and front safety signals.
• **Bus Attendant #2**—Checks tires, rear lights, and rear safety signals. Assists in fueling the bus. Records gallons and expense.
• **Personal Secretary**—Keeps track of humorous and otherwise interesting incidents as they occur en route to and during the workcamp.

- **Environmental Control Technician #1**—Ensures that center aisle and right side of bus (facing the front) are kept free of debris. Ensures that all windows on right side are closed at end of trip. Periodically passes wastebasket to messy passengers.
- **Environmental Control Technician #2**—Ensures that center aisle and left side of bus (facing the front) are kept free of debris. Ensures that all windows on left side are closed at end of trip. Keeps track of the messiest person, who must help clean the bus when we get home.
- **Security Engineer #1**—Makes sure bus is not tampered with at rest stops. Stands guard while Security Engineer #2 pursues necessary comforts.
- **Security Engineer #2**—Makes sure bus is not tampered with at rest stops while Security Engineer #1 pursues necessary comforts.
- **Sound Technician #1**—Supervises the operation of the tape deck—volume, balance, tone, rewind.
- **Sound Technician #2**—Supervises the selection of tapes, relying on passenger input and sensitivity. Checks tapes for backlash. Sees that they are placed in proper cases. Assists Sound Technician #1 with any complex operational procedures.
- **Interior Recreation Assistant #1**—Assists Recreation Director in leading games and coordinating resources for activities. Reports on right-side-of-bus non-participants in group games for public embarrassment later.
- **Interior Recreation Assistant #2**—Assists Recreation Director in leading games and coordinating resources for activities. Reports on left-side-of-bus non-participants in group games for public embarrassment later.
- **Timekeeper**—Keeps track of time from departure to arrival. Clocks the amount of time spent at rest areas, food establishments, etc.
- **Assistant Timekeeper**—Assists timekeeper by arranging chronological particulars. Helps Timekeeper with simultaneous timing of who spends the most time in the bathrooms, who sleeps the most, etc.
- **Official Nose Counter**—Counts noses to make sure no one has more than one. Reports directly to the driver when all noses are accounted for. (We do not discriminate against people without noses, but non-nosed passengers are asked to wear a reasonable facsimile in order to be counted. Plastic noses are acceptable.)
- **Odometer Orator**—Records odometer reading of miles traveled. Reports reading to Timekeeper. Lets passengers know how many miles the entire trip is, start to finish, as well as mileage between rest stops, food stops, and gas stops.
- **Assistant to the Driver**—Assists driver with map reading, conversation, and the conveying of driver's messages to passengers. Receives a percentage of all snacks intended for the driver. Enforces the prohibition of taco chips/corn chips in the bus. (Taco chips and corn chips stink in a hot bus.)
- **Recreation Director**—Protects passengers from boredom by involving them periodically in games, quizzes, skits, etc.
- **Stupidity Discouragers**—All passengers shall be employed in this capacity. Read here what is stupid:
  - It is stupid to litter inside or outside the bus.
  - It is stupid to be so loud on the bus that everyone gets a headache.
  - It is stupid to stick anything out the bus window (arms legs, heads, hands, friends, etc.).
  - It is stupid to bring soft drinks on the bus (ice water okay).
  - It is stupid to buy Big Gulps, Slurpies, or gallon-size drinks because no one's bladder is large enough to contain them.
  - It is stupid to do anything unsafe.

Knots

This fun group game requires teamwork and cooperation. If your group is larger than 10, divide into groups of 10 or less. As each group stands in a circle, all group members should grab each other's hands in the center so that there is a knot of hands at the hub of each circle. Both right and left hands should be connected with someone else. Two rules: you cannot hold hands with the person standing to your right or left; and you cannot connect both your hands with the same person.

The object of the game is now, without letting go of hands, to untangle the knot—that is, to unravel arms so that group members end up still in a circle, but holding hands with people left and right of them, not in a knot in the middle. Grips can be adjusted, but no letting go. It's amazing that, in most cases, it can be done.

Kool-Aid Koinonia

To illustrate how each member of the body of Christ is important, select three volunteers. Cover the nose of volunteer 1 and tie his hands behind his back. Blindfold volunteer 2, cover her mouth, and tie her hands behind her back. Blindfold volunteer 3, and cover her nose and mouth.

Place three drinking glasses on a table. One glass contains Kool-Aid or punch, another contains colored water and looks identical to the Kool-Aid, and the third is empty.

The object is for the three volunteers to work together to accomplish the following:
1. Select which glass has the Kool-Aid.
2. Pour the Kool-Aid into the empty glass.

3. Serve the Kool-Aid to volunteer 1.

Since volunteer 1 is the only one who can speak, he calls out instructions to the other two. Volunteer 2 is the only one who can smell, so she sniffs the glasses to determine which is the Kool-Aid. Volunteer 3 is the only one with hands free, so she pours the Kool-Aid and serves it to volunteer 1.

One entertaining way to do this is to have three groups of three try it, bringing them in, one group at a time, before the rest of you. When they come in, explain what they have to do and see which group can complete the task in the shortest time.

Lap Sit

Teaching the value of working together and of group unity, this initiative game is best with a group of 20 kids or more.

After everyone forms a circle, shoulder to shoulder, ask them to turn to their right—now they are single file, facing the same direction. They should be about six inches apart.

On the count of three, have everyone sit down in the lap of the person behind them. If it's done right, everyone in the circle will have a seat on another's lap, and no one will end up on the ground. If it's *not* done right—well, . . . So try it a few times if you fail on the first try.

If you master "Lap Sit" and the group feels like taking it a step further, ask them to attempt walking while seated in the circle. Everyone must simultaneously move their legs left, right, left, etc.

License-Plate Name Tags

Give your kids blank "license plates" (paper or cardboard in the shape of a car's plates) and marking pens, then let them design their own creative, personalized license plates (like those you see on the road: KLULESS, N LUV, SWEET16, etc.). Encourage a creative combination of numbers and letters. Limit only the number of digits or letters that can be used on the plate.

Allow your teenagers to share the significance of their plates' messages and give prizes for the most original, humorous, creative, etc. They can be worn as name tags for the rest of the event.

Lights of the Round Table

Do you want to build community with small discipleship or study groups? Ask a group of your students to commit to meeting one evening a week for Bible study and prayer. If possible, find a round table in a special place where you study by candlelight. (You can make a round table top easily out of plywood if necessary.) A round table in a secluded setting creates more intimacy and fewer distractions. You might consider also making "Lights of the Round Table" Bible covers to encourage commitment and a sense of belonging to the group.

Lines of Communication

If the body of Christ is to be strengthened, it's crucial for teenagers to visualize and evaluate the lines of communication and relationships between each other in the group as well as between them and the church community at large.

Divide your young people into groups of four to eight, each group led by a sponsor who has been prepared for this exercise. Everybody is given an envelope containing several pieces of construction paper cut into various shapes, a large (14 x 22) piece of construction paper, and a pencil. Glue should also be available.

Each group leader explains that the several pieces of construction paper in their envelopes represent those in the youth group (or the whole church). The students should creatively and honestly choose the shape or combination of shapes that they feel best represent themselves. Then they should write their own names on this shape.

Now for the large piece of paper—it represents the whole group (or church). The students should place their paper symbols of themselves where they see themselves in relation to the rest of the group (e.g., in the center of things, or on the sidelines). Next, they should choose shapes of paper that they think best represent the other people in the group or church, and then write these persons' names on them. These "people" should then be placed on the large sheet in such a way that their positions represent their relationships to you. Glue them all down.

Finally, draw the lines of communication that exist between you and the others using the following types of lines:

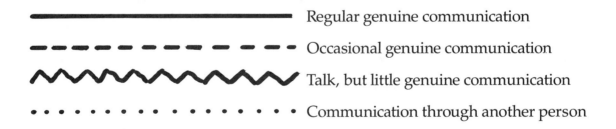

Regular genuine communication

Occasional genuine communication

Talk, but little genuine communication

Communication through another person

(show by the route of the dots which person the communication passes through)

Other types of lines can be added for other types of communication (or non-communication).

Wrap up the exercise by allowing the participants to voluntarily share and explain their sheet to the rest of their small group. Each person should also be encouraged to share which relationships they feel should be changed or where communications could be improved, and how they propose to do this.

Line Up

Whether you play "Line Up" just for fun or whether you add a debriefing afterwards in order to discuss everyone's feelings, your kids will have to use teamwork.

Draw on the floor two parallel lines that are about 12 inches apart. The group should then line up between the two lines; no one should stand on the lines. The object of the game is to reverse the order your students are standing in *without anyone stepping outside the lines*. It's tough to do without falling and requires a great deal of cooperation and hanging on to each other.

But the game's not over yet! Next have the group line up according to birth date or height or *any* classification, and the same rules apply. If you have more than one group participating, have them compete to see which group can accomplish the switch in the shortest time.

A variation: line the group up on a low wall or curb or log or plank, and the object is to rearrange the group's order without stepping off the object.

Listening Test

It can be shocking to realize how much of our energy in conversation is used for "ego-speaking" and self-expression rather than for listening. The "Listening Test" can make your kids become aware of how much they really listen to what others are saying.

First, prepare four cards:

Your favorites:
- What do you like most about school?
- What is your favorite time of year?
- What is your favorite Bible verse?

The pits:
- What bugs you the most about school?
- What is your least favorite vegetable?
- When were you last bummed out?

Exposing weaknesses:
- What is your worst personality weakness?
- What is your most annoying habit?
- What is your worst spiritual weakness?

Revealing strengths:
- What is your most positive personality trait?
- What is your greatest skill?
- What is your best spiritual strength?

Divide everyone into groups of no more than five people. Each group should be given one of the four cards. Everyone in the group then briefly answers the questions on the card. After five minutes or so the groups exchange cards, and group members have new questions to answer to each other.

After all four cards have circulated through all the groups, everyone is given a sheet of paper and told to list every fact they can remember from the answers given in their discussion group. Those with the better memories, of course, have some advantage—but those who really tuned in and listened to others in their group (rather than concentrating on their own responses) will be able to recall the most.

A discussion of the importance of listening would be a good way to wrap up this exercise. Relevant Scriptures include Proverbs 18:2,13; Proverb s 22:17; and Ecclesiastes 3:7.

Live-In Lock-In

Select a week during the school year when your entire youth group can have a week-long "lock-in" at the church. Have the kids bring a sleeping bag, pillow, alarm clock, school books and supplies, Bible, clothes for the week, trashbag for laundry, money for school lunches, and so on. Each morning, breakfast is provided and the kids leave for school as usual. But after school, they return to the church for recreation, study times (tutors, computers, etc. provided if necessary), the evening meal, an evening Bible study or lesson, and bedtime. A service project can be included (like painting classrooms at the church) or you can plan some outside activities like bowling or attending a ball game.

A "Live-In Lock-In" can be a great way to build community as it provides an extended period of time for kids to be together, plus many of the other community-building activities described in this book.

Love Target

In the middle of your circled, seated group, set one chair—the circle of students is the "target"; the center chair, the "bull's-eye."

The idea is for one individual to sit in the center chair and the rest of the group to take turns complimenting and affirming that person (the target of these words should say nothing), like "Jim, I really appreciate the way you—" or "Becky, one quality about you that really impresses me is—."

Play "Love Target" periodically as a way to allow your youths to affirm and minister to kids who are in especial need of some affirmation and encouragement.

Mailboxes

"Mailboxes" encourages communication and helps kids feel part of the group—ingredients essential to community building.

Get several wooden soda crates that are partitioned so that a soda bottle fits in each slot. Remove the bottom so you can cover it with brightly colored paper, then replace it and hang the crate near your teen meeting room. Assign everyone in the group a slot to be their own "mailbox" at church—a convenient way to distribute fliers to your regular teens as well as a nice way for them to communicate to each other if they have special notes for each other.

As your group grows, get more crates. Make sure new teens are quickly given a niche so that they feel the belonging so important to adolescents.

Make a Melody

Photocopy the musical note pattern on the next page and distribute one copy to each of your students; also distribute crayons or colored felt-tip markers. They can personalize the notes with their names and any other writing or doodles or designs they like. The final product should in some way reflect their own uniqueness. Collect the finished notes, and, finally, have the group choose a hymn or other song that they feel reflects their group.

After the meeting, find a simple arrangement of the song they've chosen. On a long sheet of butcher paper, draw a large musical staff, arrange your kids' notes on it so that they trace the melody of the group's theme song, and hang the "composition" in a prominent place. At your next get-together, talk about how poorly the song would sound with just one note missing, and how every note—every person—is important to the song.

MAKE A MELODY

Color, design, or decorate your note any way you want. Use this note as a pattern for a construction-paper note or collage a note or draw your face on it— be creative! Make it *your* note, personal and unique, just as your life is personal and unique.

Your life is part of a song to Jesus, so sing and make melody in your heart to the Lord!

Marching Band

Just for fun, lead your group in forming letters or words on a field—like a marching band does at half time—so that everyone is part of the letter or word. Position yourself as high as you can and still be heard (in order to observe the letters being formed and call for adjust-ments). When you call out the letter or words, your group should try to form them as quickly as possible. Divide larger groups into smaller units and compete for the best time. Young people *must* work cooperatively and communicate clearly in order to make this game work!

Match Mixer

Give each young person three index cards. Have everyone write one thing about themselves on each slip of paper—things like these:
- The most embarrassing thing that ever happened to me
- My secret ambition
- The person I admire most
- My biggest hang-up
- If I had a million dollars, I would—

Collect all the cards and redistribute them, three to each person, so that no one has cards they wrote themselves. At a signal everyone tries to match each card with the presumed writer of it. They mingle around the room, asking each other questions in order to determine whose cards they have. Keep track of the first youth to find owners for all her cards, and recognize her later as the winner. Let everyone else finish and then share their feelings with the rest of the group.

Meet the Press

Here's a fun game that promotes community and friendliness within the group. First let them mingle in order to find out as much as possible about each other that they didn't already know. After five minutes or so, divide the group into smaller teams or groups (unless your group is already small, then play this game individually).

One person is then chosen at random to "meet the press." While the chosen person sits at the front of the room, each team must take the next five or 10 minutes to write on a sheet of paper the chosen person's name and 20 truthful statements about him. Then collect the sheets and read them to the entire group, one at a time. The student being described judges the statements as to their truthfulness, and the team with the most correct statements is declared the winner.

In case of a tie, give extra weight to less-obvious statements—"born in Nebraska," for example, or "enjoys Shakespeare" shows more insight than "has red hair." Have as many people as you have time for "meet the press."

Mystery Gifts

Here's an activity that allows kids to give to each other, to share with each other, and to have fun all at the same time. To begin, make up some cards like the illustration at the right—so that everyone's name is on a card.

All these cards are put into a box and are randomly drawn by each person so that everyone has a name other than their own. Then they write their own name under the name they drew ("from . . . ") and write in a gift they would like to give to the person whose

name they drew. It could be any gift at all. It would be best to have the group think in terms of non-material gifts, like "perfect health for the rest of your life," etc. Kids can let their imaginations run wild with this, but the gifts should be thoughtful and suitable for each recipient.

Next, have the kids tear off the top part of the card (with the two names on it) and put it in their pocket. The bottom part of the card (with the gift) is pinned or taped to the wall or bulletin board. Everyone is then allowed to examine the board and to pick out the gift they think was given to them. They remove it from the wall and try to find the person who gave it to them. If they are wrong about the gift, then they can try to find the correct gift and trade with whoever has it. By a process of elimination, everybody eventually will come up with the right gift and giver. When they find the person who gave them the gift, they take the top part of the card from that person and sit down while others continue the search. At first there will be a lot of chaos and laughs but the results are rewarding.

You can wrap this up by discussing all that went on during the activity—how you felt about the gift that was given to you, the gifts given to others, and so on.

Name Affirmation

Give a sheet of notebook paper to each of your young people, then ask them to write their names vertically down the left side of it, one letter to a line. Pass the papers to the left. Then have each person write a compliment about the person whose name is on the paper, acrostic fashion, so that the compliment begins with one of the letters in that person's name (JAY: Joyful, Accepts others, You like to be around him. SARAH: Secret-keeper, Attractive, Really listens to you, Always helpful, Happy). Pass the sheets to the left again and repeat the procedure. Letters can be used more than once if all the letters are filled.

The last person to write on one's sheet reads aloud the list of that person's compliments. Then the paper is returned to its owner.

Negative Board

Need a way to discourage sarcasm and negativism in the youth group and to encourage affirmation instead? "Develop" a Negative Board. Take pictures of your kids with a 35mm camera, and then hang all the negatives on a bulletin board. Have the kids first try to recognize each person (negatives make that hard). Make the point that when we say negative things about each other, we're not giving an accurate picture of that person. Victims of negative talk become like the negatives on the negative board—hard to recognize.

Here's how the kids can use the negative board in a positive way in order to combat negativism in the group: whenever someone feels that someone else has said something bad about them, they should take their negative off of the negative board and present it to the offender—who must accept it and cooperate in making arrangements on the spot for a conference time with each other in order to resolve the issue. This encourages honesty and openness, as well as discourages kids from harboring ill feelings towards each other.

Nine-Legged Race

Just for fun or to demonstrate the value of working together, this variation of the three-legged race is best for large groups and lots of space.

Divide the kids into groups of eight or so (the numbers don't matter as long as the teams are even.) Place five kids on one side of the playing field, and the team's remaining three kids opposite them across the field. From the five-kid side, two of them begin a traditional three-legged race. When they reach the other side, they add another team member, turn, and run back. At each end of their course they tie up with another teammate until all eight kids are strung together at the ankles and running the last length. The first across the finish line wins. (The *real* fun is watching them figure out how to turn around—but don't tell them this.)

For heightened hilarity, use thin plastic trash-bag strips as ties, and add this rule—if a tie breaks, they have to stop and either re-tie it or replace it.

And even though you may not have specified the game as a *foot* race, the teammates cannot drop to their knees and pull themselves along with their hands.

Observers

Before your youth meeting begins, privately choose three kids to be "observers." Choose them thoughtfully—you may want to enlist one who doesn't usually get involved, one who is especially optimistic, or maybe one good at giving constructive criticism.

Throughout the entire evening, these observers are to sit back and observe what's really taking place, watching for things like these:

- How does the group work together?
- Who are the leaders?

- Were there any good ideas that were missed, ignored, or overlooked?
- Is the group positive or negative, exciting or blah?
- Do the people in the group *really* care about each other? How?
- If a visitor walked into the room, what would she think? Why?

At the end of the meeting, have the observers report their observations, then discuss what positive changes can be made.

Owl Island

This simulation can be played just for fun or used to start discussion about communication, teamwork, and cooperation. It also works well combined with a devotional about the church as the body of Christ and the importance of each member.

To introduce the game, explain that a mad scientist has cloned a deadly bacteria—and everyone in the world has been infected with it. Divide the young people into different "countries." Each country is to have theoretical biochemists, bionic men and women, and pharmacists. The theoretical biochemists are located in a top-secret lab on mysterious Owl Island. And it's here at the Owl Island lab that an effective vaccine against the bacteria has been synthesized.

What the theoretical biochemists must do is verbally relay information about the vaccine via the bionic men and women back to their own countries' pharmacists, who, with the

explanation brought to them by the bionics, then reconstruct the vaccine. The information the bionics must relay is a description of a 3-D model of the vaccine's molecular structure—made of colored toothpicks and marshmallows—which only the biochemists have seen.

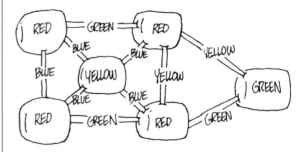

Here are the rules:
- The task must be completed within a time limit (which can be manipulated at the

leader's discretion, so that everyone or no one accomplishes their task).
- A country "dies" if the reconstructed vaccine is not exactly as the original, or if the country is not finished before the time is up.
- The men and women who carry the information must be bionic because Owl Island is surrounded by booby traps, electrified fences, dangerous animals, and similar defenses. Only bionics can therefore move between the island and home country.
- Only theoretical biochemists, and no one else, are allowed to view the structure. There should be some sort of screen set up so that no one else can see.
- The pharmacists are supplied with toothpicks and marshmallows.
- The bionics are not allowed to touch the toothpicks or the marshmallows. Only the pharmacists are allowed to touch them.

So much for the rules. Now for some suggestions:
- It's best to have about four or five in a country—one theoretical biochemist, two or three bionics, and one pharmacist.
- The biochemist should relay the information a bit at a time.
- The distance that bionics must travel between the island and home country can be varied depending on how much territory you have available and how much you want to exercise the kids. "Owl Island" is ideally suited to camps.
- The difficulty of the game is determined by the complexity of the vaccine. The more complex the model, the more time countries will need.

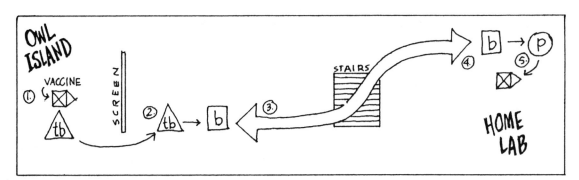

① THEORETICAL BIOCHEMIST 🔺 STUDIES VACCINE. ② 🔺 RELAYS INFO ON HOW TO BUILD TO BIONICS ⬜. ③ ⬜ GOES BACK TO HOME LAB.

④ ⬜ RELAYS INFO TO PHARMACIST ⓟ. ⑤ ⓟ RECONSTRUCTS VACCINE FOR COUNTRY.

Parable of the Shapes

Planning a meeting or discussion about love? The "Parable of the Shapes" is based on the idea that there are generally three kinds of love: "if" love, "because" love, and "in spite of" love (the best kind, of course).

Characters carry large cardboard shapes for costumes—and their shapes determine their identities. Blob, for example, carries a crumpled-up newspaper or other nondescript shape, and In Spite Of carries no shape at all.

Cast: Narrator, Blob, Circle 1, Circle 2, Star 1, Star 2, Square 1, Square 2, Triangle 1, Triangle 2, In Spite Of

Narrator:
There once was a land of If and Because
That sat on the earth as every land does.
And every person who lived in the land
Would search for a person he could understand.
Now let us together observe what takes place
When If and Because people meet face to face.

Circle 1:
As I walk along this fine sunny day,
A stranger I see coming my way.
Is he a friend or is he a foe?
Not till I look at his shape will I know.
A circle I am and a circle I stay—
A circle is needed for friendship today.

(enter Blob)

Hello my friend—Circle's my name,
And finding a friend is my kind of game.
Have you a circle to exchange with me here?
Or are you an alien shape, I fear?

Blob:
A friendly fellow you seem to be,
And circles I need for good friends to be.
What my own shape is I really don't know,
But I hope it's a circle so friendship will grow.
I'm so glad I found you, I'm so glad to see
That such a relationship can possibly be.

Circle 1:
Now wait a minute, O stranger here—
You hasten your happiness too fast, I fear.
I told you before—our two shapes must match
In order for any new friendships to hatch.
If you were a circle with roundest of frame,
We'd be friends forever because we're the same.
But I see no circle, I see nothing round.
I think that it's only a Blob that I've found.
Now think of my image, what others might say.
I can't take the risk. Away! Away!

Blob:
I'm so broken hearted, I'm in such despair.
I am not a circle. It doesn't seem fair.

(enter Circle 2)

Circle 2:
A call for a circle, is that what I hear?
I too am a circle—such joy and such cheer!
For now, brother Circle, your long vigil ends.
We've found one another. Forever we're friends!

(the two circles embrace and walk off)

Star 1:
I am a star, a beautiful star.
Better than all other shapes, by far.
And if you are the finest, I think you will see
That the shape you are holding, a star it will be.
If I'd find a star, we'd frolic in fun
And dance and play and never be done.
If you are a star, my friendship you've won.

But . . . as I look closer, I see you're not one.
You're only a Blob! We'll never go far,
Unless you can prove that you're also a star!

Blob:
My shape's not important. Myself is what
    counts.
Just give me some friendship in any amount.

Star 1:
I've no time for Blobs, so go on your way,
For I think that a star is coming this way . . .

(enter Star 2)

Star 2:
A star I am, and a star I'll stay.
O praise be to stars—it's our lucky day!

Star 1:
O star, O star, what double delight!
These shapes that we're holding, they match us just
    right.

Star 2:
At last we're together, so happy and proud.
Together we'll surely stand out in a crowd.
So Blob, adios! Farewell and goodbye!
You just don't fit in, and you needn't ask why.

Blob:
Alas—I am broken. What worse could I do
Than being rejected by each of these two?

(enter Square 1)

Square 1:
Through this crowd I now will stare
To see if there's somewhere a square.
Pardon me there, but some time could you lend?
If you are a square, I'll be your true friend.

Blob:
Oh surely, dear brother, our shape's not the same,
But I'm a sweet person—besides, what's in a name?

Square 1:
Your shape's not a square—and you talk to me so?
I can't believe all the nerve that you show.
If it's friendship you want, then friendship go get,
But not from a shape with which you don't fit!

(enter Square 2)

Square 2:
A call for a square?
I'll soon be right there!
A square I am and a square I'll be.
I'll join you in friendship, O square, just as me.
Because our fine corners do each number four,
We'll stay close together forever and more!

(both exit)

Blob:
I'm torn and I'm frazzled. What worse could there
    be
Than being rejected by each of these three?

Triangle 1:
I'm wandering to and I'm wandering fro
In search of a three-sided shape just like so. *(points)*
For if I could find one, I know we would blend,
For only a triangle can be a true friend.

Blob:
Hello there, dear fellow, I've heard all you've said.
I can't help but thinking to you I've been led.
For you need friendship and I need the same.
So on with the friendship and off with the game.

Triangle 1:
Now who is this talking? What shape do you hold?
You seem sort of strange—just what is your mold?
You sure are not pretty, you shapeless disgrace!
Why, you're just a Blob—it's all over your face!
I've no time for you, you pitiful one.
This senseless discussion is over and done!

(enter Triangle 2)

Triangle 2:
A call for triangles? Well, I'll fill the need.
We're made for each other, it must be agreed!

(exit together)

Blob:
No one understands poor shapeless me,
'Cause I'm just a Blob as you can well see.
If I were a circle or maybe a square,
Then I could be having some fun over there.
Why can't all you shapes just notice and see,
That I'm just as miserable as I can be?
With no one to laugh and be good friends with,
I'm beginning to feel just a little bit miffed.

(enter In Spite Of)

Narrator:
Now just at this moment comes into this place
A man who is different in style and in grace.
He's quiet and thoughtful and listens quite well,
Observing the stories our characters tell.
Now with me return to our tale, if you can,
And witness the ways of the In Spite Of man.

In Spite Of:
Hello. Will you be my friend?

Blob:
Oh, no. Can't you see?
I'm not a circle or square, so please leave me be.

In Spite Of:
Friend, once again to you I will say,
Will you not be my friend on this fine day?

Blob:
You humor's not funny. I'm wise to your jokes.
You're here to make fun like the rest of these folks.

In Spite Of:
Now what is the problem, my poor little man?
You seem so distressed—I just can't understand.

Blob:
I've run the whole gamut, I've pleaded and cried
To have them accept me and love me inside.
But each time I seek them, they look at my shape
And quickly reject me. It's like hearing a tape:
"You're not the right person, you've got the wrong
   shape,
The people will gossip, the people will gape."
If this shall continue from day unto day,
Alone I'll remain and depressed will I stay.

In Spite Of:
I think a great lesson's been brought to your sight.
These shapes find it hard to accept you "in spite."
They're all so possessive and selfish inside,
They wallow in vanity, ego, and pride.
But there is an answer I've found to be true,
And I've come to offer this answer to you.

Blob:
I don't understand all you're trying to say,
But you're the first person I've met here today
Who seems to accept me in spite of my form.
You break all the rule of the shape-seekers norm.

In Spite Of:
Your wisdom is growing. I think you now see
Love puts no conditions on you or on me.

Narrator:
Our moral is simple. I'll share it with you;
It's all in the Bible and known to be true.
The world offers values that dazzle your eyes,
It mixes the truth with ridiculous lies.
And we here are seeking the true meaning of
This life that we're living, this word we call
   love.
The If and Because folks are caught in a bind,
For they accept only their very own kind.
They love folks *because* and they love people *if*,
But few have discovered the *In Spite Of* gift!

Passing Out Compliments

With a sheet of paper and a pencil in each student's lap, ask them to write their names at the top and then to pass it to the person on the right. Then, on the sheets everyone just received from those on their left, have everyone write down one thing they appreciate about the person whose name appears at the top. Then pass the sheets to the right again and repeat the procedure. Sheets should go around the circle in this way until they reach their owners again.

Now ask each person three questions:
• Which was the funniest comment on your sheet?
• Which was the most heart-warming?
• Which surprised you the most?

Ask the kids to voluntarily speak a compliment openly and directly to another, a compliment that they had earlier only written to that person. When everyone's had an opportunity to do this, discuss how they feel when they are openly, publicly praised this way—do they feel awkward or proud or embarrassed or what? Ask how long it's been since they've received a compliment face to face. Discuss what keeps us from praising one another openly. End by reading 1 Thessalonians 5:8-15 together.

Positive-People Bingo

Find people who fit the descriptions found in the squares on the next page. Then have them sign their first name in the square that describes them. (The same person can sign your bingo sheet only once.) There will be two winners: one who has five signatures in a horizontal, vertical, or diagonal line; and one who has the most squares filled with signatures at the end of the time limit.

Prayer Calendar

On a blank calendar sheet, fill in the days' squares with the names and phone numbers of kids in your group (see below), then copy the sheet and distribute it among the members of your group. Sometime during each day, the kids call the teenager whose day it is, expressing their support, encouragement, and love. Be sure to include the names of the pastor, youth pastor, their wives, and sponsors. This just may help them all "bear one another's burdens."

SUNDAY	MONDAY	TUESDAY	WEDNESDAY	THURSDAY	FRIDAY	SATURDAY
JANUARY				1 JASON BOYD 941-4719	2 KATHY BOYD 941-4719	3 CHRIS BROOKS 452-4598
4 JENNI BROOKS 452-4598	5 SHONDA BROWN 471-8170	6 ALLEN CHAPIN 946-7256	7 KENNETH COLEMAN 473-5729	8 STEVE DUNN 487-2814	9 MELINDA DUNN 487-2814	10 JOHN EASTER 487-2814
11 CANDY EASTER 487-2814	12 PRISCILLA GARDNER 473-9009	13 STACY GIBSON 487-5914	14 ERIC HASERODT 473-5457	15 ALLEN HOGAN 479-1253	16 ALANA MOORMAN 477-4830	17 JORIA MOORMAN 477-4830
18 ELAINE REIKERT 941-7432	19 RIKI SMITH 472-3984	20 GAIL VORSE 487-3250	21 CRAIG WESSELS 944-8954	22 BRYAN WESSELS 944-8954	23 KEVIN WOOD 487-1059	24 JASON WOOD 487-1059
25 RANDY TROTTER 472-7455	26 DARLA TROTTER 472-7455	27 PASTOR CHAPIN 945-7255	28 REVIVAL IN MY HEART!	29 MY PARENTS!	30 MY MATH TEACHER!	31 PRINCIPAL JOHANSEN

Positive People Bingo

Find people who fit the descriptions found in the squares below. Then have them sign their first name in the square that describes them. (The same person can sign your bingo sheet only once.) There will be two winners: one who has five signatures in a horizontal, vertical, or diagonal line; and one who has the most squares filled with signatures at the end of the time limit.

A GOOD FRIEND	HAS GOOD SENSE OF HUMOR	HAS HELPED ME BEFORE	HAS A NICE SMILE	HAS LEADERSHIP QUALITIES
A SWEET PERSON	HAS GOOD IDEAS	IS EASY TO TALK TO	IS A FUN PERSON	UNDER-STANDING
AN ENCOURAGER	CARES ABOUT OTHERS	WOULD LIKE TO GET TO KNOW THIS PERSON BETTER	TALENTED	FRIENDLY
A STRONG CHRISTIAN	LOVING	HAS A GENTLE SPIRIT	SEEMS HAPPY WITH SELF	IS PATIENT
IS KIND	A GOOD PERSON	KIND OF CRAZY IN A GOOD WAY	CREATIVE	MAKES ME FEEL GOOD ABOUT SELF

Prayer Candles

This can be a moving time of prayer. Have your entire group sit in a circle, either in a darkened room or outdoors at night, with everyone holding unlit candles. When the first person lights his candle, he prays (either silently or aloud) for another member of the circle (preferably someone across the circle). After completing the prayer, that person goes over to the person he prayed for and lights her candle, then returns to his place.

The holder of the second candle lit then prays for another in the circle, etc., until all the candles are lit and the leader closes in prayer. All the candles can then be blown out simultaneously.

Progressive Worship Service

This creative service can be done in homes, at church, or on a weekend retreat. Like the progressive dinner, the worship moves from one location to the next.

Like a dinner, a worship service has a variety of elements. By concentrating on each element of worship separately and in a different location, young people are provided an opportunity to appreciate each element. Acts 2:42 and Colossians 3:16 provide a good scriptural base. Here's one way to do it:

- *Fellowship*. Begin with some kind of group interaction or sharing during which the kids get to know each other better—something that puts them in a celebrative but not rowdy mood.
- *Spiritual songs*. At the next location, have someone lead the group in a variety of well-known hymns and favorite songs of worship.
- *Prayer*. Move to a location with an atmosphere appropriate for prayer. If outside, a garden would be nice. Encourage the kids to offer prayers of petition, thanksgiving, intercession, etc.
- *Scripture reading*. At the next location, ask several kids to read a lesson from the Bible. Use a modern English translation.
- *Breaking of bread (Communion)*. The last stop can be around the Lord's Table. Conduct this however you choose, but it should be a time of celebration and joy.

Incorporate whatever other ingredients you like into your own progressive worship service, and design one that fits your group—and you can be sure that they'll never forget it.

Psychiatrist

Here's a small-group game that calls for creativity and encourages kids to get to know one another. Sit the group in a circle and choose someone to be the "psychiatrist," then ask the psychiatrist to leave the room while the game is explained.

Tell the group that their job is to assume the personality of the person on their left. All questions must be answered as if they were that person. You might want to take one minute and have everyone tell as much as they can about themselves to the person who will be them.

Then bring in the psychiatrist. His task is to figure out what's ailing these patients, and to accomplish this he can ask any question he wants. If he begins to notice the pattern, the leader yells "Psychiatrist!" and all the patients scatter to different seats—and assume anew the identity of the new person on their left. When the psychiatrist finally hits on the pattern, the game is over.

You can give the game a different sort of competitive edge by bringing in three or four kids, one at a time, and clock them to see how quickly they detect the pattern. Fastest time wins.

Put-Down Covenant

Sarcasm and other negative comments made by one person about another can undermine relationships in a youth group if they're allowed to go unchecked. Here's one way to help stem the tide.

Spend some time with your group discussing put-downs and the importance of being careful of what we say to each other (James 3:2-12). Following this study, have the kids write a Put-Down Covenant similar to the one below. You may want to distribute the example for the kids to modify or add their own thoughts to. Everyone signs the finished product, which is then hung in the meeting room as a constant reminder that, by their own agreement, put-downs are unacceptable in the youth group.

Put-Down Covenant

We would like our youth group to be a place where all teenagers can come, feel accepted, and feel good about themselves.
We know that put-downs and criticisms make people feel rejected, hurt, and bad about themselves.
We also know that hurting others in any way is wrong before God.

Therefore, we promise, with God's help, to—

- **Stop putting others down by word or action.**
- **Remind others in the group of their responsibility not to put others down.**
- **Ask forgiveness from God and from others when we fail.**
- **Forgive others when they fail.**

_____   _____
Signed   Date

Put-Down Potty

Sometimes nagging problems can be gradually solved simply by calling attention to the problem without being heavy-handed about it.

If you're having trouble with kids who constantly put each other down in youth meetings and activities, for example, try this. Get a child's toilet-training seat and label it the "Put-Down Potty." Whenever a group member (youth or sponsor) puts another person down, the culprit must pay a fine of a dime or a quarter—to be collected in the Put-Down Potty. The collected money can eventually be sent to a mission project or similar cause.

Putting Myself in a Box

This game often helps kids share deep feelings about themselves with each other, not to mention its value as a good community builder.

First you'll need to get some boxes, about shoe-box size or gift-box size, one for everybody. You'll also need some magazines, newspapers, scissors, glue, marking pens, and so on. Explain that they are to make a collage on the *inside* of the box, a collage that represents how they see themselves or feel about themselves. Their self-perceptions and feelings should be expressed through pictures, words, symbols, etc.

On the *outside* of the box, they should make a collage that represents how they think they look in others' eyes. If they want, they can let each side of the box represent how different people or groups of people see them.

Give your kids enough time to finish their boxes, then let them get into small groups and share their boxes—themselves—with each other. Non-threatening activities like this help kids open up to each other and provide chances for others to support them. Discuss the frequent difference between the inside and the outside of the boxes and how we can improve both.

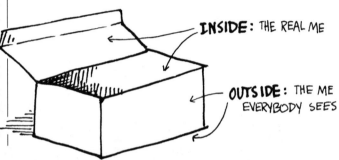

INSIDE: THE REAL ME

OUTSIDE: THE ME EVERYBODY SEES

Reciprocal Commands

Community is not just good group feelings—it requires commitment and responsibility. These "reciprocal commands" illustrate the point:

Commands about inter-relationships
- Love one another. (John 13:34; 15:12, 17; Romans 12:9-10, 13:8; Galatians 5:14; Ephesians 5:1; 1 Thessalonians 3:11-12; 4:9-10; Hebrews 13:1; James 2:8; 1 Peter 1:22; 4:8; 1 John 3:11, 23; 4:7, 11, 12, 21; 2 John 5)
- Receive one another. (Romans 15:7)
- Greet one another. (Romans 16:3-6, 16; 1 Corinthians 16:20; 2 Corinthians 13:12, 1 Peter 5:14)
- Have the same care for one another. (1 Corinthians 12:24-25)
- Submit to one another. (Ephesians 5:18-21; Hebrews 13:17; 1 Peter 5:5)
- Forbear one another. (Ephesians 5:18-21)
- Confess your sins to one another. (James 5:16)
- Forgive one another. (Matthew 5:22; 18:21-22; Ephesians 4:31-32; Colossians 3:12-13)
- Belong to one another. (Romans 12:5)
- Be of the same mind with one another. (Romans 15:5; Philippians 2:1,2)
- Accept one another. (Romans 15:7; 14:1)

Negative commands
- Do not judge one another. (Romans 14:13)
- Do not speak evil of one another. (James 4:11)
- Do not murmur against one another. (James 4:11)
- Do not bite and devour one another. (Galatians 5:14-15)
- Do not provoke one another. (Galatians 5:25-26)
- Do not envy one another. (Galatians 5:25-26)
- Do not lie to one another. (Colossians 3:9-10)

Commands about mutual edification
- Build up one another. (Romans 14:19; 1 Thessalonians 5:11)
- Teach one another. (Colossians 3:16)
- Exhort one another. (1 Thessalonians 5:11; Hebrews 3:12-13; 10:24-25)
- Admonish one another. (Romans 15:14; Colossians 3:16)
- Speak to one another in psalms, hymns, and spiritual songs. (Ephesians 5:18-20; Colossians 3:16)
- Worship together. (Psalm 133:1)
- Take material care of each other. (Deuteronomy 15:7; Romans 12:13)
- Honor one another. (Romans 12:10)

Commands about mutual service
- Be servants of one another. (Galatians 5:13-14; Ephesians 5:21; 1 Peter 4:9)
- Bear one another's burdens. (Romans 15:1; Galatians 6:2)
- Be hospitable to one another. (1 Peter 4:7-10)
- Be kind to one another. (Ephesians 4:21-22)
- Pray for one another. (John 5:16; Ephesians 6:18-19)
- Be patient with one another. (Ephesians 4:2)
- Discipline each other. (Matthew 18:15; Galatians 6:1-2; 2 Thessalonians 3:14-15)
- Bear with one another. (Ephesians 4:2)

Begin by asking the kids to study these commands individually or in pairs. With their Bibles, paper and pencil, they can follow instructions like these:
- Study the Scripture verses that deal with each of the commands.
- Write out your own definition of each command.
- Find a scriptural example (positive or negative) for each command.
- List each command's implications and applications to your personal and relational life.

Here are some questions for group discussion after the individual study:
- How many of these responsibilities are getting met in our group?
- Do any of the commands surprise you or sound unreasonable to you?
- Are there any that you find impossible to do? Why?
- Are these responsibilities optional, or are they to be expected of all Christians?
- Is there one you would like to especially see our group work on?
- How can we apply these commands to our group and make them work?

These questions and procedures are only suggestions. Revise them any way that fits your group. You might take several weeks to study these commands, perhaps by taking only one of the four commands groups each week. Find practical ways for your group to put feet to these commands.

Servant Certificates

Print copies of the certificate on the next page, give them to your youth and youth leaders, and encourage them to award another person with a certificate, to be redeemed as noted on the certificate. It's an excellent gift idea for Christmas—or it can be used anytime to encourage service and ministry in the group.

Sharing Cubes

Make a pair of large "dice" out of foam rubber or cardboard. On the six sides of each cube, write instructions for sharing. Here are some sample ones:
   Describe your week.
   Share a frustration.
   Share a prayer request.
   Compliment someone.

One at a time, each person chooses one of the cubes and "rolls it" on the floor. He or she then shares briefly, according to the instruction that turns up. If you have more than eight to ten people in your group, break into smaller groups and give each group one of the cubes.

Shirt Sharing

You'll need white T-shirts for everyone in this get-acquainted game that's perfect for retreats. You'll also need plenty of felt-tipped markers (the permanent variety work best), open space, and paper to put on the floor (and inside the shirts) in order to absorb the ink that goes through the shirts.

Give your kids instructions to write or draw

Servant Certificate

The bearer of this certificate is hereby entitled to one unabashed, unheralded gift of service to be lovingly performed by me at your point of need and time of convenience. Just let me know!

To: _____

from _____ , your humble servant

this _____ day of _____ , 19 _____ .

Mark 10:42-45

a variety of things on their shirts. Here are some suggestions:

- Write your first name somewhere on the front.
- Write your last name under the back collar.
- Write your height in your favorite color.
- Draw an animal that you would like to be.
- Draw an eye the same color as yours.
- Identify your favorite musical instrument.
- Write your birthdate on the sleeve.
- Draw the logo of your favorite sports team.
- Identify your favorite food.
- Name a Bible verse that you can quote from memory.

They can wear their shirts when they've finished, and you can direct them in a number of other customized shirt games. For example, have them group themselves by the animal or animal family (or by food or food group, by Bible book, etc.) they've drawn on their shirts.

Shuffle the Deck

Here's a simple, lively way to break a large group down into smaller ones—or to play just for fun. Distribute a deck of playing cards (or Rook cards) to the group, one per person. Then call out different combinations, like these:

- "Get in a group that adds up to 58."
- "Find three people of the same suit."
- "Find five numbers in a row, of any suit."
- "Find your whole suit."
- "Find four of you—four 3s, four 8s, etc."

For larger groups use multiple decks of cards; for smaller groups eliminate cards. Then create your own combinations!

The Sky's the Limit

After sharing or a get-acquainted mixer, play this meaningful yet fun affirmation exercise. Sit your group in a circle (if it's a large group, divide it into smaller groups). Ask the kids to pretend that they can give anything they want to others in the group—the sky's the limit. One at a time, around the circle, each student should share what they would give every other person and why.

Encourage students to think in terms of non-material as well as material gifts. For example: "Since you have so much to do in the next few months, I'd like to give you an unlimited amount of energy," or "I'd like to give you confidence in yourself as you go away to college."

Spin the Compliment

Like the old favorite Spin the Bottle, this game needs a Coke or Pepsi bottle and a circle of kids willing to affirm each other with words of appreciation. The spinner lays not a smacker but a compliment or word of encouragement on whomever the bottle points to at the end of its spin.

Spiritual Sponsors

To bring your church's adults and youths together, create a Spiritual Sponsor (or Adopt an Adolescent) program in which adults in the church are asked to sponsor (or "adopt") a teenager in the youth group—that is, they would commit to support that young person with their prayers, birthday cards, encouragement, and any other appropriate, meaningful way.

Give sponsoring adults an information card

on "their" youths; the cards are reminders as well as a source of information. At the end of the school year, organize a sponsor- appreciation banquet as a thank-you to these adults.

Name: Brian Mellan

Address: 1245 E. Depot

City: Renton, Virginia

Phone: 835-9487

Birthdate: 9/16/73

Friends: Kevin, Teresa, Josh

Hobbies: Waterskiing, girls, baseball, *Sports Illustrated*

Comments: Brian is a junior at Renton North High School; he likes school enough to want to go to college, but unsure as yet where. Parents are Robert and Shirley, members of our church; they moved here five years ago from Milwaukee with brother Tim and sister Tammy.

Spy Game

This simulation for large groups teaches players how they are one, even though they may not realize it. Introduce it simply as a game to be played for fun— keep your group unaware that they'll learn something valuable from the game! The apparently elaborate instructions only disguise the actual simplicity of the game. You can call the game Spy Game, Double Agent, or any name you choose.

Before the game:
- Prepare enough slips of paper to enable everyone in the crowd to have one. Select about four sets of numbers, such as:

53	121	207	129
219	107	21	101
21	49	119	47
107	123	53	123

- Fold the papers and shuffle them so they are all mixed up. The important thing is that all the number sets add up to the same sum. (In this case 400.) The players are unaware of this, of course.
- Get enough pennies for everyone to have one. Part of the game involves flipping coins.
- Also have golf pencils on hand for everyone who needs one.

Say to your kids:
- "You are all spies. In a moment you will receive a slip of paper with numbers on it. By adding the numbers, you will know the code number of the country you are spying for. The person next to you could be an enemy spy or he might be a friend from your country. You don't know. Don't reveal your code number until you have to, and make sure you add the number correctly."
- "The object of the game is to 1) eliminate enemy spies from the game, 2) locate and team up with your fellow spies, and 3) avoid being eliminated from the game. In other words, whichever country survives without being eliminated is the winner."
- "You will also receive a coin and a pencil with your code number. When the game begins, add up your numbers and write the

total on the paper. Next, go up to any person on the field (or in the room). Before you both flip your coins, one of you calls odd, the other even. If both coins turn up the same, whoever called 'even' is the *aggressor*; the other is the *responder*. If the coins land one heads and the other tails, whoever called odd becomes the aggressor."

- "After you determine who the aggressor is, the aggressor asks, 'Friend or foe?' The responder must then show his code number. If it is the same as the aggressor's, the responder remains in the game because he is a friendly spy. He now joins the aggressor by holding onto his waist and following behind. If the responder's code number is different from the aggressor's number, the responder is out of the game."
- "As long as you are in the game and can find other survivors, repeat the process. If you have a fellow spy behind you, then you work as a group. You are the spokesman for the group, however, if you were the original

aggressor. You approach another individual or group, flip coins, and eliminate, be eliminated, or form a larger group."

- "Repeat this procedure until only one group is left—the winning country."

Play the game:
- Make sure there is enough room for the snake-like groups to form and move about. As the game progresses, of course, no one will be eliminated, and all will be absorbed into one long group.
- Keep the game moving. Before the game is over, players will eventually discover that there aren't any enemy spies. It doesn't take long for Spy Game to be played.

After the game:
- Sit the group down and ask them, "What did you assume about the game? Was it true? How did you feel when you discovered that everyone was on the same team? How is this game a lot like real life?"

Strength Voting

How do your students' opinions of themselves compare with others' opinions of them? This affirmation exercise helps them see themselves through their classmates' eyes.

Ask everyone to write their names at the top of a sheet of paper, as well as three things about themselves that they consider their strengths. Warn them against excessive modesty—if they think they're good at something, tell them to be honest and write it down (e.g., "good listener," "sense of humor").

When your kids are finished listing their virtues, ask them to pass the sheets around the room so that others in the group can "vote" on

the strengths listed for each person. As a teen's sheet makes the rounds through the room, other group members mark a check by those qualities that they agree are prominent strengths. But if a friend thinks that a person has a strength not on the sheet that ought to be in the top three, then that friend should write in the quality. When the sheets finally circulate throughout the room, they'll have lots of checks and probably lots of write-in votes.

And when the papers return to their owners, your kids will have a fairly clear idea about which strengths others see in them.

Surprise Package

It's no secret that young people tend to judge others almost entirely according to appearance. This simple object lesson helps teens understand that, first, appearances are deceiving and, second, everyone has great value regardless of appearances.

First, play any game that produces one winner. Announce that the winner gets to choose one of two prizes, both of which are displayed: one is large and elegantly gift-wrapped or in an expensive-looking container. The other, smaller one is in a brown paper bag.

Expect the winner to choose the expensive-looking gift—and expect his disappointment when he opens it and finds either nothing or else even trash. The best gift, of course, is in the brown bag. It will be easy to move from this to the fact that "God looks upon the heart, not outward appearances" and to apply this to relationships in the group. For what God finds in each of us—his "packages"—are individuals, each with infinite worth and value.

Teen of the Week

To make your kids feel important—and also to help everyone to get to know each other better—choose a Teen of the Week who is the honored guest at that week's youth meeting.

Contact the chosen teen's parents secretly and have them provide you with family photos, baby pictures, awards, report cards, toys, articles of clothing, or anything that would be of interest to the group. One bulletin board in the church can be set aside for the Teen of the Week, and all those items can be hung up on the board. When the young people arrive for the meeting, they'll all head straight for the Teen of the Week board to find out who it is that week.

Furthermore, the chosen young person can be honored in some special way during the meeting. It's a good way to have fun and to let kids know that they're special.

Thanksgiving Exchange

If your students know each other fairly well, plan to do this exercise that teaches gratitude and affirmation. Ask them to write their names at the top of a sheet of paper, then collect the papers and redistribute them so that they all have someone else's paper. Now have everyone write on the sheet what they would be thankful for *if they were the person named on the sheet*. They can list as many things as they want.

Your young people can exchange sheets several times, so that several people have a chance to add to the list. The sheets should eventually be returned to the person named on the paper.

Give everyone time to read the comments on their sheets, then allow those who want to share their lists with the entire group.

> **Kristen**
> can be thankful for—
> • Having a sister
> • Good health
> • Doesn't need glasses
> • Has lots of friends
> • Got a summer job

The Tie That Binds

Add some fun to a banquet when your group is seated at either long tables or round tables—and there are even some lessons to be learned from the fun.

Tie everyone's wrists together all the way down (or around) the table—right wrist to the next person's left, and so on. When the food is served, you all have a problem to solve. In order to eat, you must all cooperate with those sitting on each side of you. Both arms, of course, must move at the same time as those at your table dine.

Follow up at your next meeting with a discussion or program about cooperation and inter-dependency.

Tinker-Toy Unity

Resurrect someone's old Tinker Toys (or buy a new set!) for an exercise that symbolizes group unity in a fun, creative way. You'll need a large enough set for each person in the group to build at least a simple object.

Assignment: your young people are to create small symbols or representations of themselves. They can make simple stick figures that resemble a human figure or abstract Tinker Toy sculpture that needs interpretation.

When everyone is finished, have the first teenager share her creation with the group, describing how she feels about it, what it represents, etc., and placing the creation on the table when she's finished talking. After the next student shares, he attaches his Tinker Toy self-symbol to the previous one, as do all the youths in their turn. The objects are all eventually interconnected to each other and form a giant Tinker Toy sculpture.

Display it for a few weeks as a reminder to the group of their unity and oneness.

Trust Test

Here's a good exercise to build trust within the group. Break into groups of six to eight. Each group forms a close circle with one person in the center. The person stands stiff, keeps feet together, and doesn't bend his knees. He falls (keeping his body in this fixed position) toward the people in the circle. He must trust each member of the circle to keep him from falling as they push him around from person to person, back and forth across the circle. Follow-up with a discussion of the experience.

Trust Walk

This outdoor exercise, done either in pairs or in larger groups, has been used for years to teach trust and dependence upon one another. The idea is simple: one person takes the hand of a blindfolded person (who in turn holds the hand of another blindfolded player if this activity is done in more than pairs), who must follow the leader on a walk, preferably over unfamiliar terrain. Leaders, of course, can warn their "blind" followers—"Look out for the curb coming up," "We're coming to a stairway," "There's a low branch coming up in a few feet—you'll have to duck."

The path can be as difficult or easy as you want to make it, but the idea is for followers to trust their leaders and for leaders to ensure the safety of the followers who trust them. Give everyone the chance to lead as well as follow, and discuss the experience afterwards.

T-Shirt Solidarity

Having special T-shirts printed for your group builds a sense of group identity. Find someone who'll create an attractive design for your group name; then have the design printed onto good quality T-shirts, whether commercially or silk-screened by hand yourselves. You can probably find a T-shirt shop in your city who will do this for you at a reasonable cost.

To make the most of your shirts, throw a Back-to-School Party, and tell the youths to wear their school colors. Toward the end of the evening, give out the shirts. As school begins, they'll undoubtedly become involved in many other activities than the youth group, but the shirts will remind them that they remain a special part of your group and that you hope to see them throughout the year. Have everyone put on the shirts, take a group picture, and have copies made for everyone.

Unity Soup

Here's a delicious way to demonstrate group unity. Ask everyone to bring a can of soup (any kind they want) to a meeting at which dinner will be served. At the meeting pour all the soup into the same big pot for cooking. It probably won't look too good, but it will taste—well, interesting. Actually, it's usually fairly tasty.

At another meeting have everyone bring a can of their favorite soda pop and mix it all together. Now that's unity!

Unwanted Guest

Most youth groups don't easily make new people feel welcome. Assimilating strangers can be made easier, however, with this tried-and-tested project. Arrange for a kid from another youth group (far away enough so as not to be recognized) to come and spend a Sunday at your church. No one in your group should know about the set-up—they'll think the teen is simply a typical visitor. Your guest should be dressed normally but not stylishly, should be friendly but quiet, and should speak only when spoken to. (This may take some acting.) He should come to Sunday school, church, maybe a softball game that afternoon (that you'll need to set up in advance), and a get-together after church that night.

That evening let your group know that the visitor was a "plant." Introduce him to the group and let him report to your kids how he was received and treated. If you want to get really heavy, have him share with the group how some went out of their way to either accept or ignore him. Some kids will want to crawl under the tables, and others will feel as if they have finally done something right.

Uppers and Downers

Lead your group in filling out a chart similar to the one on the next page. First ask them to think of a time when someone said something to them that made them feel bad—a "downer"—a put-down, angry comment, etc. Then have them recall a time when someone gave them an "upper" and made them feel great. Encourage them to write down several entries for the first two columns.

Next, have the students do the same thing in the third and fourth columns—only this time they should record times when they said an upper or downer to someone else.

Chances are, if your group is typical, that your young people will think of many more downers than uppers. Discuss what this means. Talk about how easy it is to discourage or put down others without a second thought—how damaging our tongue can be, and how the damage takes so long to repair.

Follow up with a look at Hebrews 10:23-25 (which deals with encouragement), and then discuss ways to practice it. You might want to continue with another affirmation exercise from this section.

You can also help kids identify the things they say to each other as uppers or downers, a practice that will encourage them to be careful about what they say. Are you at a retreat? Then challenge them to confront each other during the weekend if they hear someone giving someone else a downer. This can help eliminate the negativism that often ruins youth-group meetings and activities.

OTHERS		ME	
Upper	Downer	Upper	Downer

"US" Quiz

Quiz your group with 25 silly-to-serious questions like those below. The person with the most correct answers wins a snapshot of the entire group. This is a good way to publicize your group among newcomers in the room as well as to remind the regulars of what the group is all about.

1. Name the event when we stayed overnight in a barn.
2. Who is our pastor?
3. Name two people in our group who are related.
4. What's the name of our church newsletter?
5. Where did we enjoy the refreshments last week?
6. Name two service projects that our group did last year.

Valentine Candy

This affirmation exercise works best with Valentine heart candies (SWEET HEART, BE MINE, etc.), yet it can be done any old time with any kind of candy. With a handful of candy, each player tries to give away all his candy to others in the group (one per person)—but not without a compliment or affirming word.

This exercise encourages not only affirmation, but giving and sharing as well. And everyone both gives and receives. (It's unlikely that anyone will be neglected in this exercise, but you'll want to be on the lookout for those who are.)

Verbal Puzzle

This game is not only a lot of fun, but it's effective at illustrating the difficulty of following and understanding verbal directions. Choose three to six couples, then have each pair sit back to back so they cannot see each other's work.

One partner in each pair holds a diagram of the completed jigsaw-type puzzle, and the other partner has the puzzle pieces themselves, scrambled and waiting to be arranged

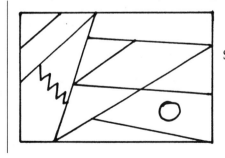

Suggested Puzzle Design

into the picture or design. The partner with the diagram describes the pieces and their intended location to the other. The couple to finish first wins. Allow the others to finish, and then discuss as a group what they learned about communication.

You may want to start the discussion with questions like these:
- How did you feel? Confused, frustrated, angry, rushed?
- What causes us to misunderstand what others say or mean?
- React to this statement: "What I heard you say is not what you meant."

Welcome Coupon Book

Welcome a new church-staff member, youth sponsor, or young person this way: have all this kids write a letter to the new person introducing themselves, and enclose a "coupon" that can be redeemed for something. Coupons may say, for example, "I will deliver a pie at your request" or "If you want two free guitar lessons, call me" or "I'll buy lunch for you any Saturday." All the letters and coupons are then presented to the newcomer—and they'll really feel wanted and accepted.

Welcome Questionnaire

Another way to help a new person fit in (especially those who have moved in from out of town) is to give them the results to a questionnaire that your group took earlier—or poll your teenagers verbally with the newcomer in attendance. Here are the sort of questions you can ask that new kids usually like knowing the answers to:
- Where can you get the best and cheapest hamburgers in town?
- Where is the best place to sit and talk?
- What's the best radio station?
- Where is the least expensive movie theater?
- Where do you go if you want to run into your friends?
- What should teenagers be sure not to miss if they can spend only one day in town?
- What's the best thing about our youth group?
- What's the best event that our youth group does every year?

What Are My Gifts?

The atmosphere for this activity is crucial—the group needs to be relaxed, unhurried, and comfortable with each other. Photocopy the list of character traits on the next page (add others if you want to) and distribute them among your group members. Ask them to read the list and then check three gifts they believe are their own strongest traits. Next, ask them write an R beside those character qualities that they think best apply to the person sitting on their immediate right. Finally, have them write an L next to those traits that best apply to those on their left.

Now, one at a time, have the two students on either side of one member read their lists that presumably describe her. Then let the member herself read her own self-description. Ask the member described how she felt about the others' description of her, and open the discussion up to the entire group before moving on to the next person.

This may take some time—so if you have a large group, do a few people each meeting for several weeks.

What Others Think of Me

"What do they think of me?" Few questions are quietly asked inside teenagers as often as this one, and this exercise can give them some solid, objective data to help answer the question. Give each student a long sheet of paper, 3 inches by 8 inches or so, and instruct them to write their names at the bottom and a one-word self-description at the top. They then fold the paper down from the top twice in order conceal their word. The paper should look like the example.

Now the kids exchange sheets two or three times so that they lose track of their own papers. Then each of them writes at the top of the page a one-word description of the person named at the bottom. The kids should be honest, constructive, and as helpful as possible to the one they're describing. (If they don't know the person, they should leave it blank.) The sheets' tops should again be folded down before the sheets are exchanged again for another round. The process is repeated until the sheets are full of one-word descriptions of the student named at the bottom.

When the students get their own sheets back, give them a few minutes to look over their lists. Open a discussion in which kids can comment on the differences and similarities between their self-image and others' views of them.

Top folded down twice to conceal the word written there

Name written at bottom

Whopper

Do your kids need to know each other better? Give each one a sheet of paper or a note card and a pencil, and ask them to write down four statements about themselves—three of them true, but one of them a "whopper."

One at a time, the group members read their four statements while everyone else tries to guess which one is the lie. When everyone's

Traits

___ compassion
___ listening
___ trustworthiness
___ loyalty
___ sympathy
___ caring
___ cheerfulness
___ ability to cheer up others
___ helpfulness
___ ability to make some- one who's hurting feel better
___ ability to mediate between two people or groups
___ encouragement
___ teaching
___ humor
___ ability to get things done
___ vision for what the future can be
___ hospitality—making people feel comfortable
___ perseverance/tenacity— ability to hang in there

___ directness—doesn't play games
___ independence—is not easily influenced by fads or trends
___ nurturing—ability to help people grow
___ organization
___ creativity
___ acceptance—ability to accept others without judgment
___ diplomacy—ability to see two sides of an issue
___ spirituality
___ humility
___ hopefulness
___ optimism
___ charity—ability to give everything freely
___ faithfulness
___ forgiveness
___ sensitivity
___ perception—ability to see beyond the superficial level

had a guess, the reader tells which one's the whopper, and the kids score themselves this way: the reader gets one point for every incorrect guess, and the guessers get one point if they guess correctly. Whoever has the most points at the end of the game wins.

For even more fun, play "Whopper" in reverse—each person writes down three *false* statements and only one true one. (After all, inventing fabrications about yourself is more fun than thinking of true ones!) The object becomes to choose the sole truth.

Yarn Sharing

Here's a simple game to get your group to open up and share their feelings and Christian experience. Tell your group that they will be part of an experiment: you will throw a ball of yarn (holding one end of it) to someone in the circle. When one catches the ball, she should share one of the following experiences:
• What God has done for her.
• What God has done for someone she knows.
• What God has done for all of us (Christ's death, given us his Word, etc.).
• Something she is thankful for.

After sharing, she throws the ball of yarn to someone else in the circle (while holding onto a length of yarn), who catches it and repeats the process. When everyone has shared several times (or, for large groups, at least once), you'll discover that the group has woven a web of sorts. Then proceed to one or more of the following suggestions:

• Ask "What is this yarn doing for us physically?" Most groups say something like "Holding us together." Note for the kids that in order for an intricate, even beautiful pattern to emerge, everyone had to participate.
• Ask a member or two to loose their hold on the yarn. The center of the web, of course, will immediately slacken, and the group will tend to step back from each other in order to take up the slack. The question "What happens to the group when someone drops their yarn?" now becomes timely.

Finish with a brief talk about how the Bible instructs us to bear each other's problems, to share our happinesses and sorrows, to be thankful, etc. The yarn symbolizes the network of ties and relationships between you that, to mean something, must be maintained by everyone.

Youth-Group Covenant

If rules and discipline are sore points in your youth group, this idea may help the youths to negotiate standards of group behavior with each other. Rules and regs are much easier to abide by and enforce when they're arrived at by consensus than by decree.

First, let your teenagers brainstorm all the rules they think should be included in a youth-group covenant as you or a student lists them on a chalkboard or overhead projector. You can suggest rules for consideration as well.

Next, divide into smaller groups and instruct the kids to choose the top five or so—the ones they think are the most important. When the large group reconvenes, members nominate their choice of rules. Then let the

discussion flow. It's probably wise to set a limit of rules—five is a good number; 10 is probably the maximum needed for any group. The purpose of the nominations and discussions, of course, is to eliminate as many rules as you can before settling on the handful that can be reasonably kept and enforced.

After the nominations, put the rules up to a vote of the group; when the winning rules have been chosen, have someone write them up on a poster or parchment (like the Bill of Rights) and have all sign their names. This Youth-Group Covenant can then be posted on the wall as a reminder of everyone's responsibility to abide by the rules that they formulated themselves.

Youth-Group Letterhead

Make each person in your youth group feel special by designing a youth-group letterhead that includes the names of all group members. Then use the letterhead for correspondence, regular mailings, announcements, etc. Be sure to update the letterhead regularly, adding and subtracting names as necessary.

St. Matthew Youth
St. Matthew United Methodist Church

Christine Addison
Pam Bailey
Susan Boismenue
Jeannie Bibby
Becky Brown
Terri Burkarth
Chris Carl
Dana Clifton
Adam Corbitt
David Corbitt
Susan Davinroy
Jeff Dickinson
Cathy Downing
Amy Dunck
Kristi Dunck
Lynda Eastwood
Jason Fischer
David Flowers
Jason Franklin
Mike Greer

Sarah Napier
Kelli Nickel
Jamie Palmer
Larry Patton
Karen Petri
Tim Price
Brett Pyles
Kristi Ratliff
Steve Ratliff
Chris Reed
Eric Rhodes
Kathy Richards
Aimee Sally
Chris Shannon
Lisa Sigman
Chrissy Smith
Kim Towns
K.C. Roeckel
Bill Wiggs
Mike Wilson

Zip Zap

Learn each other's first names with this circle game. Players must first learn who is seated on either side of them. To everyone's left is "Zip"; to their right is "Zap." From the center of the circle, the leader points to a student and says, "Zip!" (or "Zap!") and then counts to five reasonably fast. The teen pointed to must shout the name of the person to his left (or right) before the leader counts to five—otherwise he takes the leader's place in the center and the leader takes that student's seat.

Section Three

Community Building—
A Curriculum

This section provides a 13-week TalkSheet curriculum for groups that are serious about community building. These TalkSheets walk students through key concepts of Christian community and help them to put these concepts into practice in their youth group. This user-friendly curriculum requires only a copy machine. The students work from the reproducible TalkSheets in this section.

What are TalkSheets? Simply put, they are ready-to-use discussion starters. Each TalkSheet focuses on one topic, raising questions that help the kids think through an idea before they have to discuss it with the group. Here's how they work.

1. Make a photocopy of the TalkSheet original for each person in your group.
2. Give your students a few minutes to write out their answers to the questions on the TalkSheet.
3. Lead the youths to discuss their answers to the questions with the group. The question-by-question guide accompanying each TalkSheet can help you avoid lecturing and instead assist kids in discovering truth on their own.

Although most of the sessions could go longer, each one is designed to be used in a one-hour meeting. You might want to divide some sessions in two—do one half one week and the other half the next week. You won't bore the kids—every session has a lot of activity and good discussion material. If you can spend more time on each topic, so much the better.

On the other hand, you don't need to cover everything each session suggests. Although four TalkSheets are provided in some sessions, you may only want to use two of them. Adapt each session to fit your group's needs.

How Each Session Works

Goals and Objectives tells you what you can accomplish with the session. **Things You Will Need for This Session** provides a list of the items you'll want to have ready for the session. The TalkSheets mentioned here are found in the back of this book. **Publicity for This Session** gives you creative ways to grab your group's attention and get them excited about the session. **To Introduce This Session** helps each group member focus his or her thinking on the session's topic. After handing out and discussing the appropriate TalkSheets, use **To Close This Session** to encourage your young people to apply whay they've learned.

Each session has room for more than discussing the TalkSheets. I suggest additional activities in the leader's guide accompanying each TalkSheet and recommend ideas from Section Two. But you can add other activities, visual aids, or teaching strategies as you wish. In fact, it's a good idea to vary the sessions, including plenty of opportunities for fun, movement, and variety. Keep your meetings upbeat and interesting.

Introduce the topic in a non-threatening manner—a game, an intriguing object lesson, or an ice-breaker, for instance—and then get to work after everyone feels comfortable. After the discussion and Bible study, wrap up the session using the suggestions in the leader's guide or your own ideas.

How To Use TalkSheets

TalkSheets are easy to use.

1. Make clear copies of the TalkSheet original. Any method of duplicating will work—so long as the students can read the printing and can write on the paper.

Keep in mind that you are able to make copies of the TalkSheets for your group because the publisher has given you permission to do so. U.S. copyright laws haven't changed. It is still illegal to make copies of published material without the publisher's permission. You may make copies of the TalkSheets for your group only. Thanks for your cooperation.

2. Try the TalkSheet yourself first. Fill it out as if you were one of the kids in your group. This role playing will give you firsthand knowledge of what you will ask your students to do. As you fill out the TalkSheet, you may think of additional questions, activities, or applicable Scriptures.

3. Give students time to work on their TalkSheets. Kids can work on their TalkSheets individually or in small groups—whatever you decide. Or lead the whole group to answer one question at a time. Whatever your plan, be sure to allow enough time for the kids to thoughtfully answer each question in writing *before* the discussion.

4. Lead the discussion. A TalkSheet is not a quiz. Let your kids know that you are asking for opinions. Explain that not only are all opinions worthwhile, but that the students are responsible to contribute their opinions to the rest of the group. This climate of acceptance and respect demonstrates what community is all about.

Here are some additional tips on leading effective TalkSheet discussions.

• *Divide large groups*. If your group is larger than 15 or 20 kids, you may want to divide into three groups of four or five with a facilitator in each group who leads the discussion.

• *Don't feel pressured to spend time on each question*. For a short meeting, focus discussion on the questions you feel are more important.

• *Keep the group on the topic*. Gently redirect the discussion if the group wanders from the topic.

• *Affirm everyone who contributes*. Even if you don't agree with some of the comments and ideas the kids share, let them know that you appreciate their thoughtful openness. It's better to remain neutral than to shut off the flow of dialogue by judging an opinion as right or wrong. Just thank kids for sharing, and do it sincerely.

• *Don't set yourself up as an authority*. Be a co-learner and facilitator. Give input when it's appropriate, but save outright teaching until an appropriate time.

• *Actively listen to each person*. Look the kids in the eyes when they talk. Rephrase their comments sometimes just to show that you really are listening.

• *Don't force anyone to talk*. Everyone has the right to pass. You can nudge the group by asking certain kids for their opinions; but if they are reluctant, don't push them.

• *Don't allow one person to monopolize the discussion*. Most groups have a motormouth who likes to talk. Direct questions to some of the others and encourage everyone to participate.

• *Allow humor when appropriate*. A good laugh loosens up a tense discussion.

• *Don't be afraid of silence*. If no one has anything to say right away, just wait. Sometimes rephrasing the question starts the flow of talk, but don't be intimidated by silence. You may even want to discuss the silence itself.

5. Provide a notebook. Giving kids a three-ring binder—or some other kind of notebook—can encourage them to value their completed TalkSheets.

Leader's Guide for Session 1
UNITY

When Jesus prayed for the church he said, "May they be one." More than anything else, Jesus wanted his followers to be *one*, to experience Christian unity. This first session lays the foundation for the entire course as students discover the meaning of Christian unity.

Goals and Objectives for Session 1
This session will help the students—
• Become familiar with some of the main Bible passages concerning unity and oneness and apply these passages to their church or youth group.
• Recognize that even though they are all uniquely different from each other, they also have much in common.
• Identify ways to become more one with each other and to live out Christian unity in the youth group.

Things You Will Need for This Session
1. In the back of this book are the Talk-Sheets for this session (Session 1/UNITY/TalkSheet #1 and #2). Photocopy enough TalkSheets for all your students.
2. Make sure everyone has a Bible and a pen or pencil.
3. Reserve an overhead projector or bring in a chalkboard or dry-erase board.
4. Don't forget whatever props you need for any additional activities you decide to use (see Section Two).

Publicity for This Session
Mail each group member one piece of a jigsaw puzzle, along with a letter explaining that she is an important part of the youth group—just as the puzzle piece is an important part of the puzzle. Ask students to bring their puzzle pieces to the meeting.

Take time before or after the meeting to actually put the puzzle together with the group. (Choose a puzzle with approximately the same number of pieces as group members.) If some kids are absent, the incomplete puzzle shows how absence affects the group. You might stop right then to pray for those absent members.

For a different twist, cut a photo of the group into small pieces—like a puzzle—and mail out one piece to each person.

To Introduce This Session
"The Spy Game" (page 84), a quick simulation game that demonstrates unity, is a good opener for this session. Other ideas are listed under "Unity" in the categorical index before Section Two (page 29).

Before handing the TalkSheets to the kids, say something like *Unity is an important biblical concept. It means to be one, and it makes up half of the word* community. *More than anything else, a Christian community is group of people who have been made one in Jesus Christ.*

To Close This Session
Close this session with a prayer, not only for an increase in group unity but also for the entire course of study on Christian community.

Question #1: Draw a "Unity Meter" on the chalkboard, and ask some of the kids to indicate where they marked their X. Let them elaborate on their opinions, but don't let them turn it into a gripe session. Keep things positive by asking about specific times when the group experienced unity, even for a short time. Most groups discover a definite need for improvement. If the consensus is that the group is strong in unity, then affirm them and help them discover more about what their unity means.

Question #2: Allow the group to share their opinions on the meaning of unity. Of the four answers provided, the best choice is "being friends with others even though we have differences." The whole idea behind Christian unity is that people who are very different from each other can be one in Christ. We aren't all the same, and we don't always agree on everything, but we can still be one.

Question #3: List on the board the attitudes, actions, or circumstances that the kids feel hinder community. Guide the discussion away from overly negative or personal remarks.

Question #4: Lead the kids to discover that when Jesus was on earth he prayed for *us*. Jesus desired unity for all those who would believe on him—*that's us!* He didn't pray that we would win the whole world to Christ or that we would make the world a better place to live. He prayed for unity. Encourage the kids to share their opinions on why they do or do not believe that Jesus' prayer has been answered.

Question #5: After a close reading of the passage, ask them to call out the "ones" they found while you list them on the chalkboard.

Question #6: Add any additional "ones" suggested by your group to the list on the board.

Question #1: This question helps the students identify the things that divided people in the church at Galatia.

Question #2: Have fun brainstorming all the possibilities here— for example, "Neither sophomore nor senior." On most high-school campuses, seniors and sophomores don't mix much. Ask the kids what other groupings divide them from each other.

Question #3: Before students begin to write this passage in their own words, encourage them to specify the divisions that exist within their group without mentioning names. The purpose of this exercise is to identify areas that need improvement, not to accuse individuals. Invite several people to read their completed letters.

Question #4: Discuss the meaning of *humility* and why it is important to Christian unity. Get the kids thinking by asking, "Why is humility difficult for most people? Do people today think humility is a virtue? What makes you say that? Do you know any humble people? How can you tell they are humble?"

Question #5: Ask a few volunteers to share the actions and words they feel would show that they consider someone "better than themselves." Urge them to be specific and practical.

Unity

Neither Nor

1 *Read Galatians 3:26-28.* List all the "neither/nors" in this passage.

neither _____ nor _____

neither _____ nor _____

neither _____ nor _____

2 If you were to list a few "neither/nors" that would promote unity in your youth group, what would they be? (For example, "neither sophomore nor senior")

neither _____ nor _____

neither _____ nor _____

neither _____ nor _____

3 *Read 1 Corinthians 1:10-13.* Paul wrote this appeal to the Christians at the church at Corinth. If Paul were to write a letter to your church or youth group, what might he say? Rewrite the passage in your own words, applying it to your church or youth group.

To:
From: Paul
Message:

4 *Read Philippians 2:1-4:* According to this passage, what is the key to unity?

5 List a few ways you could consider others better than yourself:

_____

_____

Leader's Guide for Session 2
THE BODY OF CHRIST

The most common word picture of the church in Scripture is the picture of the human body. This picture helps us to understand the value of each individual in the church working together in unity.

Goals and Objectives for Session 2
This session will help the students—
• Understand how their youth group fits into the body of Christ.
• Realize that they are important parts of the body of Christ.

Things You Will Need for This Session
1. In the back of this book are the Talk-Sheets for this session (Session 2/THE BODY OF CHRIST/TalkSheets #1, #2, and #3). Photocopy enough TalkSheets for all your students.
2. Make sure everyone has a Bible and a pen or pencil.
3. Reserve an overhead projector or bring in a chalkboard or dry-erase board.
4. Don't forget whatever props you need for any additional activities you decide to use (see Section Two).

Publicity for This Session
Draw a human figure on a sheet of paper and put the head of Jesus on it. Then write the name of each youth-group member somewhere on the body. Title it "Body Beautiful." Mail out copies to the group with an invitation to come and find out what it means to be part of Christ's Body.

For something quick and simple, send out postcards that read, "Are you a toenail, an armpit, or a kneecap? Find out this week at youth group!"

To Introduce This Session
If you have time, play the "Body Balloon Burst" game (page 34). It takes about 10 minutes to play. Or try "Body Life Skit" (page 34) or "Brother Hood Hour" (page 36).

To Close This Session
One additional point to make in closing: The body of Christ is a metaphor, but it is not *just* a metaphor. The church is literally Christ's body—the physical presence of Christ in the world today. Just as Jesus brought healing and did many good works when he was physically on earth, so now his body, the church, must continue to bring healing and good works to the world. We are literally the hands and feet of Jesus Christ in the world.

Close with a prayer that your youth group will truly be the body of Christ in your neighborhood.

Question #1: In case students are not familiar with the term *metaphor*, explain that it compares something that you don't understand with something that you do understand. For example, the church is like a football team. Not literally, of course— most churches have more than eleven in the congregation—but figuratively. It is a metaphor.

In this exercise, the metaphors for the church that do not appear in the Bible are a garden, a rock, and a river. All the others are in the Bible. You might want to go over them with your students:

1. *A bride* (2 Corinthians 11:2; Ephesians 5:25; Romans 7:4). We are the bride; Christ is the bridegroom.
2. *A flock of sheep* (John 10:11-15). We are the sheep; Christ is the Good Shepherd.
3. *A family* (Hebrews 2:11, Galatians 4:1-7). We have been adopted into God's forever family. We are brothers and sisters in Christ; God is our heavenly Father.
4. *Salt* (Matthew 5:13). We are the salt of the earth. Salt is used both as a preservative and a seasoning.
5. *Branches on a vine* (John 15:1-8). Jesus is the vine, we are the fruit-bearing branches.
6. *A kingdom* (Colossians 1:13) We are citizens of the Kingdom of God; Jesus is the king, we are his subjects.
7. *A building* (Ephesians 2:19-22). We are a building "not made with hands" (2 Corinthians 5). We are a holy temple of God, with Christ as the cornerstone.

Ask the group to think of any modern metaphors that could describe the church— a zoo, a football team, a tossed green salad, a rock band. Have them explain why their metaphor is fitting.

Question #2: Ask the group to brainstorm as many comparisons between the church and a human body as they can think of. Encourage them to think of some not mentioned in the Scripture. For example, "A healthy body grows big and strong; a healthy church also grows big and strong."

Question #3: All four answers are true. Although the body of Christ can be thought of as the church universal, its most common application is the local body of believers— even the youth group.

Question #4: As your students think about their group as the body of Christ, they'll form an opinion about its well-being. If students don't feel like the body is healthy right now, ask them to explain why and to prescribe a cure.

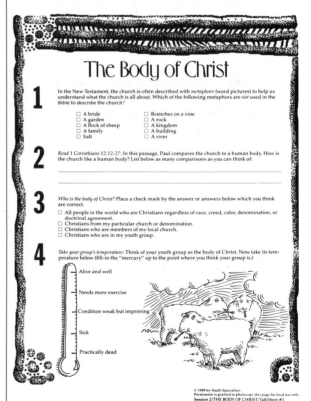

If your group is larger than 15 people, divide into groups of 10 or less. Ask someone to read aloud the instructions on the TalkSheet. Tell them to first write their own name, and then the names of *the people in their small group only*. This will save time if your group is large.

After the kids have worked on their TalkSheets for a few minutes, ask several to tell where they wrote their names. It will be interesting for all to see how they place themselves and how they are placed by others.

Find out how many kids thought to write Jesus' name on the head of the body. If they didn't, ask them to do that now. Ask them what they think that means. You might want to refer to Ephesians 4:15 and Philippians 2, especially verse 5, which talks about having the "mind of Christ." What does this mean for the body of Christ?

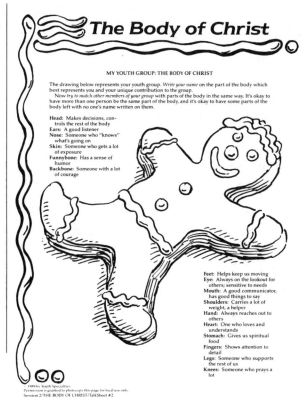

The Body of Christ

MY YOUTH GROUP: THE BODY OF CHRIST

The drawing below represents your youth group. *Write your name* on the part of the body which best represents you and your unique contribution to the group.

Now *try to match other members of your group* with parts of the body in the same way. It's okay to have more than one person be the same part of the body, and it's okay to have some parts of the body left with no one's name written on them.

Head: Makes decisions, controls the rest of the body
Ears: A good listener
Nose: Someone who "knows" what's going on
Skin: Someone who gets a lot of exposure
Funnybone: Has a sense of humor
Backbone: Someone with a lot of courage

Feet: Helps keep us moving
Eye: Always on the lookout for others; sensitive to needs
Mouth: A good communicator, has good things to say
Shoulders: Carries a lot of weight, a helper
Hand: Always reaches out to others
Heart: One who loves and understands
Stomach: Gives us spiritual food
Fingers: Shows attention to detail
Legs: Someone who supports the rest of us
Knees: Someone who prays a lot

Either allow the kids to work on these case studies—or "tension getters"—in small groups, or simply read them aloud to the entire group and ask them for possible endings. Telling what should happen next helps students apply the principles in the 1 Corinthians 12 passage. The discussion should help them see that thinking of the church or the youth group as the body of Christ is not merely an interesting perspective, but knowing that we are a body motivates us to make practical changes in the way we respond to each other. (If you like, add additional case studies—real or imaginary—that are closer to the actual experience of your youth group.)

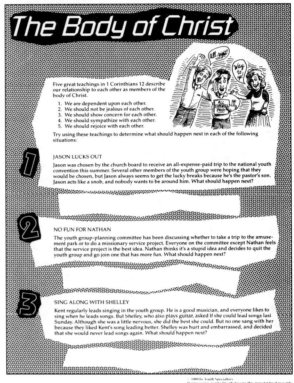

Leader's guide for Session 3
SPIRITUAL GIFTS

The body of Christ functions well as its members use their spiritual gifts "so that the body of Christ may be built up until we all reach unity in the faith . . . and become mature" (Ephesians 4:13). Session 3 focuses on Ephesians 4 and other passages of Scripture that name and explain the use of spiritual gifts that God gives to each Christian.

Goals and Objectives for Session 3
This session will help the students—
• List the various spiritual gifts mentioned in the Bible.
• Realize and appreciate that God has given to each of them special gifts for his ministry.
• Find ways to discover their own personal spiritual gifts.

Things You Will Need for This Session
1. In the back of this book are the Talk-Sheets for this session (Session 3/SPIRITUAL GIFTS/TalkSheets #1, #2, and #3). Photocopy enough TalkSheets for all your students.
2. Make sure everyone has a Bible and a pen or pencil.
3. Reserve an overhead projector or bring in a chalkboard or dry-erase board.
4. Don't forget whatever props you need for any additional activities you decide to use (see Section Two).

Publicity for This Session
To stimulate anticipation for this session, mail everyone a postcard that says: "You may be the lucky winner of a fabulous free gift! Bring this card to youth group this week and find out!" At the youth group meeting, you can actually give away some inexpensive gifts, or you can explain to everyone "Yes, you actually are the lucky recipient of a free gift! And it's a lot better than any toy or trinket. It's a spiritual gift that you are going to learn about tonight!"

Another way to publicize this meeting is to wrap a gift in beautiful paper and fancy bows, display it in a prominent place, and post a sign that reads: "Tonight at youth group . . . GIFTS FOR EVERYONE! Be there!" Open the display gift at the meeting (maybe a box of candy for everyone to share) and then announce that the study is on the fabulous gifts of the Spirit.

To Introduce This Session
Although several activities in Section Two highlight spiritual gifts, the "Give and Get Game" (page 54) especially illustrates the point of this session: When everyone is giving, then everyone is receiving.

Another opener is a short reader's theatre, "Gifts of Beauty" (page 52).

Introduce your group to the idea of spiritual gifts by saying something like *Gifts are great! Everyone likes to receive gifts, not only because of the gift itself but because the giving of a gift shows that another person cares a great deal for you.*

God cares a great deal about each one of us, and so he has given to us many wonderful gifts. Some of those gifts—health, shelter, and daily food—we take for granted. Other gifts we don't particularly appreciate—a little brother or sister, a demanding teacher, or liver and onions. Another kind of gift God gives us is a spiritual gift. *In fact, to each one of us in the body of Christ God gives one or more spiritual gifts for the benefit of the church. If you are part of the body of Christ, then you are blessed with spiritual gifts.*

To Close This Session
The young people in your youth group are not the church of tomorrow—they are the

church of right now. God has empowered them with gifts that can make a difference in the church and in the world.

Close with a prayer asking God to open the eyes of the young people to the gifts he has given them and to alert them to use their gifts to build up Christ's body and to glorify God.

Instructions for TalkSheet #1

Question #1: A gift has special significance because it's connected with the giver. Allow the students to share with each other some of the gifts they have received and why those gifts are meaningful to them.

Question #2: Brainstorm with the kids about good things that they have or that they have experienced. Help them see that God is the only source of goodness and the giver of good gifts.

Question #3: Read the listed Scriptures aloud with the group. Ask a few kids to share how they think a person discovers his spiritual gift. The correct answers that should emerge are these: (1) People in the church will tell you that they think you have that particular gift. (2) Sometimes you stumble across your spiritual gift by trying to do something and experiencing success with it. (3) If you *like* doing something, that could be it. When God gives someone a spiritual gift, he plants the desire to use it inside that person.

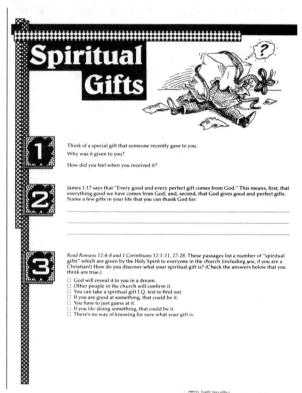

Spiritual Gifts

1 Think of a special gift that someone recently gave to you.
Why was it given to you?

How did you feel when you received it?

2 James 1:17 says that "Every good and every perfect gift comes from God." This means, first, that everything good we have comes from God; and, second, that God gives good and perfect gifts. Name a few gifts in your life that you can thank God for:

_____

_____

_____

3 Read *Romans 12:4-8 and 1 Corinthians 12:1-11, 27-28*. These passages list a number of "spiritual gifts" which are given by the Holy Spirit to everyone in the church (including *you*, if you are a Christian!) How do you discover what your spiritual gift is? (Check the answers below that you think are true.)

☐ God will reveal it to you in a dream.
☐ Other people in the church will confirm it.
☐ You can take a spiritual gift I.Q. test to find out.
☐ If you are good at something, that could be it.
☐ You have to just guess at it.
☐ If you *like* doing something, that could be it.
☐ There's no way of knowing for sure what your gift is.

After students match up as many words and definitions as they can, alone or in pairs, discuss with your group all the spiritual gifts specifically mentioned in the Bible. Don't get sidetracked debating the more unusual gifts with your kids. (If you need more information, consult a Bible dictionary or a resource like *Your Spiritual Gifts Can Help Your Church Grow* by C. Peter Wagner [Ventura: Regal Books, 1979].)

Spiritual Gifts

WHAT DO THEY MEAN?

Below is a list of spiritual gifts found in Romans 12, 1 Corinthians 12, and other passages in the New Testament. Do you know what they mean? See if you can match the name of the gift on the left with its meaning on the right.

f	1. Prophecy	a. To take the Gospel to another place or culture
o	2. Pastor	b. The ability to discover and clarify information
g	3. Teaching	c. To speak in an unknown language by the power of the Holy Spirit
b	4. Wisdom	d. To guide and direct others to use their gifts
w	5. Knowledge	e. To perform powerful acts in the name of Christ
p	6. Encouragement	f. To deliver a divine message from God
y	7. Discerning of spirits	g. To communicate information that helps others learn
r	8. Giving	h. To assist others in using their gifts
h	9. Helps	i. To provide an open house and friendship to those in need
n	10. Mercy	j. To suffer, even to the point of death, for Christ
a	11. Missionary	k. To identify and to solve unmet needs in the church
x	12. Evangelist	l. To be in authority over a number of churches
i	13. Hospitality	m. To cure illness and restore health in the name of Christ
q	14. Faith	n. To feel compassion for others and to help them
d	15. Leadership	o. To assume responsibility for a group of believers
u	16. Administration	p. To give words of comfort, affirmation, and counsel to others
e	17. Miracles	q. To have extraordinary confidence in God
m	18. Healing	r. The ability to contribute material resources to the body
c	19. Tongues	s. To pray for others regularly and effectively
t	20. Interpretation	t. To translate the message of one speaking in tongues
l	21. Apostle	u. To set goals and to devise and execute plans to fulfill those goals
v	22. Celibacy	v. To remain single and to resist sexual temptations
s	23. Intercession	w. To have special insights given by the Holy Spirit.
j	24. Martyrdom	x. To share the good news with unbelievers
k	25. Service	y. To know whether something is of God or Satan

After the group completes the exercise, ask a few volunteers to share their discoveries. Prompt interaction by asking, "Did any of you find yourself to be strong in more than one of the gifts?" and "Did any of you have trouble finding any one of these gifts that you were strong in?" and "When you were reading the descriptions of the spiritual gifts, did someone else's name in the group come to mind?"

Point out that the list on the TalkSheet does not define all of the spiritual gifts listed in the Bible. God may have given one in your group the gift of pastoring, of being a missionary, or of healing. In fact, many scholars believe that the Bible itself does not give an exhaustive list of spiritual gifts. One of your kids, for instance, may be gifted with a sense of humor or with creativity. The important thing is to find out what gift God has given to you to benefit the body of Christ.

Spiritual Gifts

Do you know what your spiritual gift is? (You may have been given more than one!) For each of the eight listed below, circle a number to indicate whether you feel weak or strong in any of them.

The Gift of Service
God has given me a special ability for helping out whenever a need arises. If there is a job that needs to be done, I am willing to do it if I can.

1   2   3   4   5   6   7   8   9   10
Weak   Strong

The Gift of Teaching
God has given me a skill for helping others to learn. I am good at motivating people to learn and grow in the Christian faith.

1   2   3   4   5   6   7   8   9   10
Weak   Strong

The Gift of Speaking God's Truth (Evangelism)
God has given me a gift for communicating the Gospel to others. When I explain the Good News, God seems to use my words to bring insight and understanding about his grace.

1   2   3   4   5   6   7   8   9   10
Weak   Strong

The Gift of Encouragement
God has given me the ability to see the best in others. I find it easy to compliment people and to point out their strengths.

1   2   3   4   5   6   7   8   9   10
Weak   Strong

The Gift of Leadership
God has given me a gift for organization. I can get things done. I find it easy to take responsibility and direct others.

1   2   3   4   5   6   7   8   9   10
Weak   Strong

The Gift of Kindness (Mercy)
God has given me the ability to be compassionate and understanding whenever someone is in trouble or needs help. I enjoy being able to minister to someone who is feeling down.

1   2   3   4   5   6   7   8   9   10
Weak   Strong

The Gift of Generosity (Giving)
God has given me a freedom to share myself with others. I find it easy to give whatever I can to others or to God's work whenever a special need arises.

1   2   3   4   5   6   7   8   9   10
Weak   Strong

The Gift of Faith
God has given me complete confidence and trust in him. Whenever I pray, I believe and fully expect that God will answer my prayer.

1   2   3   4   5   6   7   8   9   10
Weak   Strong

The Gift of Helps
God has given me the desire and ability to assist other members of the body to use their spiritual gifts. I enjoy helping other people to be more effective in their ministries.

1   2   3   4   5   6   7   8   9   10
Weak   Strong

Leader's Guide for Session 4
CHRISTIAN LOVE

Paul ended his teaching about spiritual gifts to the Corinthian church by saying, "Earnestly desire the best gifts," but immediately added, "And I show you a more excellent way." What follows is one of the most eloquent statements on Christian love ever written. Romans 12 and Ephesians 4 are also followed by practical guidelines for demonstrating love in the body. The implication is clear: Contributing to the common good of the church by practicing spiritual gifts is important—but unless genuine love is the motivation, Christian community will not be the result. Session 4 focuses on the importance of love in the Body of Christ.

Goals and Objectives for Session 4
This session will help the students—
• Recognize the difference between Christian love and other kinds of love.
• Realize the importance of putting love into action.
• Consider practical ways to express love in the body of Christ.

Things You Will Need for This Session
1. In the back of this book are the Talk-Sheets for this session (Session 4/CHRISTIAN LOVE/TalkSheets #1, #2, and #3). Photocopy enough TalkSheets for all your students.
2. Make sure everyone has a Bible and a pen or pencil.
3. Reserve an overhead projector or bring in a chalkboard or dry-erase board.

4. Don't forget whatever props you need for any additional activities you decide to use (see Section Two).

Publicity for This Session
Send everyone in the group a valentine with the message, "This week at youth group: How to be become a great lover." That should raise a few eyebrows and motivate everyone to come!

Or create an announcement incorporating the words of a popular rock song. For example: *Tina Turner wants to know: "What's love got to do with it?" — Get the answer to that and other questions about true love this week at youth group!*

To Introduce This Session
Toss this question out to the group as a quick opener: "What is *love*? We hear a lot about love in music, at the movies, in our literature. But what is it? How would you define it?"

After some of the kids share their answers, say something like *Tonight we'll explore the concept of love a little bit—especially Christian love—and find out how we can become better lovers.*

To Close This Session
Have the group select two applications from the last exercise and commit together to begin practicing them right now. Close with a prayer thanking God for his great love and committing the group to be more loving, especially within the body of Christ.

Question #1: Designing a bumper sticker lets the group think about love in a non-threatening way. Just for fun, ask kids to share their bumper stickers with the group.

Question #2: Composing a definition requires kids to dig deeper into their perceptions of love. Of the answers volunteers share aloud, ask the group which ones they agree with the most.

Question #3: Review aloud the definitions of *philos*, *eros*, and *agape* from the TalkSheet, pointing out that in English our one word for *love* means all three types. Statements #3 and #6 illustrate *philos*; #2 and #4, *eros*; #1 and #5, *agape*.

The Bible never condemns either *philos* or *eros* love. In fact, the Bible assures us that they are good, natural, and even necessary for our well-being. But it is God's love, *agape*, that makes them complete. *Agape* enriches our love for our families and our ethnic heritage (*philos*) and enhances intimacy with the person we give *eros* love to—we become better lovers because we accept the person we love unconditionally and give ourselves to them. *Agape* completes beauty and intimacy. Without *agape*, *philos* and *eros* alone will not satisfy the longing of the human heart.

The discussion of the three loves leads into the skit "Parable of the Shapes" on page 73. (If they don't have time to memorize lines, several students can present it readers-theatre style.) The three loves are described there as "If" love, "Because" love, and "In Spite Of" love.

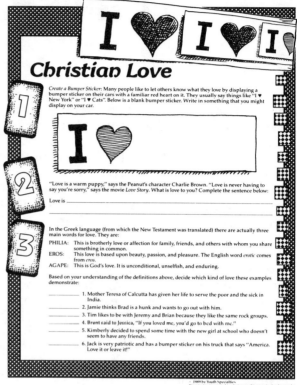

Question #1: Give the kids time to decide (on the basis of these brief descriptions) which of the young people on the list would be easy to love or hard to love. Ask for a show of hands on each one. Don't allow remarks that associate any of these kids with actual kids in the youth group. Make the point that not everyone is easy to love. Love doesn't happen automatically. We must be committed to Love itself (to God himself), and then we will be able to love those who seem unlovable.

Christian love, one has said, "is love that just sprays out there. Anyone who walks in front of it gets loved." In other words, Christian love is not choosy about who gets loved or dependent upon the desirable qualities of the object of that love.

Question #2: Ask how many people marked *true* and how many marked *false*. Normally we think of loving someone only after we like them a lot. But Christian love reverses the order. We love first and let liking develop later, if ever. "Christ never asked us to like our neighbor," writes C.S. Lewis in *The Four Loves*. "But he did ask us to love even the people we don't like." Christian writer Frederick Buechner adds,

In Jesus' terms we can love our neighbors without necessarily liking them. In fact, liking them may stand in the way of loving them by making us overprotective sentimentalists instead of reasonably honest friends. When Jesus talked to the Pharisees, he didn't say, "There, there, everything's going to be all right." He said, "You brood of vipers! How can you speak good when you are evil!" (Matthew 12:34) And he said that to them because he loved them. This does not mean that liking may not be a part of loving, only that it doesn't have to be. (*Wishful Thinking*, Harper & Row, 1973)

Question #3: After reading aloud this passage, ask the kids to read their statements on why it is important for Christians to love. The 1 John passage makes three main points: First, love is the test of real Christianity, the mark of the Christian; second, we should love others because God first loved us; third, if we love each other, God lives in us and his love is made complete in us.

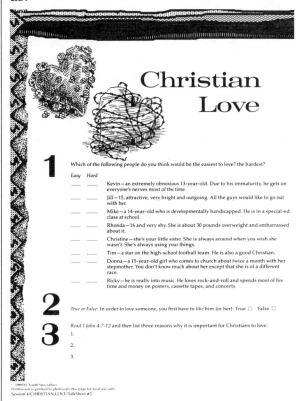

Christian Love

1 Which of the following people do you think would be the easiest to love? the hardest?

Easy Hard

____ ____ Kevin—an extremely obnoxious 13-year-old. Due to his immaturity, he gets on everyone's nerves most of the time.

____ ____ Jill—15, attractive, very bright and outgoing. All the guys would like to go out with her.

____ ____ Mike—a 14-year-old who is developmentally handicapped. He is in a special-ed class at school.

____ ____ Rhonda—16 and very shy. She is about 30 pounds overweight and embarrassed about it.

____ ____ Christine—she's your little sister. She is always around when you wish she wasn't. She's always using your things.

____ ____ Tim—a star on the high-school football team. He is also a good Christian.

____ ____ Donna—a 15-year-old girl who comes to church about twice a month with her stepmother. You don't know much about her except that she is of a different race.

____ ____ Ricky—he is really into music. He loves rock-and-roll and spends most of his time and money on posters, cassette tapes, and concerts.

2 *True or False*: In order to love someone, you first have to *like* him (or her). True ☐ False ☐

3 *Read 1 John 4:7-12* and then list three reasons why it is important for Christians to love:

1.

2.

3.

Question #1: The third phrase, "you demonstrate it" is the point of the Scripture. Love must be put into action.

Question #2: Give the kids enough time to thoughtfully apply these Scriptures about Christian love to their youth group. Sometimes working in groups stimulates more practical applications than an individual will think of. Start them thinking with questions like, "What are the changes that need to be made?" or "What must we stop doing?" or "What must we start doing or continue doing?" or "How can we demonstrate Christian love more in our youth group?" Allow the kids to share their conclusions with the entire group while you write them down on the chalkboard or on newsprint.

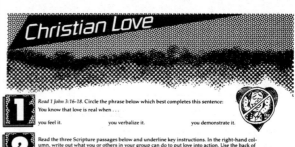

Christian Love

1 Read 1 John 3:16-18. Circle the phrase below which best completes this sentence:
You know that love is real when . . .

you feel it.   you verbalize it.   you demonstrate it.

2 Read the three Scripture passages below and underline key instructions. In the right-hand column, write out what you or others in your group can do to put love into action. Use the back of this sheet if needed.

Romans 12
Love must be sincere. Hate what is evil; cling to what is good. Be devoted to one another in brotherly love. Honor one another above yourselves. Never be lacking in zeal, but keep your spiritual fervor, serving the Lord. Be joyful in hope, patient in affliction, faithful in prayer. Share with God's people who are in need. Practice hospitality.
Bless those who persecute you; bless and do not curse. Rejoice with those who rejoice; mourn with those who mourn. Live in harmony with one another. Do not be proud, but be willing to associate with people of low position. Do not be conceited.
Do not repay anyone evil for evil. Be careful to do what is right in the eyes of everybody. If it is possible, as far as it depends on you, live at peace with everyone. Do not take revenge, my friends, but leave room for God's wrath, for it is written: "It is mine to avenge; I will repay," says the Lord. On the contrary: "If your enemy is hungry, feed him; if he is thirsty, give him something to drink. In doing this, you will heap burning coals on his head."
Do not be overcome by evil, but overcome evil with good.

1 Corinthians 13
Love is patient, love is kind. It does not envy, it does not boast, it is not proud. It is not rude, it is not self-seeking, it is not easily angered, it keeps no record of wrongs. Love does not delight in evil but rejoices with the truth. It always protects, always trusts, always hopes, always perseveres.

Ephesians 4
Therefore each of you must put off falsehood and speak truthfully to his neighbor, for we are all members of one body. "In your anger do not sin": Do not let the sun go down while you are still angry, and do not give the devil a foothold. He who has been stealing must steal no longer, but must work, doing something useful with his own hands, that he may have something to share with those in need.
Do not let any unwholesome talk come out of your mouths, but only what is helpful for building others up according to their needs, that it may benefit those who listen. And do not grieve the Holy Spirit of God, with whom you were sealed for the day of redemption. Get rid of all bitterness, rage and anger, brawling and slander, along with every form of malice. Be kind and compassionate to one another, forgiving each other, just as in Christ God forgave you.

(Example:)
1. It seems like we argue a lot in this group — usually about stuff that really doesn't matter. We need to listen more and argue less.

Leader's Guide for Session 5
FORGIVENESS

Love knits the body of Christ together as believers exercise their spiritual gifts for the benefit of the whole body. Love also leads to forgiveness. God forgives us because he loves us, and our love for each other is the foundation for forgiving each other when there is conflict. This is the emphasis of Session 5.

Goals and Objectives for Session 5

This session will help the students—
• Understand the complete and unconditional nature of God's love.
• Recognize their responsibility to practice Christian forgiveness toward each other.
• Commit themselves to practicing forgiveness whenever conflict arises in the youth group.

Things You Will Need for This Session

1. In the back of this book are the Talk-Sheets for this session (Session 5/FORGIVENESS/TalkSheets #1, #2, and #3) photocopy enough TalkSheets for all your students.
2. Make sure everyone has a Bible and a pen or pencil.
3. Reserve an overhead projector or bring in a chalkboard or dry-erase board.
4. Don't forget whatever props you need for any additional activities you decide to use (see Section Two).

Publicity for This Session

If you plan to use the story of Hosea and Gomer (TalkSheet #2), consider this announcement: "Would God want *you* to marry a prostitute? Find out this week at Youth Group!" Or mail the group postcards that read, "Question of the week: *Who was Gomer*—a character on the *Andy Griffith* show, a famous prostitute, or a stand-in for Pee-Wee Herman? Get the answer this week at Youth Group!"

For something more to the point, you could send out a mailer with the headline: "ALL'S FORGIVEN! Find out more this week at Youth Group!"

To Introduce This Session

Show the group forgiveness and judgment in action by playing the game "Forgivers and Judgers" (page 50), or bring them face to face with forgiveness by role playing a confrontation with one of the kids.

Before the meeting secretly arrange for one of the students to disrupt your lesson by repeatedly talking to a friend or by saying something offensive. Then you get mad and threaten to call his parents or even send him out of the room for the rest of the meeting. The student begs for forgiveness. You ignore him. He continues to beg and plead. You ask the group if *they* think you ought to forgive him. If the acting is convincing, the group should be stunned into readiness for realistically discussing forgiveness.

To Close This Session

Read Matthew 5:9 again as you encourage your kids to practice forgiveness. Remind them that a good place to start is to forgive or to ask forgiveness from the person whose initials are written on their TalkSheets. Close with prayer.

Question #1: This exercise is a good warm-up activity that's fun and gets kids thinking about confession. In pairs the kids read their three statements to each other, guessing which is the true confession. Find out how many students scored two points.

Question #2: God forgives us because he loves us and because Jesus paid for our sins on the cross. Other statements are true statements (God wants us to love him, for instance), but they are not the reasons why he forgives us. Emphasize to your students that sin *is* a big deal and that sins are *not* easy for God to forgive. They cost the suffering and death of God's Son, Jesus Christ. But because of the price that was paid, God is "faithful and just to forgive us for our sins."

Question #3: Have the kids share their answers. The main idea is that *Christians should forgive in response to and in the same spirit as God's forgiveness.*

Question #4: Let two of your kids role-play this parable. Cast one of them as the king and another as the servant who owed 10,000 talents. The scene starts with verse 32, when the king calls the servant in. The servant must convince the king that what he did (not forgiving the fellow servant's small debt) was right.

Jesus taught that we are obligated to forgive each other in light of the forgiveness that God has given to us. Have the kids share their answers to the questions and their interpretations of the parable's moral. Record them on the chalkboard so that everyone can see them during the remainder of the session.

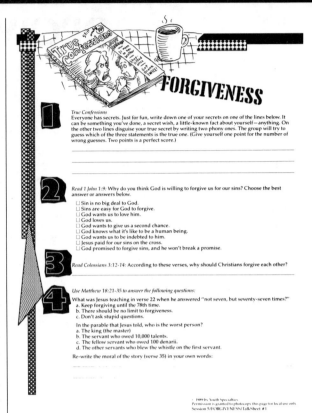

Instead of distributing this TalkSheet, you can read the story of Gomer and Hosea to the group and lead a discussion afterward asking these or other questions.

1. What is your impression of Hosea? Of Gomer?
2. Why do you think Hosea did what he did?
3. How do you think Gomer felt about Hosea?
4. Who do you identify with the most, Gomer or Hosea? Why?
5. What do you think is the main point of this story?

(Even if you duplicate and pass out this TalkSheet, you may still want to read the story while the kids follow along.)

Hosea's story shows that God loves us and forgives us and sticks with us, even though we are sinners and run away from him. The book of Hosea was written to the people of Israel who, like Gomer, were unfaithful to God. Yet God would not give up on Israel. He still has not given up on them—or us. Make sure this point comes through.

Forgiveness

The Old Testament book of Hosea describes God's forgiveness in the story of the prophet Hosea and his wife, Gomer. One Christian writer, Frederick Buechner, has re-told the story in modern language. Read his version and answer the questions that follow.

GOMER

She was always good company—a little heavy with the lipstick maybe, a little less than choosy about men and booze, a little loud, but great on a party and always good for a laugh. Then the prophet Hosea came along wearing a sandwich board that read "The End is at Hand" on one side and "Watch Out" on the other.

The first time he asked her to marry him, she thought he was kidding. The second time she knew he was serious but thought he was crazy. The third time she said yes. He wasn't exactly a swinger, but he had a kind face, and he was generous, and he wasn't all that crazier than everybody else. Besides, any fool could see he loved her.

Give or take a little, she even loved him back for a while, and they had three children whom Hosea named with queer names like Not-pitied-for-God-will-no-longer-pity-Israel-now-that-it's-gone-to-the-dogs so that every time the roll was called at school, Hosea would be scoring a prophetic bulls-eye in absentia. But everybody could see the marriage wasn't going to last, and it didn't.

While Hosea was off hitting the sawdust trail, Gomer took to hitting as many night spots as she could squeeze into a night, and any resemblance between her next batch of children and Hosea was purely coincidental. It almost killed him, of course. Every time she raised a hand to him, he burst into tears. Every time she raised one to him, he was the one who ended up apologizing.

He tried locking her out of the house a few times when she wasn't in by five in the morning, but he always opened the door when she finally showed up and helped get her to bed if she couldn't see straight enough to get there herself. Then one day she didn't show up at all.

He swore that this time he was through with her for keeps, but of course he wasn't. When he finally found her, she was lying passed out in a highly specialized establishment located above an adult bookstore, and he had to pay the management plenty to let her out of her contract. She'd lost her front teeth and picked up some scars you had to see to believe, but Hosea had her back again and that seemed to be all that mattered.

He changed his sandwich board to read "God is love" on one side and "There's no end to it" on the other, and when he stood on the street corner belting out

How can I give you up, O Ephraim!
How can I hand you over, O Israel!
For I am God and no man,
The Holy One in your midst.
(Hosea 11:8-9)

nobody can say how many converts he made, but one thing that's for sure is that, including Gomer's, there was seldom a dry eye in the house. (Hosea 1-3, 11)

(Reprinted by permission from *Peculiar Treasures* by Frederick Buechner, copyright 1979 by Frederick Buechner, Harper & Row Publishers, San Francisco.)

This story is, in my opinion:

☐ ridiculous   ☐ funny   ☐ impossible
☐ I don't get it   ☐ disgusting   ☐ heavy
☐ sad   ☐ incredible   ☐ touching

What do you think is the main point of this story?

Question #1: Ask a few volunteers to honestly share their responses to the situations. Probably no one will choose "forgive and forget" in all of these situations. Ask the group, "What do you think Jesus would do in each case?"

A good point to make here is that it is possible to still love someone without loving what they have done. C.S. Lewis wrote, "For a long time, I used to think this is a silly, straw-splitting distinction," writes C.S. Lewis in *The Four Loves.* "How could you hate what a man did and not hate the man? But years later it occurred to me that there was one man to whom I had been doing this all my life—namely myself. However much I might dislike my own cowardice or conceit or greed, I went on loving myself. There had never been the slightest difficulty with it."

Another point is that the option "Talk to the person about it" is always a good one. Matthew 18:15-19 gives some guidelines. Confront them lovingly and offer forgiveness. If the person won't accept it, then walk away from it. *Read Romans 12:17-21 to the group.* Our other option as believers is to overcome evil with good.

Question #2: Talk briefly about why some chose forgiving (or asking forgiveness) as the more difficult. The point is that both require effort.

Question #3: There is a difference between peace-makers and peace-lovers. Most think of themselves as peace-lovers, but it is only the peace-makers who are blessed, says Jesus. Forgiving qualifies you as a peace-maker and results in blessing from God.

The flip-side is if we *don't* forgive, we receive the opposite of blessing—unhappiness, bitterness, resentment, hatred, and anger. The choice is ours.

Question #4: Since the answer to this question is personal, don't ask your kids to share unless they want to. Open discussion by asking, "What steps might you take to make peace with the person whom you have identified on your sheet?"

Forgiveness

1 *What would you do?* Read the situations below and decide how you would most likely respond. (Be honest!) Write in the letter of your probable response:

a. Hold a grudge.
b. Get mad.
c. Get even.
d. Get depressed.
e. Avoid that person in the future.
f. Throw a tantrum.
g. Laugh.
h. Nothing.
i. Forgive and forget.
j. Talk to the person about it.
k. Pray.
l. Other: _____

_____ Someone starts a nasty rumor about you that is not true.
_____ Someone tells your folks about something bad you did.
_____ Someone cuts you down or calls you a derogatory name.
_____ Someone steals something from you.
_____ Someone copies your homework or test.
_____ Someone plays a practical joke on you that makes you look dumb.
_____ Someone spills ink on your best outfit.
_____ Someone borrows something from you and then damages it or doesn't return it.
_____ Someone goes out with your steady boyfriend or girlfriend.
_____ Someone lies to you.
_____ Someone physically hits or threatens you.

2 Which is most difficult for you:
☐ To forgive someone?
☐ To ask for their forgiveness?

3 *Read Matthew 5:9.* Now check the statement that best applies to you.
☐ I always do whatever I can to make peace with others.
☐ I sometimes try to make peace with others.
☐ I rarely try to make peace with others.
☐ I never try to make peace with others.

4 *Read Ephesians 4:31-32.* Is there a person you need to forgive? A person you need to ask for forgiveness? Write their initials here: _____

Leader's Guide for Session 6
SERVANTHOOD

Today we talk a lot about rights: civil rights, human rights, women's rights, children's rights, even gay rights. We're supposed to stand up for ourselves. Jesus, however, made it clear that we have the right to give up our rights in service to him and to each other. In fact, he said it is the only way to really live.

Goals and Objectives for Session 6
This session will help the students—
- Define greatness as "serving each other."
- Evaluate specific ideas and examples of serving each other.
- Explain how humility and self-sacrifice contribute to unity in the body of Christ and to better relationships with others.

Things You Will Need for This Session
1. In the back of this book are the Talk-Sheets for this session (Session 6/SERVANTHOOD/TalkSheets #1, #2, #3, and #4). Photocopy enough Talk-Sheets for all your students.
2. Make sure everyone has a Bible and a pen or pencil.
3. Reserve an overhead projector or bring in a chalkboard or dry-erase board.
4. Don't forget whatever props you need for any additional activities you decide to use (see Section Two).

Publicity for This Session
Send a postcard to each member of the group announcing that this week's meeting will feature "service with a smile." Or use the slogan "Get Real!" or ask "What is Real?" suggesting the excerpt from *The Velveteen Rabbit*.

For another approach, sponsor a "Who Is the Greatest?" contest at the youth group: "Find out this week if YOU qualify for greatness!"

To Introduce This Session
Choose three students to introduce this session by performing the following skit.

One Fine Day
in the Insane Asylum

Actors 1 and 2: patients in an insane asylum.
Actor 3: a doctor making her rounds to check on the patients.

Actors one and two are sitting in chairs picking flowers out of the air and looking vacantly insane.

Actor 1: (*jumping up all of a sudden, beating on his chest, and shouting*) I am the greatest! I am the king of the universe! I am the greatest! There is no one alive greater than me! (*He keeps this up, while Actor 2 sits passively ignoring him*)

Actor 3: (*enters and tries to quiet Actor 1*) Hey, let's quiet down! You're disturbing the other patients. Besides, what makes you think you're the greatest person alive, anyway?

Actor 1: God told me!
Actor 2: (*jumps up and yells*) I did not!!

After the actors leave the stage, you can say something like *You don't have to be a nobody! God wants you to do great things and to become a truly great person! Tonight we're going to discover the real meaning of greatness—from God's perspective.*

To Close This Session
Focus your closing prayer on some of commitments the group made to practice the servanthood of Jesus (from TalkSheet #3). Sing "Servant of All" (in Maranatha

Music's *Praise* songbook and as well as in the Songs and Creations *Songs* songbook) or listen to Bob Dylan's "Gotta Serve Somebody" from the album *Slow Train Comin'*.

In another meeting create a youth-group coupon book made up of services contributed by members of the youth group. For example, "I will come to your house and straighten up your bedroom. Redeem any weekend" or "I will come to your house and mow your lawn for you. You provide the lawn mower" or "This coupon good for one free guitar lesson."

Another idea to reinforce the teaching in this session is "Servant Certificates" (page 81).

Instructions for TalkSheet #1

Question #1: Have each person share the name of his nominee and his reason for nominating this person to receive the Nobel Prize for Greatness.

Question #2: Ask the kids to tell their top three choices of great actions. What are some other actions the group considers great. Ask who decides what greatness is for each of them as individuals. Who do they most want to impress? Friends at school? Teachers? Parents? Themselves? God? Does this make a difference in what they do?

Question #3: Read the Scripture aloud before the kids write out a definition of greatness according to Jesus. Allow them to share their definitions as well as the words they have chosen to describe what Jesus meant by *servant*. Stimulate further discussion by asking, "Why do you think the disciples were arguing about who was the greatest? How do you think the disciples felt when Jesus answered them the way he did?"

Question #1: When the kids have read the Scripture and completed the questions, invite them to share their answers. Some teachers suggest the towel as a symbol for leadership in the church; for it was with the towel that Jesus washed the feet of the disciples, demonstrating his teaching that the leader's role is that of a servant. Mention that, unlike communion, Jesus did not institutionalize foot-washing as a ritual in the church. It is instead a metaphor for any act of servanthood. Explain also that humbly accepting the servanthood of others is a mark of a leader. Sometimes—like Peter—we are reluctant to allow others to serve us. But one way we serve others is to gratefully allow them to serve us.

Discuss what today's equivalent to foot-washing might be. You may want to actually wash someone's feet to demonstrate how the disciples might have felt when Jesus washed their feet.

Question #2: Put each quality to a vote—agree or disagree—and record on the chalkboard a group definition of *humility* and *sacrificial love*. This dramatic description of Jesus also describes how we should live. "Let this mind be in you" means that we should follow Jesus' example. The next TalkSheet will put some practical handles on this.

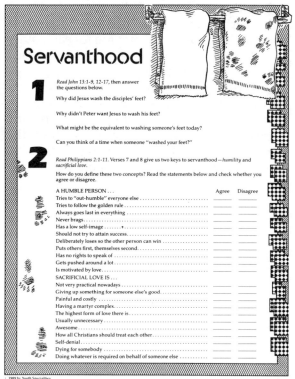

Instructions for TalkSheet #3

Question #1: As you discuss each one of the verses, encourage the kids to suggest strategies for actually praying for each other or sharing possessions or forgiving or disciplining each other.

Question #2: Of the strategies discussed during question #1, invite the kids to thoughtfully choose three. List specific ideas that the group comes up with on the board, and ask each young person to choose one that she will practice *this week*.

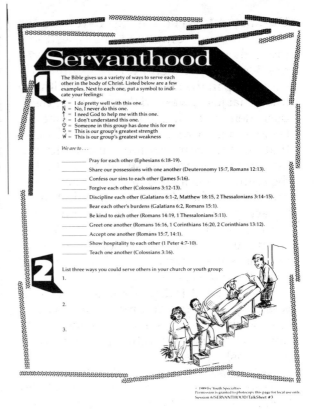

Servanthood

1 The Bible gives us a variety of ways to serve each other in the body of Christ. Listed below are a few examples. Next to each one, put a symbol to indicate your feelings:

★ = I do pretty well with this one.
N = No, I never do this one.
↑ = I need God to help me with this one.
? = I don't understand this one.
♡ = Someone in this group has done this for me
S = This is our group's greatest strength
W = This is our group's greatest weakness

We are to . . .

_____ Pray for each other (Ephesians 6:18-19).

_____ Share our possessions with one another (Deuteronomy 15:7, Romans 12:13).

_____ Confess our sins to each other (James 5:16).

_____ Forgive each other (Colossians 3:12-13).

_____ Discipline each other (Galatians 6:1-2, Matthew 18:15, 2 Thessalonians 3:14-15).

_____ Bear each other's burdens (Galatians 6:2, Romans 15:1).

_____ Be kind to each other (Romans 14:19, 1 Thessalonians 5:11).

_____ Greet one another (Romans 16:16, 1 Corinthians 16:20, 2 Corinthians 13:12).

_____ Accept one another (Romans 15:7, 14:1).

_____ Show hospitality to each other (1 Peter 4:7-10).

_____ Teach one another (Colossians 3:16).

2 List three ways you could serve others in your church or youth group:

1.

2.

3.

Instructions for TalkSheet #4

Use this optional TalkSheet in conjunction with question #2 on TalkSheet #2 to give a clearer picture of sacrificial love. This excerpt from *The Velveteen Rabbit* is a powerful parable describing the self-giving nature of love. (You may choose to use this TalkSheet without reproducing it. Simply read the story to the kids and allow them to verbally respond to the questions.)

Servanthood

"WHAT IS REAL"
(from *The Velveteen Rabbit*
by Armand Eisen)

"What is REAL?" asked the Rabbit one day, when they were lying side by side near the nursery fender, before Nana came to tidy the room. "Does it mean having things that buzz inside you and a stick-out handle?"

"Real isn't how you are made," said the Skin Horse. "It's a thing that happens to you. When a child loves you for a long, long time, not just to play with, but REALLY loves you, then you become Real."

"Does it hurt?" asked the Rabbit.

"Sometimes," said the Skin Horse, for he was always truthful. "When you are Real you don't mind being hurt."

"Does it happen all at once, like being wound up," he asked, "or bit by bit?"

"It doesn't happen all at once," said the Skin Horse. "You become. It takes a long time. That's why it doesn't often happen to people who break easily, or have sharp edges, or who have to be carefully kept. Generally, by the time you are Real, most of your hair has been loved off, and your eyes drop out and you get loose in the joints and very shabby. But these things don't matter at all, because once you are Real you can't be ugly, except to people who don't understand."

1 Questions to think about:
How does this story make you feel? Why?

2 What do you think about "being real"? What does it mean?

3 When or how have you experienced "being real"?

4 Write out what you think is the moral of the story below.

Leader's Guide for Session 7
MY SELF

Jesus said that the second greatest commandment is "Love your neighbor as yourself" (Matthew 22:39). If this statement guides us how to love our neighbor, it also instructs us how to love ourselves. The Bible has much to say about how God thinks of us and many clues about how we should think of ourselves. In this session your kids will examine some of these clues and discuss how their own self-images affect the quality of life in the body of Christ.

Goals and Objectives for Session 7
This session will help students—
• List things that influence their self-concept.
• Recognize the relationship between a healthy self-image and community building.
• Move toward changing their self-images to conform to God's image of them.

Things You Will Need for This Session
1. In the back of this book are the Talk-Sheets for this session (Session 7/MY SELF/TalkSheet #1, #2, and #3). Photocopy enough TalkSheets #1 and #2 for each person in your group. TalkSheet #3 is optional.
2. Make sure everyone has a Bible and a pen or pencil.
3. Reserve an overhead projector or bring in a chalkboard or dry-erase board.
4. Don't forget whatever props you need for any additional activities you decide to use (see Section Two).

Publicity for This Session
Here's a fun mailer idea. Draw a life-size face on a piece of paper and cut out the eyes so that a person can look through the page. Then print the announcement for the next meeting above, below, or around the face *in reverse type* so that it can be read only in a mirror. Attach a note to the mailer instructing the reader to hold the announcement up to a mirror and look through the eye holes to read what it says.

— "Do you sometimes feel like a turkey? Join the crowd this week at Youth Group and discover the real you! Gobble it up!"

To Introduce This Session
Illustrate the power that other people's labeling of individuals has to influence self-image by playing "Identity Masks" (page 61).

Following the game, say something like *Your self-image—how you think of yourself—influences how you relate to others. If you can't stand yourself, chances are that no one else will* be able to stand you either. On the other hand, if you feel comfortable with yourself and accept yourself as you are, others more easily accept you and feel comfortable getting to know you.

To Close This Session

The first step in developing friendships and loving others with *agape* love is to accept God's deep love for us and so learn a healthy self-love. We are each one special and wonderful in God's eyes—so special that he sent his Son to die for us. When we receive God's great love, the possibility for genuine community exists. We will consider others worthy of our love because God has especially loved each one of them.

Either lead the group in one of the affirmation exercises in Section Two or close with prayer. Thank God for his love and for creating each person in the group with special gifts, talents, and abilities. Pray that all group members might become more aware of their own self-worth, as well as the worth of others.

Instructions for TalkSheet #1

Question #1: Choosing one word of the pair gets kids thinking about what kind of people they are. After students have made their choices, pick out a few of the word pairs and ask a few kids to tell why they picked the words they did. Have some fun with this question.

Question #2: Ask several kids to tell who they would like to be and why they chose that person. Their choices identify what they value. Notice how many physically appealing, wealthy, powerful, or famous people they choose. Comment on what these choices reveal. Do your students desire lasting, God-honoring qualities, or do their choices reflect that they are self-centered and short-sighted? Without criticizing your kids for their choices, point out that the best people to imitate are those who value godly priorities. You may want to have the kids select one person from all those named as the person most worthy of patterning their lives after.

Question #3: If your group is larger than 10, divide into groups of five or less for this question. Ask each person to share any *three* of the completed sentences on their TalkSheet with the rest of the group they are in. They can choose to share the ones they are most comfortable with.

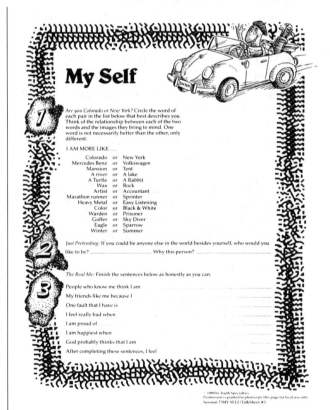

My Self

Are you *Colorado* or *New York*? Circle the word of each pair in the list below that best describes you. Think of the relationship between each of the two words and the images they bring to mind. One word is not necessarily better than the other, only different.

I AM MORE LIKE . . .

Colorado	or	New York
Mercedes Benz	or	Volkswagen
Mansion	or	Tent
A river	or	A lake
A Turtle	or	A Rabbit
Wax	or	Rock
Artist	or	Accountant
Marathon runner	or	Sprinter
Heavy Metal	or	Easy Listening
Color	or	Black & White
Warden	or	Prisoner
Golfer	or	Sky Diver
Eagle	or	Sparrow
Winter	or	Summer

Just Pretending: If you could be anyone else in the world besides yourself, who would you like to be? _____ Why this person? _____

The Real Me: Finish the sentences below as honestly as you can.

People who know me think I am _____
My friends like me because I _____
One fault that I have is _____
I feel really bad when _____
I am proud of _____
I am happiest when _____
God probably thinks that I am _____
After completing these sentences, I feel _____

Instructions for TalkSheet #2

Question #1: Most students have been on one side or the other of Jeremy's situation. In small groups discuss Jeremy's problem and their answers to the printed questions. Ask them also to arrive at a consensus on the question "What advice would you give to Jeremy?" and then share their advice with the total group.

Question #2: As the kids look up these Scripture passages concerning self-image and complete the sentences, discuss the meaning of each passage. The questions that follow allow kids to respond to the Scripture. Do they feel better or worse after discovering what the Bible says about them? How should they feel? Do they really believe what the Bible says about them? Do they believe kids at school or television or themselves more than God?

Question #3: This question helps students understand the relationship between loving themselves in a healthy way and loving others in a healthy way. The correct answers are *a*, *d*, and *f*. Explain that the Bible does not advocate becoming obsessed with loving ourselves but assumes that we do love ourselves. We need to love others like we love ourselves. Only God's *agape*—unselfish love—makes us able to do that.

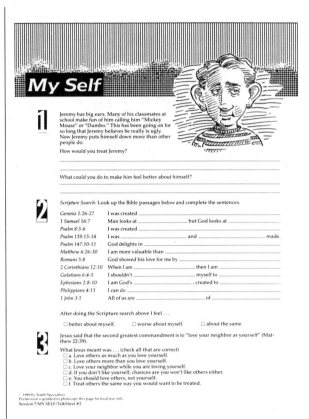

My Self

1 Jeremy has big ears. Many of his classmates at school make fun of him calling him "Mickey Mouse" or "Dumbo." This has been going on for so long that Jeremy believes he really is ugly. Now Jeremy puts himself down more than other people do.

How would you treat Jeremy?

_____

What could you do to make him feel better about himself?

_____

2 *Scripture Search:* Look up the Bible passages below and complete the sentences.

Genesis 1:26-27	I was created _____
1 Samuel 16:7	Man looks at _____ but God looks at _____ .
Psalm 8:3-6	I was created _____
Psalm 139:13-14	I was _____ and _____ made.
Psalm 147:10-11	God delights in _____
Matthew 6:26-30	I am more valuable than _____
Romans 5:8	God showed his love for me by _____
2 Corinthians 12:10	When I am _____ then I am _____
Galatians 6:4-5	I shouldn't _____ myself to _____
Ephesians 2:8-10	I am God's _____ , created to _____ .
Philippians 4:13	I can do _____
1 John 3:1	All of us are _____ of _____

After doing the Scripture search above I feel . . .

☐ better about myself.   ☐ worse about myself.   ☐ about the same.

3 Jesus said that the second greatest commandment is to "love your neighbor as yourself" (Matthew 22:39).

What Jesus meant was . . . (check all that are correct)
☐ a. Love others as much as you love yourself.
☐ b. Love others more than you love yourself.
☐ c. Love your neighbor while you are loving yourself.
☐ d. If you don't like yourself, chances are you won't like others either.
☐ e. You should love others, not yourself.
☐ f. Treat others the same way you would want to be treated.

This optional TalkSheet can close session 7. Either duplicate or read aloud the parable, then discuss these questions.
- What is the moral or underlying truth behind this parable?
- How was Humpty Dumpty's self-concept influenced by the King?
- Who do you think Humpty Dumpty represents? The King?
- How much are you like Humpty Dumpty?

My Self

HUMPTY DUMPTY REVISITED
by Vic Pentz
(Reprinted from *The Wittenburg Door*, June 1972)

Humpty Dumpty sat on the wall.
Humpty Dumpty had a great fall.
All the king's horses and all the king's men
Couldn't put Humpty back together again.

But soon the King himself heard of Humpty's fate. And he was deeply disturbed. So, setting aside his royal finery, disguised as a common peasant, the King slipped unnoticed through the majestic palace gates and into the rough and tumble street life of his kingdom.

The King meandered through the back streets and alleys in search of Humpty. After several days and nights the persistent King found him. Humpty's shattered body was scattered over a ten-foot circle amidst the broken glass and flattened beer cans of a back alley. Though weak from his recent journey, the King was overjoyed at the sight of Humpty. He ran to Humpty's side and cried, "Humpty! It is I—your King! I have powers greater than those of my horses and men who failed to put you together again. Be at peace, I am here to help!"

"Leave me alone. I've gotten used to this new way of life. I kind of like it now," Humpty's mouth retorted.

"But . . ." was all the King could get out before Humpty continued.

"I tell you I'm fine. I like it here. That trash can over there. The way the sun sparkles on the broken glass. This must be the garden spot of the world!"

"I assure you, my kingdom has much more to offer than this back alley. There are green mountains, rolling surf, exciting cities."

But Humpty would hear none of it. And the saddened King returned to the palace.

A week later one of Humpty's eyes rolled skyward only to see once again the concerned face of the King looking over his body.

"I've come to help," firmly stated the King.

"Look, leave me alone, will you?" said Humpty. "I've just seen my psychiatrist, and he assures me that I'm doing a fine job of coping with my environment as it is. You're a cop-out. A man has to deal with life as it comes. I'm a realist."

"But wouldn't you rather walk?" puzzled the King.

"Look," Humpty's mouth frowned, "once I get up and start walking I'll have to stay up and keep walking. At this point in my life I'm not ready to make a commitment like that. So if you'll excuse me, you're blocking my sun."

Reluctantly the King once again turned and walked through the streets of his kingdom back to the palace. It was over a year before the King ventured to return to Humpty's side.

But sure enough, one bright morning one of Humpty's ears perked up at the sure, steady strides of the King. This time he was ready. Humpty's eye turned toward the tall figure just as his mouth managed the words, "My King!"

Immediately the King fell to his knees among the broken glass. His strong, knowing hands gently began to piece together Humpty's fragments. After some time, his work completed, the King rose to full height, pulling up with him the figure of a strong young man.

The two walked hand in hand throughout the kingdom. Together they stood atop lush green mountains. They ran together along deserted beaches. They laughed and joked together as they strolled the gleaming cities of the King's kingdom. This went on forever. And to the depth, breadth, and height of their friendship there was no end.

Once while walking together down the sidewalk in one of the King's cities, Humpty overheard a remark that made his heart leap with both the joy of his new life with the King and the bitter memory of his former, shattered life in the back alley. Someone said, "Say, who are those two men?"

Another replied, "Why, the one on the left is old Humpty Dumpty. I don't know the one on the right, but they sure look like brothers!"

Leader's Guide for Session 8
MY FRIENDS

Friendships are the roots of community in a youth group. If a young person has no real friends in the youth group, then that group is not his community. Session 8 defines Christian friendship and explores ways to build more meaningful friendships within the youth group.

Goals and Objectives for Session 8
This session will help the students—
• Reflect upon those things that they already consider to be important in friendships.
• List biblical principles and characteristics of friendship.
• Examine the levels of friendship in their current relationships.

Things You Will Need for This Session
1. In the back of this book are the Talk-Sheets for this session (Session 8/MY FRIENDS/TalkSheet #1, #2, and #3). Photocopy enough TalkSheets for each person in your group.
2. Make sure everyone has a Bible and a pen or pencil.
3. Reserve an overhead projector or bring in a chalkboard or dry-erase board.
4. Don't forget whatever props you need for any additional activities you decide to use (see Section Two). The "Phone a Friend" activity suggested in **To Introduce This Session** requires an amplified telephone system.

Publicity for This Session
For a daring approach to your publicity this week (and one that will definitely grab your kids' attention), send out a mailer with this bold headline: "THIS WEEK AT YOUTH GROUP—FIND OUT WHAT THE "F" WORD REALLY MEANS!" Be sure to explain in the mailer that the "F" word in this case is *Friendship* or you may get a few phone calls from parents.

To Introduce This Session
Stir the group up to talk about friendship by playing "Phone a Friend." Hook up an inexpensive phone amplifier to a phone in the room (Radio Shack has a suction cup pick-up that works with any amplifier) so that everyone in the room can hear the phone conversation. Or amplify a speaker phone with a microphone.

Choose one person in the group to phone a friend who is not at the meeting. She has three minutes to convince her friend to do one of the following because of "true friendship."

• Go on a blind date with her distant cousin. When asked about his looks, the student can say only that he has a great personality.

• Come help her change a diaper on the baby she's baby-sitting.

• Go in her place to a funeral of a distant relative.

Give a prize to anyone who can convince his friend to do one of these in less than a minute.

Lead into the TalkSheet exercise by saying something like *Friends are fantastic. Everybody needs friends. The happiest, healthiest, and most successful people have a network of friends around them. But sometimes it's hard to make friends. We either don't have time to develop friendships, or we don't know how. Good friendships aren't accidental. Although following rules and step-by-step methods doesn't guarantee friendship, making friends and keeping them does require time, effort, and skill. Everyone can make friends if they know how—and that includes you. This session will help us to examine our friendships and to understand what it takes to be a friend.*

To Close This Session
Below are five steps for deepening friendships, suggested by Alan Loy McGinnis in his book *The Friendship Factor*. Describe them to your kids in closing, and ask them to apply them to a particular friendship that they would like to deepen.

1. *Assign top priority to your relationships.* Don't take them for granted. Deep friendships require much time and effort.
2. *Cultivate transparency.* Be open and honest with others. Let them see what is in your heart.
3. *Talk about your affection.* Tell your friends that you like them and care about them. Communicate your feelings in words.
4. *Learn the gestures of love.* Put friendship into action. Do things regularly for the other person that affirm the friendship.
5. *Create space in your relationship.* Don't smother or try to control the other person. Allow him to be himself.

Encourage your young people to take advantage of the possibilities for friendship that exist in the youth group. Introduce them to the idea of making friends with adults, too. Let your kids know that you want to be their friend as well as their youth leader or authority figure. In addition, remind them that Jesus also wants to be their friend and that, based upon the qualities of friendship that we have discussed, he is a perfect friend who will "never leave us nor forsake us" and "sticks closer than a brother." Close this session with a prayer that each person will develop more and better friendships during the coming weeks and months.

Question #1: "Buying" a friend reveals the kids' priorities in a friendship. Everyone will spend their money differently, so let several describe their purchases and why they spent their quarter as they did. They can add any other qualities not on the list, and those qualities are free.

You can extend this activity if you want to by having the kids check off all those listed qualities that their best friend possesses. Then have add up the listed prices for the "total value" of that friendship. Have them do the same thing for themselves—what is their friendship worth to someone else? Allow some of the kids to share their totals.

Question #2: Summarize some of the kids' definitions of friendship on the chalkboard. Then create a group definition of friendship. (The dictionary defines *friend* as "a person attached to another by feelings of affection or personal regard; a person who is on good terms with another; not hostile.")

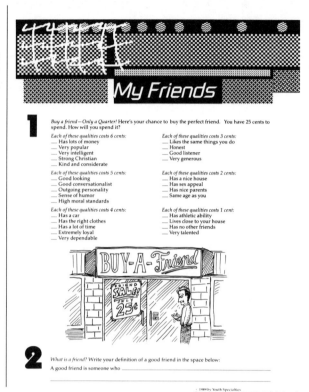

My Friends

1 Buy a friend—Only a Quarter! Here's your chance to buy the perfect friend. You have 25 cents to spend. How will you spend it?

Each of these qualities costs 6 cents:
___ Has lots of money
___ Very popular
___ Very intelligent
___ Strong Christian
___ Kind and considerate

Each of these qualities costs 5 cents:
___ Good looking
___ Good conversationalist
___ Outgoing personality
___ Sense of humor
___ High moral standards

Each of these qualities costs 4 cents:
___ Has a car
___ Has the right clothes
___ Has a lot of time
___ Extremely loyal
___ Very dependable

Each of these qualities costs 3 cents:
___ Likes the same things you do
___ Honest
___ Good listener
___ Very generous

Each of these qualities costs 2 cents:
___ Has a nice house
___ Has sex appeal
___ Has nice parents
___ Same age as you

Each of these qualities costs 1 cent:
___ Has athletic ability
___ Lives close to your house
___ Has no other friends
___ Very talented

2 What is a friend? Write your definition of a good friend in the space below:
A good friend is someone who _____

Shading the names of friends written in the circle makes the kids evaluate the depths of the friendships they currently have. Debrief in small groups where kids can share what they learned from this activity about themselves and their friendships.

Instructions for TalkSheet #3

Question #1: After someone reads aloud the suggested Scriptures describing the friendships of David and Jonathan and Jesus and Lazarus, list with the kids the characteristics of friendship evident in these scriptural accounts. Some of the more obvious qualities are oneness in spirit, *agape* love, commitment, gift-giving, protection, help, assistance, defending, empathy, compassion, emotional attachment.

Question #2: This passage of Scripture teaches that a good friend acts like a good friend. If you don't show yourself friendly, the friendship will die. List with the kids actions that show that a person is friendly.

Question #3: When the kids have listened to Colossians 3, lead them to discuss how they feel about each of the eight listed characteristics of friendship. Which ones do they feel they need the most work on? Which ones do they think are the most important? How can they improve in these areas?

My Friends

1 *Good Friends:* Read about the Bible friendships below.

David and Jonathan — 1 Samuel 18:1-4, 19:1-6
Jesus and Lazarus — John 11:11-14, 30-36

List as many qualities of friendship as you can find in those Scriptures:

_____   _____
_____   _____
_____   _____
_____   _____

2 *Read Proverbs 18:24.* How do you "show yourself friendly?" In other words, what do you do to keep your friendships alive and well?

_____

3 *Read Colossians 3:12-14.* Rate yourself on each of the eight characteristics of friendship described in Colossians by circling a number between one (low) and ten (high).

COMPASSION: I try to see things from my friends' point of view.
1   2   3   4   5   6   7   8   9   10

KINDNESS: I take every opportunity to do nice things for my friends.
1   2   3   4   5   6   7   8   9   10

HUMILITY: I try to build up and encourage my friends.
1   2   3   4   5   6   7   8   9   10

GENTLENESS: I treat my friends as I would want to be treated. I avoid hurting them.
1   2   3   4   5   6   7   8   9   10

PATIENCE: I am willing to go the second mile with my friends.
1   2   3   4   5   6   7   8   9   10

BEARING: I try to help my friends whenever they need me.
1   2   3   4   5   6   7   8   9   10

FORGIVING: I forgive rather than hold a grudge or get even.
1   2   3   4   5   6   7   8   9   10

LOVING: I let my friends know that I really care a lot about them.
1   2   3   4   5   6   7   8   9   10

Leader's Guide for Session 9
MY COMMUNITY

Unity, love, forgiveness, and service characterize the members of the body of Christ. Christian friendships and a biblical estimation of self-worth also shape our Christian life in community. Scripture uses many word pictures to help us understand the nature of the church and of Christian living. In Session 9 we'll study Christian community through the biblical word picture of the family.

Goals and Objectives for Session 9
This session will help the students—
• Compare the Christian community to a family.
• Become more aware of each person's place in the youth group.
• Identify ways their youth group can become more like a family.

Things You Will Need for This Session
1. In the back of this book are the Talk-Sheets for this session (Session 9/MY COMMUNITY/TalkSheets #1 and #2). Photocopy enough TalkSheets for all your students.
2. Make sure everyone has a Bible and a pen or pencil.
3. Reserve an overhead projector or bring in a chalkboard or dry-erase board.
4. Don't forget whatever props you need for any additional activities you decide to use (see Section Two).

To Introduce This Session
Divide into small groups and do the "Football Stadium" exercise (page 48). Or toss out this question to the kids: "What are some characteristics of a healthy family?" The kids will probably mention things like closeness, love, togetherness, commitment to each other, and so on.

After they have shared their ideas, say something like *Just about every day you choose to be with friends who have interests in common with you. You are also surrounded daily by people who you* don't *choose to be with—you merely go to the same school or live in the same neighborhood with them. You usually have very little to do with these people.*

Then there are your relatives! You didn't choose them, but you can't stop being related to them because you are in the same family with them. And often you can count on them even when you don't share the same interests. God created our families to support and help us while we are growing up. And at the same time we support and help other family members as well.

The church and the youth group also support and help us while we are growing up. Maybe that's why God speaks of becoming a Christian as being born again. He gives us a new family—the church—to help us live and grow as Christians. Every Christian is part of God's family, and each member bears a resemblance to the heavenly Father.

In this session we will look at our church family—this youth group—and find out how we can strengthen it so that all of us are being as helpful and supportive of each other we can.

To Close This Session
Ask the group this question: "As result of what we have discussed in this session, what do you think we need to do now? What is the most important action that we can take as a group to become a better youth group, a closer community, a healthier family? List and prioritize the suggestions of the group. Make this list as practical and specific as possible. Rather than suggesting that the group simply care more about each other, refine the idea to a weekly prayer

meeting to pray for each other. Close with a prayer of thanksgiving for the group and a prayer of commitment to *do* the things that you have listed.

Another way to close the session is to create a larger coat of arms for the group on poster paper using colored pens, paints, photos, and so on. Then hang it on the wall.

You might even take some of the best ideas and choose someone to create an official youth-group coat of arms which can be printed on T-shirts, letterhead, etc.

Another good idea is to take a "family portrait" of the youth group and then enlarge and duplicate it for each member of the group.

Instructions for TalkSheet #1

Question #1: Write the kids' sentence completions on the chalkboard or overhead. Ask them to focus their answers on positive qualities of the group ("friendliness," "helps kids grow in Christ," "makes everyone feel included," rather than "has comfortable chairs" or "fun ski trips").

Question #2: Since some of the statements in the list are personal, not all will feel comfortable sharing their responses. As you read each statement aloud, comment on them and ask if anyone would like to explain their feelings about a particular statement. Rather than taking a poll on each statement, you might ask how the group can improve in that particular area. For instance, you might ask how the group can make individuals feel like they are an important part of the group.

Question #3: After studying the Scriptures, ask the kids how the church is like a family. Talk over applying these ideas to the youth group.

Question #4: Listen to the kids' responses to the questions and discuss each one. Ask several to recall for the group how people in the church or youth group have shown brotherly love, motherly care, or fatherly guidance to them.

My Community

1 Complete this sentence: The best thing about our youth group is

2 Your Opinion Please: Read the statements below and put a check next to all those you agree with. Cross out the ones you disagree with.
- I feel like I'm an important part of our youth group.
- The youth group is important to me.
- Our youth group is about the right size.
- I have a lot of good friends in our youth group.
- There are too many cliques in our youth group.
- I look forward to our youth group meetings and activities.
- I wouldn't come to this youth group if I had a choice.
- Our youth group has good leaders.
- I am doing my part to make our youth group better.
- I would be comfortable inviting my friends to our youth group.
- Our youth group has helped me become a better Christian.
- Our youth group is like a family to me.

3 Scripture Search: Read any four of the Scriptures below and answer the question that follows:
Psalm 68:62   Corinthians 6:17   Ephesians 2:19
Ephesians 3:15   Galatians 6:10
Hebrews 2:11   Philippians 2:151   Peter 4:17

How is the church like a family?

4 Read 1 Thessalonians 2. In this letter to the church at Thessalonica, Paul describes various relationships in the Christian community with words we use to talk about family. Study this chapter and answer the following questions:
1. Why would Paul call these Christians brothers?
2. What are some characteristics of motherly care as mentioned in verses 7-8?
3. What are some characteristics of fatherly guidance as mentioned in verses 10-12?

Instructions for TalkSheet #2

After everyone has had time to create his coat of arms, allow the kids to share their creations with each other in small groups. Then with the entire group, debrief the activity by asking the kids questions like:

- What did you learn from this activity?
- How do you feel about our group after doing this activity? Encouraged? Discouraged? Frustrated? Excited?

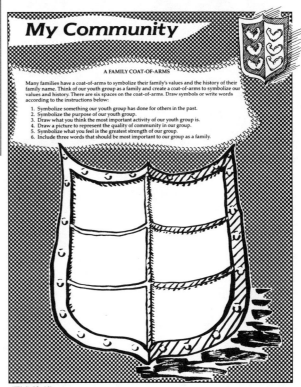

My Community

A FAMILY COAT-OF-ARMS

Many families have a coat-of-arms to symbolize their family's values and the history of their family name. Think of our youth group as a family and create a coat-of-arms to symbolize our values and history. There are six spaces on the coat-of-arms. Draw symbols or write words according to the instructions below:

1. Symbolize something our youth group has done for others in the past.
2. Symbolize the purpose of our youth group.
3. Draw what you think the most important activity of our youth group is.
4. Draw a picture to represent the quality of community in our group.
5. Symbolize what you feel is the greatest strength of our group.
6. Include three words that should be most important to our group as a family.

Leader's Guide for Session 10
COMMUNICATION

Communication and *community* come from the same root word. They go together. There can be no real community without good communication. The ability to communicate well, however, is not something that people are born with (although a crying baby is certainly communicating), nor is communication a theological or philosophical concept to be understood. It is a skill that needs to be developed. People learn how to communicate by communicating. Unfortunately for a lot of young people, they have grown up with the idea that they should be seen and not heard, and this retards their development as effective communicators.

This session introduces the skill of communication and helps young people to understand its importance in building Christian community.

Goals and Objectives for Session 10

This session will help students—
• Realize the importance of communication in building community.
• Recognize the difference between good or positive communication and bad or negative communication.
• Identify ways to improve communication in the youth group.

Things You Will Need for This Session

1. In the back of this book is the TalkSheet for this session (Session 10/COMMUNICATION/TalkSheet #1). Photocopy enough TalkSheets for all your students.
2. Make sure everyone has a Bible and a pen or pencil.
3. Reserve an overhead projector or bring in a chalkboard or dry-erase board.
4. Don't forget whatever props you need for any additional activities you decide to use (see Section Two).

Publicity for This Session

One way to publicize this session is to send out an outrageously false announcement communicating the wrong date, the wrong time, the wrong place, and promising an incredible program featuring famous superstars. The only thing right is at the bottom of the page: "For more information, call"— and list your name and phone number. Then when people call, you can tell them the correct time and place and that the meeting is about communication.

To Introduce This Session

Do as many communication exercises with the kids as time permits, discussing their feelings, experiences, and insights after each exercise. There is only one TalkSheet, for this session should be more interactive and participatory than the previous sessions.

Kick off a series of communication games with the "Gossip Game." Divide into teams and assign the first person on each team to quickly memorize a Bible verse or other statement and to whisper it in the next person's ear. The second person must repeat it for the third person on the team, and so on. The object is for the last person on the team to accurately repeat the verse or statement from memory. The last person's version of the statement is usually mixed up and illustrates how gossiping distorts truth.

Two games requiring advance preparation are "Owl Island" (page 72) and "Verbal Puzzle" (page 89). *Play It!* by Wayne Rice and Mike Yaconelli (Zondervan/Youth Specialties) has more ideas.

Before handing out the TalkSheet say something like *Everyone of us has been misunderstood when we shared something with someone else. And we have misunderstood others who have talked to us. Sometimes communication is positive and improves relationships between people, and sometimes it is negative and builds walls between people. In this session we want to look at communication in our youth group. How do we communicate with each other? Is it positive or negative? Does it help or hurt our relationships? Does it build bridges of friendship or walls of alienation and bitterness?*

Healthy communication grows out of the Christian values of honesty, love, and forgiveness. We've already studied some of these things, now let's practice using them to improve our communication skills.

To Close This Session
Encourage the kids to communicate their feelings or needs with each other in a sharing time, and then close the meeting with prayer.

You might also want to brainstorm with the group a list of practical ideas for improving communication among themselves. Write these on the chalkboard and decide which ones to implement immediately.

Instructions for TalkSheet #1

Question #1: When individuals have identified characteristics of good and bad communication, allow them to share their answers as you record them on the chalkboard or overhead.

Question #2: Invite the kids to share the names of the people whom they feel are good communicators and to explain why. Stimulate them to evaluate how well they communicate with others by asking, "How many people do you think might name *you* as a person who communicates well with them?"

Question #3: As you read aloud the list of statements, ask the kids for their responses. If there is wide disagreement, talk about why. If students agree that a negative issue is a problem for the group (like "There is a lot of gossip"), stop and discuss it, avoiding griping and name-calling. Asking "Why do you think this is true?" or "What do you think can be done to improve in this area?" can guide the group to constructive discussion. Remind kids that they can pass on any of the items if they don't want to reveal their answers.

Question #4: All of these Scripture verses deal with communication—talking, slander, gossip—showing biblical recogni-

tion of positive communication as essential for followers of Christ and negative communication as deadly. Allow the kids to share the sentences they wrote. Especially the book of James has strong words on this, calling the tongue the deadliest of weapons.

Many other strategies teach kids about effective communication and guide them to practice their own communication skills. Role playing works well. Ask two kids to discuss a controversial issue in front of the group. Person A, for instance, could role-play a group member who believes that all the money from a youth-group fund-raiser should be used to go to an amusement park. Person B could play the role of a group member who thinks that the money should be used for a mission project or given to a hunger-relief organization. Following a two-to-three-minute discussion, debrief with the group focusing on the pair's communication process, not the issue discussed. What constructive and helpful ways did they communicate? In what ways were they negative and hurtful? (An excellent role-playing resource is the communication game Roll-a-Role, published by Youth Specialties.)

Another strategy, "Personal Encounter," allows kids to practice verbal communication one on one with each member of the group. Set up two rows of chairs facing each other and positioned in the following manner:

Side A   X X X X X X X X X X X X
Side B   X X X X X X X X X X X X

If the number of people is uneven, then the leader should participate. After everyone is seated, give the following instructions to the group:

1. When the leader gives the signal, everyone move one chair to the right.
2. After you have moved, you will have one minute to carry on a conversation with the person across from you, asking and answering the following questions:
   Person on Side A: "Right now, while talking to you, I feel—" (finish the sentence)
   Person on Side B: "Why?"
   Person on Side A: "Because—"
   Person on Side B: "What can I do that would improve our relationship as members of the Christian family?"
   Person on Side A: (Responds to above question)

After the group has returned to their original chairs, talk about the following questions:

1. How did you feel talking to different people?
2. What did you learn from the experience?
3. Did you communicate differently with different people? Why?

The book *One-on-One* (whose subtitle is *The Face-to-Face Encounter Book That Helps You Talk About the Really Important Things*) is a worthwhile Youth Specialties Talk Box resource. It effectively brings kids together in lively dialogue.

Since this session also deals with negative communication—put-downs, sarcasm, thoughtless remarks—spend some time dealing with it. Section Three contains several ideas for confronting negativism: "Negative Board," "Put-Down Covenant," "Uppers and Downers."

Sharing Cubes: try this idea on page 81.

Leader's Guide for Session 11
LISTENING

Good communication is two-way communication: it involves not only talking and sharing, but also careful listening. *Hearing* comes naturally, as other senses do. But *listening* is a skill requiring effort and concentration. Session 11 focuses on developing the insights and skills necessary for careful and effective listening.

Goals and Objectives for Session 11
This session will help the students—
• Experience the contribution careful listening makes to building community.
• Identify characteristics of non-listening and effective listening.
• Practice effective listening.

Things You Will Need for This Session
1. In the back of this book is the TalkSheet for this session (Session 11/LISTENING/ TalkSheet #1). Photocopy enough Talk-Sheets for each person in your group.
2. Make sure everyone has a Bible and a pen or pencil.
3. Reserve an overhead projector or bring in a chalkboard or dry-erase board.
4. Don't forget whatever props you need for any additional activities you decide to use (see Section Two).

Publicity for This Session
To advertise this session on listening, try sending everyone a copy of a cassette tape with a message on it. Instead of a simple announcement of the meeting, record a lengthy one containing lots of details. Inform the group that they will be asked questions at the meeting concerning the information on the tape, and whoever has the most correct answers wins a prize. If you ask tricky true-false questions, chances are your kids will miss a number of them.

Use this as a kick-off to your session on listening.

To Introduce This Session
Open this session with some of the listening activities in Section Two. Try "Interrogation" (page 63), "Interview Mixer" (page 63), or "Listening Test" (page 67).

Your opening comments to the group can include something like *How many times have you heard or said, "Nobody listens to me?" You can't communicate well with people who won't listen to you. God created us with one mouth and two ears. Perhaps that's his way of saying to us, "Listening is more important than talking!" Even God had trouble communicating with people who wouldn't listen to him. "Son of man," God said to Ezekiel, "you are living among a rebellious people. They have ears to hear, but they do not hear!"*

Good friends listen to each other. When one person listens—really listens—to another, she communicates to the speaker that he is a significant person. In this session we'll examine principles of effective listening and learn to become better listeners.

To Close This Session
Listening is one of the best gifts one person can give to another. It affirms and validates a person and lets that person know that she is important. In a Christian community we treat each other with dignity and respect by listening to each other. Remind the kids that God listens attentively to each one of us. Certainly if the Creator of the universe feels that each person is important enough to be listened to, so should we.

Close with prayer thanking God that he listens to us. Pray that each person might listen more closely to God and to each other.

Question #1: Explore with the kids why they listen to the people they underlined and to any additional people they listed. Invite them to name some specific people as well. List their choices on the chalkboard or overhead. Next, have volunteers tell who listens to *them*, and ask this question: "How do you know that this person is really listening to you?" Again make a list on the chalkboard.

Question #2: Use this question to allow kids to share how they feel when they aren't being listened to. They may add other words to the list. Probably no one will choose one of the positive feelings because when we fail to listen, we are hurting the one speaking to us. This can be a tough lesson to learn.

Question #3: As you read this list of statements aloud, ask kids to raise their hands to tell their response. Allow anyone to pass. You may want to comment on these as you go along. Every other one (a,c,e,g,i) is a desirable listening habit, and the others are bad listening habits. The bad news is that the negative habits—letting your mind wander, tuning out, interrupting—are more natural than the positive ones. To cultivate thriving relationships, we need to work on developing good listening habits and breaking the negative ones.

Question #4: This question is designed to help the kids apply these passages from Scripture. Allow the kids to share their completed sentences.

As with the previous session on communication, this one needs to be more interactive and participatory than earlier sessions. Include activities that give the kids practice in listening. Besides those already listed in **To Introduce This Session**, consider the following activity.

Before asking several in the group to participate in role playing, write on the board and briefly explain these three keys to effective listening.

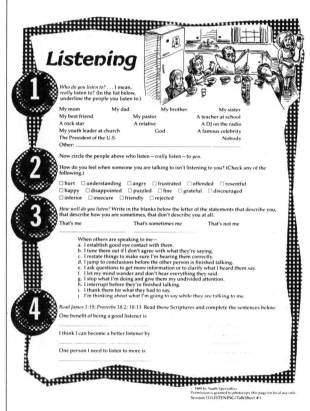

1. *Listen for what the other person is actually saying, meaning, or feeling*. Don't jump to conclusions. Often a person says one thing and actually means another. Or she'll have a hidden agenda that you need to explore. And sometimes he is expressing a feeling, and actual words are not that important. Try to capture the essence of what a person is saying.
2. *Give the other person some feedback so that he knows you are listening and trying to understand what he is saying*. This not only helps the person communicate more effectively, but it ensures that you are receiving the correct message. Ask questions, restate what the person has said.

3. *When you respond, build upon what the speaker has said.* Don't respond as if the other person hasn't said anything at all. Before you add your own ideas, comment on what you heard or thank the person for sharing that information with you.

Depending on the size of the group, choose two to role-play while the rest of the group watches; or divide into groups of 10 or fewer, assigning each group to do the same role play at the same time.

Each student plays her role seriously while the observers compare the action to the three keys listed on the board. The observers may even want to take notes during the role play to jog their memory for the discussion to follow.

After two people have been selected for each role play, give them the description of the role, the situation, and the task. The instructions usually tell which person should begin the role play. Keep in mind that role plays are not skits with scripts to follow. Instead, kids spontaneously interact the way they think their characters would behave in the given situation. Allow each role play to go for about three minutes or until it reaches a dead end.

After the role plays discuss how the actors did or did not apply the keys to effective listening, then move on to the next role play until all three are finished. Switch actors for each role play.

Role Play #1
What To Do on Friday Night

Person A

Role:
You like to go out and do fun things on weekend nights, but you don't like to spend much money or be seen with the wrong kind of people.

Situation:
You and your friend are trying to decide what to do on Friday night.

Task:
Try to convince your friend to go to a shopping mall to hang out and buy some frozen yogurt.

Person B

Role:
You like to spend weekend nights having lots of fun. You like doing things that are exciting or active, and you aren't too concerned about what kind of place you go or how much it costs.

Situation:
You and your friend are trying to decide what to do on Friday night.

Task:
Try to convince your friend to go see a new exciting adventure movie or go to the local arcade to drive the race cars and play video games. You begin the conversation by asking your friend, "Hey, what do you want to do Friday night?"

Role Play #2
The Unfair History Teacher

Person A

Role:
You like school and get good grades. Sometimes your friends think you like school too much. You really like history and English, and you like teachers who give you group projects to work on.

Situation:
You just sat down to lunch with a student who is in your history class. You start to discuss a group project that the teacher assigned.

Task:
Try to convince the other person that the class, the teacher, and the project are all worthwhile, and that he should try hard to do a good job. You begin the conversation by saying, "I really like our history class, don't you?"

Person B

Role:

You are an average student. You don't like school, but you don't hate it either. You do the best you can and get average grades. You like classes like math and science a lot more than history and English. You prefer a teacher to give you a list of things to learn or solve rather than a group project. In fact, you *hate* group projects.

Situation:

You just sat down to lunch with a student who is in your history class. You start to discuss a group project that the teacher assigned.

Task:

Try to convince the other person how lost you feel in the class and how frustrated you are with the group project. Try to get her to agree with you that the teacher is unfair and that you shouldn't have to do the group project.

Role Play #3
Parent-Youth Late Night

Person A

Role:

You are 16 years old. You enjoy having a good time and going out with your friends. You try to live within the standards you and your parents agreed upon. You have been out with your friends and lost track of time; although you agreed to be back at 11 p.m., you didn't get home until 12:30 in the morning.

Situation:

You have just come into the house an hour and a half late. This is the second time this month you have been late. One of your parents is waiting up for you.

Task:

Begin with the statement, "Sorry I'm late, Mom [or Dad]. I really didn't know what time it was getting to be." Try to keep the conversation from turning into a fight.

Person B

Role:

You are a parent. You respect your 16-year-old's attempts to be responsible, but you are concerned about him being out too late—past the agreed-upon time.

Situation:

Your teenager has just come home. He was supposed to be home at 11 p.m., but it is now 12:30 in the morning.

Task:

Try to figure out why your teenager is late. Convince him of the importance of doing what was agreed upon. Try to get him to understand your concern about being late. You may (if you feel it is necessary) promise him a penalty for being late.

Leader's Guide for Session 12
RESOLVING CONFLICT

Every group experiences conflict and disharmony. And most groups attempt to solve their problems one way or the other. Resolving conflict without leaving permanent scars, however, depends on positive communication and effective listening. Session 12 guides students and leaders to attack group problems with the love and forgiveness we've already talked about and to manage conflict through healthy communication.

Goals and Objectives for This Session
This session will help students—
• Realize that conflict is inevitable and that it isn't always bad.
• Realize that conflict cannot be avoided; therefore, it must be managed.
• Realize how the inability to manage conflict can damage the quality of Christian community.
• Identify ways to manage conflict personally and within the youth group.

Things You Will Need for This Session
1. In the back of this book is the TalkSheet for this session (Session 12/RESOLVING CONFLICT/TalkSheet #1). Photocopy enough TalkSheets for all your students.
2. Make sure everyone has a Bible and a pen or pencil.
3. Reserve an overhead projector or bring in a chalkboard or dry-erase board.
4. Don't forget whatever props you need for any additional activities you decide to use (see Section Two).

To Introduce This Session
An excellent way to introduce this session is by reading aloud "The Zax" by Dr. Seuss (from *Sneetches and Other Stories*), a story available in your local public library or book store. It is a delightful story about two people who get into an ridiculous argument, with neither side willing to give an inch. Because of their stubbornness, they both lose. Ask the kids to discuss who was at fault, who won, and what makes this story so ridiculous.

Begin the session by saying something like *"Why can't you kids get along with each other?"* How many times have you heard that? It seems that ever since we were little kids, we have been finding ways to argue, disagree, and create conflict with each other. Of course, the problem is not new. Adam and Eve's kids, Cain and Abel, had an argument, and Cain ended up putting his brother six feet under. But that's not the best way to handle conflict, is it?

In our group we have been exploring together how we might become more of a family—a Christian community of good friends. Now community and conflict are not compatible, right? You can't have harmony and disharmony at the same time. Or can you? The fact is there is disharmony and conflict even in the Christian community, just as in any family. But when conflict becomes dominant, community is eventually destroyed. The question is, can conflict be managed? Can it be controlled? What does the Bible have to say about it? What can YOU do? This session will answer these and other questions about resolving conflict.

To Close This Session
As the kids reflect on what they learned during this session, ask volunteers to complete this sentence aloud: "The most important thing I learned about conflict today is—"

Close by reading Psalm 133:1—"Behold, how good and pleasant it is when brothers [and sisters!] live together in unity!" Pray that God will not permit conflict to damage or destroy the unity that is developing within the group.

Question #1: Ask the kids to picture a specific conflict they experienced in the youth group, in their circle of friends, or in their family. How did they respond? Allow them to share what they usually do in a conflict and then to choose a better response from the TalkSheet.

Question #2: In this "tension getter," the group tackles an actual conflict and decides how it should be handled. Discuss each solution to the problem that is volunteered. You might want to vote for the best solution offered.

Another idea is to divide the group in half, with everyone whose last name begins with the letter A through L being the "youth council" and those with initials M through Z being the "skiers." Give them 10 minutes to come up with a plan to resolve the issue. You might want to use "How To Resolve Conflicts" (below) at this point in the session. Explain the three principles, and then have the kids utilize them to arrive at some possible solutions to the problem.

Question #3: Allow kids to share their summaries with the group. If you have time, divide into groups and have each group prepare a short skit or role play to illustrate the teaching found in each Scripture. They may want to use the following sentences as first lines for their skits:

Matthew 5:38-42—"Boy, would I like to get even with Leroy for what he did to me!"

Matthew 7:1-5—"There's one guy in our group who really ought to be straightened out!"

Matthew 18:15-17—"Jim, I want to talk to Jack about a problem. Will you go with me?"

1 Corinthians 1:10-13—"There's one subject that we just can't discuss in this group. It always starts an argument."

Galatians 5:26-6:5—"I've been concerned about Mac lately. Have you noticed . . . ?"

Ephesians 4:25-27—"If there's one thing that really makes me mad, it's every time Eva . . . "

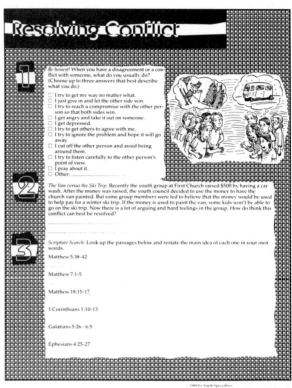

How To Resolve Conflict.

Teach this simple 3-step model for conflict resolution to the group whenever you feel it is appropriate to do so.

Step One:

    Identify the conflict. This may seem obvious at first, but sometimes the issues need to be clarified or verbalized before you can work together to resolve the conflict. Or sometimes one person believes there is a conflict, but the other person is unaware of it.

Step Two:

    Brainstorm alternative solutions. At this stage the solutions are not to be judged as to their rightness or wrongness; any solution is acceptable as a possibility, even if it seems incredible or unworkable. Think of as many possible solutions as you can and write them all down.

Step Three:

Decide on a plan. The solution may be so obvious at this point that you may be able to settle the problem once and for all with one of the alternatives listed. But most of the time those in conflict need to negotiate and compromise in order to devise a plan that will satisfy all sides in the dispute. This step is simply a commitment by all parties to put a plan into effect that will hopefully solve the problem.

If your group is aware of ongoing conflicts, lead them in trying out these three steps to resolving conflicts, either in small groups or with the entire group.

How To Give and Take Criticism.

Introduce the following list of ideas on the subject of criticism during this session if you wish to.

Giving criticism. When feel you have a legitimate criticism or complaint, following these rules will make the most of your complaint without damaging your relationship.

1. Complain to the person you think is harming you, not to anyone else.
2. Don't object to someone's behavior in front of other people.
3. Don't compare one person's performance with anyone else's.
4. Make your complaint in person as soon as you can, and as soon as you can clearly talk about it.
5. Don't repeat a point once you have made it and the other person has thought about it.
6. Object only to actions that the person can change.
7. Make only one complaint at a time.
8. After making your complaint in good faith, don't apologize for it.
9. Avoid sarcasm.
10. Avoid words like *always* and *never.*
11. If you never compliment the other person, don't expect him to be open to

your criticism.

Taking criticism. It's not easy to take criticism, but these guidelines can help you to deal with it more effectively. They will also help defuse the situation, preventing long-term damage to relationships.

1. Be quiet while you are being criticized, and make it clear that you are listening.
2. Look directly at the person talking to you.
3. Under no condition find fault with the person who has just criticized you.
4. Don't create the impression that the other person is destroying your spirit.
5. Don't make fun or jokes.
6. Don't change the subject.
7. Don't imply or assume that the person criticizing you has ulterior or hostile motives.
8. Don't criticize the criticism, or get even by leveling a criticism of your own at the other person.
9. Don't jump to conclusions about the criticism. Ask questions that clarify the criticism like, "How has this offended you?" or "What do you think I should do?"
10. Convey to the other person that you understand her objection and will thoughtfully consider her criticism.

Discuss these two lists with the group, asking them if they agree or disagree with any of the suggestions. You might have the group role-play a few situations to practice the ideas. For example, two kids can role play a situation like this:

Person A:

You are a little overweight and know it. But it has never really been an issue until recently. One of the kids in the youth group (Person B) has been making fun of you, calling you "Tubby" and making other hurtful wise-cracks about your weight. You have decided that the next time it happens, you will confront this person.

Person B:

You are a fun-loving kid in the youth group who likes to give people nicknames and make jokes about everything. Person A is a little overweight, so you have occasionally called him "Tubby." Sometimes you kid Person A about eating too many enchiladas, but it's all in fun. You really don't mean to be unkind. Next time you see Person A, you say,

"Hey Tubs, I hear you've been on a sea-food diet—if you see food, you eat it! Ha, ha, ha!"

This role play is only a sample. Your kids may be able to come up with better ones that are closer to actual experience. Give your group a chance to give and receive criticism and to practice dealing with it in a constructive, biblical manner.

Leader's Guide for Session 13
COMMITMENT TO COMMUNITY

This final session wraps up the entire course. It identifies some of the highlights, and directs kids to commit themselves to put what they have learned into practice.

Goals and Objectives for Session 13

This session will help students—
• Recall some of the main ideas learned throughout this course of study.
• Identify what they have learned and how they have changed as a result of this course.
• Make a commitment to work together in the future to promote unity in their youth group.

Things You Will Need for This Session

1. In the back of this book is the TalkSheet for this session (Session 13/ COMMITMENT TO COMMUNITY/ TalkSheet #1). Photocopy enough Talk-Sheets for all your students.
2. Make sure everyone has a Bible and a pen or pencil.
3. Reserve an overhead projector or bring in a chalkboard or dry-erase board.
4. Don't forget whatever props you need for any additional activities you decide to use (see Section Two).

To Introduce This Session

Lively crowd breakers and mixers fill Section Two. Don't stop using them now! After 13 sessions you can see what they have done to build community among your kids.

Introduce the last TalkSheet by saying something like *For several months we've studied what it means to be a Christian community, a family, the body of Christ. It's time to ask ourselves, "Now what?" Was this just a lot of information to be filed away, or will what we have learned make a difference in our lives and in our youth group? A lot of people think that it can make an important difference, but the difference that it actually makes is up to you. In fact Session 13 is not the end of our learning about Christian community—IT'S JUST THE BEGINNING!*

To help us remember what we've learned so far and to give us an idea of what we are committing ourselves to, let's take a little test—a "final exam" covering all 12 sessions that we've studied. Don't worry. Just answer all the questions the best you can, and everybody gets an A!

To Close This Session

Any of the following options effectively bring this session to a close.
• *Youth-Group Wish*: On the back of their "final exams," have the kids write out a wish for the youth group—something that could possibly happen within the next year. In small groups or in the larger group, have the kids share their wishes and then pray that they might become a reality.
• *Group Photo*: Have the group pose for a photo. Either enlarge and frame it for the room, or duplicate it for each member of the group.
• *Declaration of Inter-dependence*: Have the kids write a Declaration of Inter-dependence that begins, "We the members of _____ youth group, in order to form a more perfect unity in Christ . . . " When they complete it, ask a calligrapher to write it on parchment for each member to sign. Frame and display it in a prominent place.
• *Youth-Group Motto*: Have the kids create a youth-group motto or slogan that reflects their desire to be one in Christ. Imprint group letterhead or T-shirts with the motto.
• *Worship and Communion*: Conduct a short worship service, with Scripture songs and readings, and then celebrate communion together. Close with a prayer of commitment.

This general questionnaire reminds kids of some main points from each session. The questions are worded so that even those kids who missed sessions can still take a stab at answering them.

Give the kids 10 minutes or so to write their answers. Then let volunteers share their answers with the group. Discuss each question, clarifying the main point. There are many possible correct answers, so review the first 12 sessions to prepare for guiding the discussion.

Summarize the discussion by asking the kids to reflect on these questions.

- What one thing do I want to remember from this study about Christian community?
- What one thing would I like to see improved in our youth group during the next 12 months?
- What one thing can I do to help our youth group become the kind of Christian community that God want us to be?

Commitment to Community

**UP CLOSE AND PERSONAL
FINAL EXAM**

1 How would you define *Christian unity*?

2 What does it mean to be a part of the *body of Christ*?

3 What are *spiritual gifts* and why are they important?

4 How is *Christian love* different from other kinds of love?

5 Why do you think Christians should be *forgiving*?

6 How can Christian young people *serve* each other?

7 Why is having a positive *self-image* important?

8 Name one characteristic of a really good *friend*.

9 How is the Christian *community* like a family?

10 Give an example of *good communication*.

11 How can a person become a better *listener*?

12 When people are having *conflict* in the group, what are some steps that can be taken to resolve it?

1989 by Youth Specialties
Permission is granted to photocopy this page for local use only.
Session 13/COMMITMENT TO COMMUNITY/TalkSheet #1

Unity

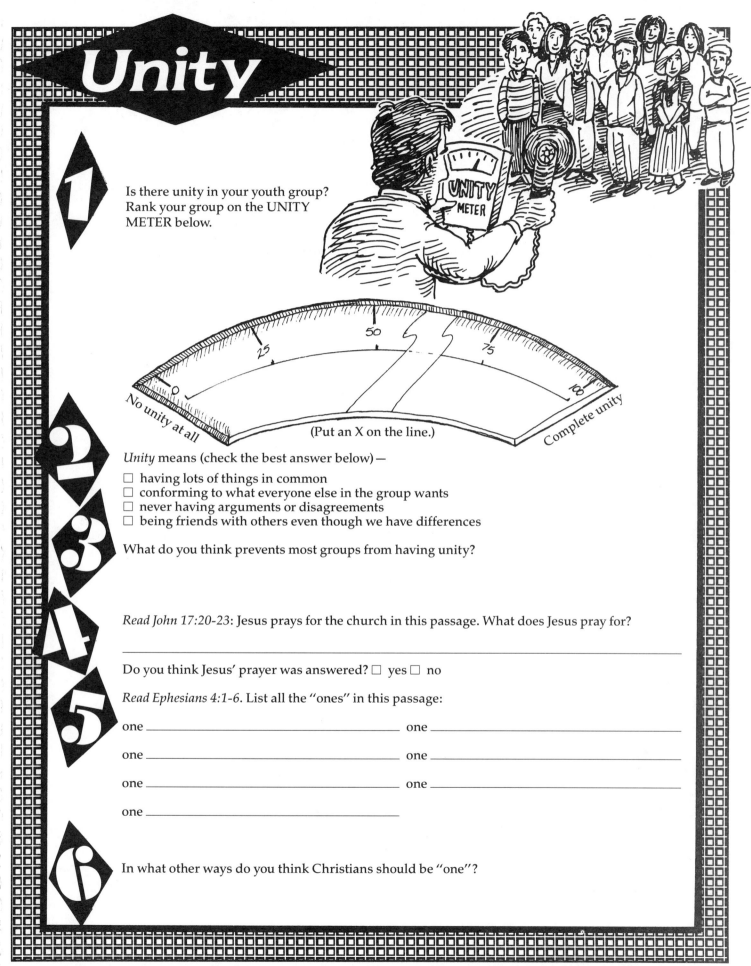

1 Is there unity in your youth group? Rank your group on the UNITY METER below.

25   50   75

0   180

No unity at all   (Put an X on the line.)   Complete unity

Unity means (check the best answer below) —

☐ having lots of things in common
☐ conforming to what everyone else in the group wants
☐ never having arguments or disagreements
☐ being friends with others even though we have differences

2 What do you think prevents most groups from having unity?

3 *Read John 17:20-23*: Jesus prays for the church in this passage. What does Jesus pray for?

_____

Do you think Jesus' prayer was answered? ☐ yes ☐ no

4 *Read Ephesians 4:1-6.* List all the "ones" in this passage:

one _____   one _____

one _____   one _____

one _____   one _____

one _____

5

6 In what other ways do you think Christians should be "one"?

Unity

Neither Nor

1 *Read Galatians 3:26-28*. List all the "neither/nors" in this passage.

neither _____ nor _____

neither _____ nor _____

neither _____ nor _____

2 If you were to list a few "neither/nors" that would promote unity in your youth group, what would they be? (For example, "neither sophomore nor senior")

neither _____ nor _____

neither _____ nor _____

neither _____ nor _____

3 *Read 1 Corinthians 1:10-13*. Paul wrote this appeal to the Christians at the church at Corinth. If Paul were to write a letter to your church or youth group, what might he say? Rewrite the passage in your own words, applying it to your church or youth group.

To: _____
From: Paul
Message:

4 *Read Philippians 2:1-4*: According to this passage, what is the key to unity?

_____

5 List a few ways you could consider others better than yourself:

_____

_____

_____

The Body of Christ

1 In the New Testament, the church is often described with *metaphors* (word pictures) to help us understand what the church is all about. Which of the following metaphors are *not* used in the Bible to describe the church?

☐ A bride   ☐ Branches on a vine
☐ A garden   ☐ A rock
☐ A flock of sheep   ☐ A kingdom
☐ A family   ☐ A building
☐ Salt   ☐ A river

2 *Read 1 Corinthians 12:12-27*: In this passage, Paul compares the church to a human body. How is the church like a human body? List below as many comparisons as you can think of:

_____

_____

3 *Who is the body of Christ?* Place a check mark by the answer or answers below which you think are correct.

☐ All people in the world who are Christians regardless of race, creed, color, denomination, or doctrinal agreement.
☐ Christians from my particular church or denomination.
☐ Christians who are members of my local church.
☐ Christians who are in my youth group.

4 *Take your group's temperature*: Think of your youth group as the body of Christ. Now take its temperature below (fill in the "mercury" up to the point where you think your group is.)

Alive and well

Needs more exercise

Condition weak but improving

Sick

Practically dead

The Body of Christ

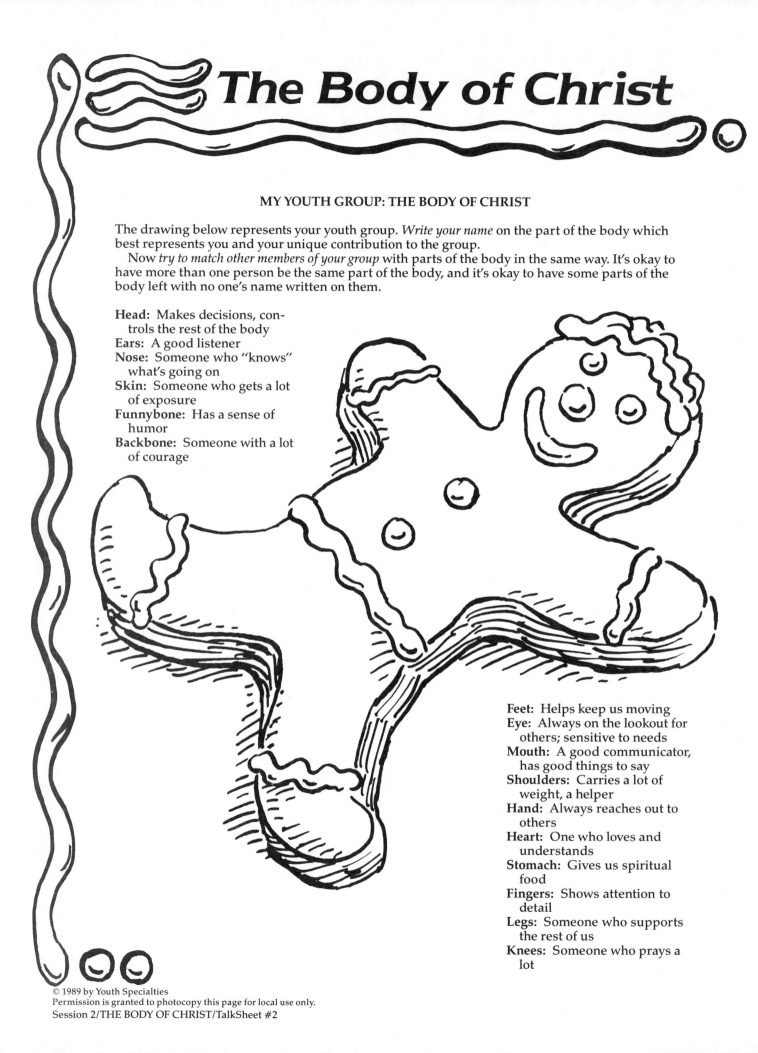

MY YOUTH GROUP: THE BODY OF CHRIST

The drawing below represents your youth group. *Write your name* on the part of the body which best represents you and your unique contribution to the group.

Now *try to match other members of your group* with parts of the body in the same way. It's okay to have more than one person be the same part of the body, and it's okay to have some parts of the body left with no one's name written on them.

Head: Makes decisions, controls the rest of the body
Ears: A good listener
Nose: Someone who "knows" what's going on
Skin: Someone who gets a lot of exposure
Funnybone: Has a sense of humor
Backbone: Someone with a lot of courage

Feet: Helps keep us moving
Eye: Always on the lookout for others; sensitive to needs
Mouth: A good communicator, has good things to say
Shoulders: Carries a lot of weight, a helper
Hand: Always reaches out to others
Heart: One who loves and understands
Stomach: Gives us spiritual food
Fingers: Shows attention to detail
Legs: Someone who supports the rest of us
Knees: Someone who prays a lot

The Body of Christ

Five great teachings in 1 Corinthians 12 describe our relationship to each other as members of the body of Christ.

1. We are dependent upon each other.
2. We should not be jealous of each other.
3. We should show concern for each other.
4. We should sympathize with each other.
5. We should rejoice with each other.

Try using these teachings to determine what should happen next in each of the following situations:

JASON LUCKS OUT

Jason was chosen by the church board to receive an all-expense-paid trip to the national youth convention this summer. Several other members of the youth group were hoping that they would be chosen, but Jason always seems to get the lucky breaks because he's the pastor's son. Jason acts like a snob, and nobody wants to be around him. What should happen next?

NO FUN FOR NATHAN

The youth group-planning committee has been discussing whether to take a trip to the amusement park or to do a missionary service project. Everyone on the committee except Nathan feels that the service project is the best idea. Nathan thinks it's a stupid idea and decides to quit the youth group and go join one that has more fun. What should happen next?

SING ALONG WITH SHELLEY

Kent regularly leads singing in the youth group. He is a good musician, and everyone likes to sing when he leads songs. But Shelley, who also plays guitar, asked if she could lead songs last Sunday. Although she was a little nervous, she did the best she could. But no one sang with her because they liked Kent's song leading better. Shelley was hurt and embarrassed, and decided that she would never lead songs again. What should happen next?

Spiritual Gifts

1 Think of a special gift that someone recently gave to you.

Why was it given to you?

How did you feel when you received it?

2 James 1:17 says that "Every good and every perfect gift comes from God." This means, first, that everything good we have comes from God; and, second, that God gives good and perfect gifts. Name a few gifts in your life that you can thank God for:

_____

_____

_____

3 *Read Romans 12:4-8 and 1 Corinthians 12:1-11, 27-28.* These passages list a number of "spiritual gifts" which are given by the Holy Spirit to everyone in the church (including *you*, if you are a Christian!) How do you discover what your spiritual gift is? (Check the answers below that you think are true.)

☐ God will reveal it to you in a dream.
☐ Other people in the church will confirm it.
☐ You can take a spiritual gift I.Q. test to find out.
☐ If you are good at something, that could be it.
☐ You have to just guess at it.
☐ If you *like* doing something, that could be it.
☐ There's no way of knowing for sure what your gift is.

Spiritual Gifts

WHAT DO THEY MEAN?

Below is a list of spiritual gifts found in Romans 12, 1 Corinthians 12, and other passages in the New Testament. Do you know what they mean? See if you can match the name of the gift on the left with its meaning on the right.

_____ 1. Prophecy	a. To take the Gospel to another place or culture
_____ 2. Pastor	b. The ability to discover and clarify information
_____ 3. Teaching	c. To speak in an unknown language by the power of the Holy Spirit
_____ 4. Wisdom	d. To guide and direct others to use their gifts
_____ 5. Knowledge	e. To perform powerful acts in the name of Christ
_____ 6. Encouragement	f. To deliver a divine message from God
_____ 7. Discerning of spirits	g. To communicate information that helps others learn
_____ 8. Giving	h. To assist others in using their gifts
_____ 9. Helps	i. To provide an open house and friendship to those in need
_____ 10. Mercy	j. To suffer, even to the point of death, for Christ
_____ 11. Missionary	k. To identify and to solve unmet needs in the church
_____ 12. Evangelist	l. To be in authority over a number of churches
_____ 13. Hospitality	m. To cure illness and restore health in the name of Christ
_____ 14. Faith	n. To feel compassion for others and to help them
_____ 15. Leadership	o. To assume responsibility for a group of believers
_____ 16. Administration	p. To give words of comfort, affirmation, and counsel to others
_____ 17. Miracles	q. To have extraordinary confidence in God
_____ 18. Healing	r. The ability to contribute material resources to the body
_____ 19. Tongues	s. To pray for others regularly and effectively
_____ 20. Interpretation	t. To translate the message of one speaking in tongues
_____ 21. Apostle	u. To set goals and to devise and execute plans to fulfill those goals
_____ 22. Celibacy	v. To remain single and to resist sexual temptations
_____ 23. Intercession	w. To have special insights given by the Holy Spirit.
_____ 24. Martyrdom	x. To share the good news with unbelievers
_____ 25. Service	y. To know whether something is of God or Satan

Spiritual Gifts

Do you know what your spiritual gift is? (You may have been given more than one!) For each of the eight listed below, circle a number to indicate whether you feel weak or strong in any of them.

The Gift of Service
God has given me a special ability for helping out whenever a need arises. If there is a job that needs to be done, I am willing to do it if I can.

1   2   3   4   5   6   7   8   9   10
Weak   Strong

The Gift of Teaching
God has given me a skill for helping others to learn. I am good at motivating people to learn and grow in the Christian faith.

1   2   3   4   5   6   7   8   9   10
Weak   Strong

The Gift of Speaking God's Truth (Evangelism)
God has given me a gift for communicating the Gospel to others. When I explain the Good News, God seems to use my words to bring insight and understanding about his grace.

1   2   3   4   5   6   7   8   9   10
Weak   Strong

The Gift of Encouragement
God has given me the ability to see the best in others. I find it easy to compliment people and to point out their strengths.

1   2   3   4   5   6   7   8   9   10
Weak   Strong

The Gift of Leadership
God has given me a gift for organization. I can get things done. I find it easy to take responsibility and direct others.

1   2   3   4   5   6   7   8   9   10
Weak   Strong

The Gift of Kindness (Mercy)
God has given me the ability to be compassionate and understanding whenever someone is in trouble or needs help. I enjoy being able to minister to someone who is feeling down.

1   2   3   4   5   6   7   8   9   10
Weak   Strong

The Gift of Generosity (Giving)
God has given me a freedom to share myself with others. I find it easy to give whatever I can to others or to God's work whenever a special need arises.

1   2   3   4   5   6   7   8   9   10
Weak   Strong

The Gift of Faith
God has given me complete confidence and trust in him. Whenever I pray, I believe and fully expect that God will answer my prayer.

1   2   3   4   5   6   7   8   9   10
Weak   Strong

The Gift of Helps
God has given me the desire and ability to assist other members of the body to use their spiritual gifts. I enjoy helping other people to be more effective in their ministries.

1   2   3   4   5   6   7   8   9   10
Weak   Strong

Christian Love

1 *Create a Bumper Sticker*: Many people like to let others know what they love by displaying a bumper sticker on their cars with a familiar red heart on it. They usually say things like "I ♥ New York" or "I ♥ Cats". Below is a blank bumper sticker. Write in something that you might display on your car.

2 "Love is a warm puppy," says the Peanut's character Charlie Brown. "Love is never having to say you're sorry," says the movie *Love Story*. What is love to you? Complete the sentence below:

Love is _____

_____

3 In the Greek language (from which the New Testament was translated) there are actually three main words for love. They are:

PHILIA: This is brotherly love or affection for family, friends, and others with whom you share something in common.

EROS: This love is based upon beauty, passion, and pleasure. The English word *erotic* comes from *eros.*

AGAPE: This is God's love. It is unconditional, unselfish, and enduring.

Based on your understanding of the definitions above, decide which kind of love these examples demonstrate:

_____ 1. Mother Teresa of Calcutta has given her life to serve the poor and the sick in India.

_____ 2. Jamie thinks Brad is a hunk and wants to go out with him.

_____ 3. Tim likes to be with Jeremy and Brian because they like the same rock groups.

_____ 4. Brent said to Jessica, "If you loved me, you'd go to bed with me."

_____ 5. Kimberly decided to spend some time with the new girl at school who doesn't seem to have any friends.

_____ 6. Jack is very patriotic and has a bumper sticker on his truck that says "America. Love it or leave it!"

Christian Love

1 Which of the following people do you think would be the easiest to love? the hardest?

Easy *Hard*

_____ _____ Kevin—an extremely obnoxious 13-year-old. Due to his immaturity, he gets on everyone's nerves most of the time.

_____ _____ Jill—15, attractive, very bright and outgoing. All the guys would like to go out with her.

_____ _____ Mike—a 14-year-old who is developmentally handicapped. He is in a special-ed class at school.

_____ _____ Rhonda—16 and very shy. She is about 30 pounds overweight and embarrassed about it.

_____ _____ Christine—she's your little sister. She is always around when you wish she wasn't. She's always using your things.

_____ _____ Tim—a star on the high-school football team. He is also a good Christian.

_____ _____ Donna—a 15-year-old girl who comes to church about twice a month with her stepmother. You don't know much about her except that she is of a different race.

_____ _____ Ricky—he is really into music. He loves rock-and-roll and spends most of his time and money on posters, cassette tapes, and concerts.

2 *True or False*: In order to love someone, you first have to *like* him (or her). True ☐   False ☐

3 *Read 1 John 4:7-12* and then list three reasons why it is important for Christians to love:

1.

2.

3.

Christian Love

 Read 1 John 3:16-18. Circle the phrase below which best completes this sentence:

You know that love is real when . . .

you feel it.   you verbalize it.   you demonstrate it.

 Read the three Scripture passages below and underline key instructions. In the right-hand column, write out what you or others in your group can do to put love into action. Use the back of this sheet if needed.

Romans 12

Love must be sincere. Hate what is evil; cling to what is good. Be devoted to one another in brotherly love. Honor one another above yourselves. Never be lacking in zeal, but keep your spiritual fervor, serving the Lord. Be joyful in hope, patient in affliction, faithful in prayer. Share with God's people who are in need. Practice hospitality.

Bless those who persecute you; bless and do not curse. Rejoice with those who rejoice; mourn with those who mourn.
1. Live in harmony with one another. Do not be proud, but be willing to associate with people of low position. Do not be conceited.

Do not repay anyone evil for evil. Be careful to do what is right in the eyes of everybody. If it is possible, as far as it depends on you, live at peace with everyone. Do not take revenge, my friends, but leave room for God's wrath, for it is written: "It is mine to avenge; I will repay," says the Lord. On the contrary: "If your enemy is hungry, feed him; if he is thirsty, give him something to drink. In doing this, you will heap burning coals on his head."
Do not be overcome by evil, but overcome evil with good.

1 Corinthians 13

Love is patient, love is kind. It does not envy, it does not boast, it is not proud. It is not rude, it is not self-seeking, it is not easily angered, It keeps no record of wrongs. Love does not delight in evil but rejoices with the truth. It always protects, always trusts, always hopes, always perseveres.

Ephesians 4

Therefore each of you must put off falsehood and speak truthfully to his neighbor, for we are all members of one body. "In your anger do not sin": Do not let the sun go down while you are still angry, and do not give the devil a foothold. He who has been stealing must steal no longer, but must work, doing something useful with his own hands, that he may have something to share with those in need.

Do not let any unwholesome talk come out of your mouths, but only what is helpful for building others up according to their needs, that it may benefit those who listen. And do not grieve the Holy Spirit of God, with whom you were sealed for the day of redemption. Get rid of all bitterness, rage and anger, brawling and slander, along with every form of malice. Be kind and compassionate to one another, forgiving each other, just as in Christ God forgave you.

(Example:)
1. It seems like we argue a lot in this group - usually about stuff that really doesn't matter. We need to listen more and argue less.

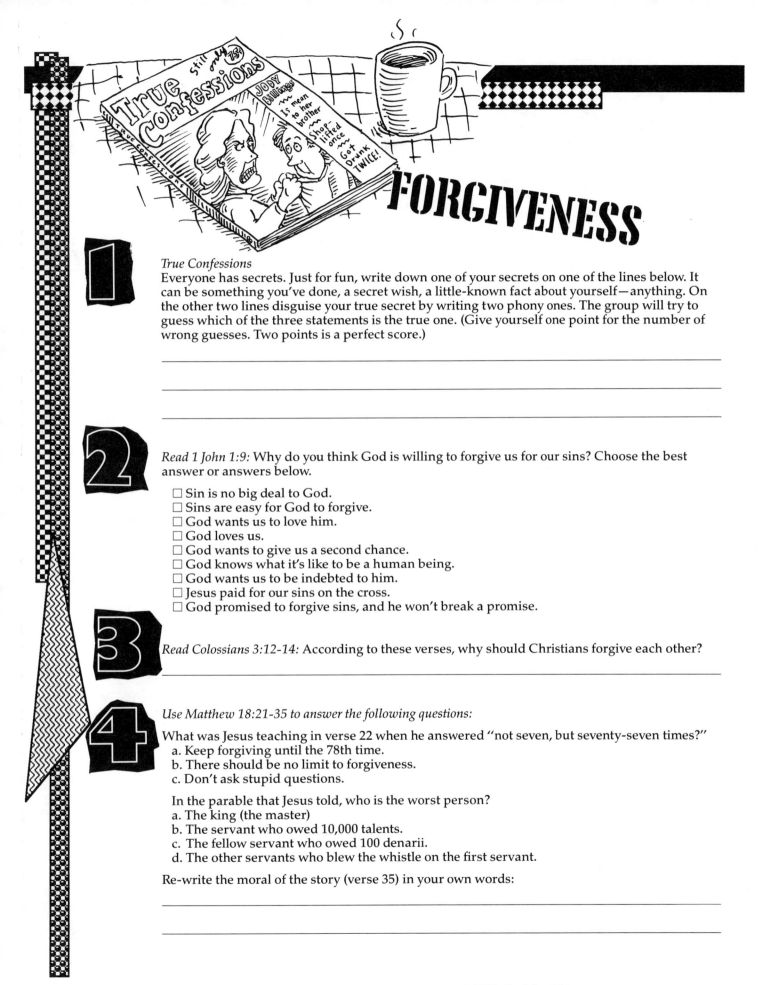

FORGIVENESS

1 *True Confessions*
Everyone has secrets. Just for fun, write down one of your secrets on one of the lines below. It can be something you've done, a secret wish, a little-known fact about yourself—anything. On the other two lines disguise your true secret by writing two phony ones. The group will try to guess which of the three statements is the true one. (Give yourself one point for the number of wrong guesses. Two points is a perfect score.)

_____

_____

_____

2 *Read 1 John 1:9:* Why do you think God is willing to forgive us for our sins? Choose the best answer or answers below.

☐ Sin is no big deal to God.
☐ Sins are easy for God to forgive.
☐ God wants us to love him.
☐ God loves us.
☐ God wants to give us a second chance.
☐ God knows what it's like to be a human being.
☐ God wants us to be indebted to him.
☐ Jesus paid for our sins on the cross.
☐ God promised to forgive sins, and he won't break a promise.

3 *Read Colossians 3:12-14:* According to these verses, why should Christians forgive each other?

_____

4 *Use Matthew 18:21-35 to answer the following questions:*

What was Jesus teaching in verse 22 when he answered "not seven, but seventy-seven times?"
a. Keep forgiving until the 78th time.
b. There should be no limit to forgiveness.
c. Don't ask stupid questions.

In the parable that Jesus told, who is the worst person?
a. The king (the master)
b. The servant who owed 10,000 talents.
c. The fellow servant who owed 100 denarii.
d. The other servants who blew the whistle on the first servant.

Re-write the moral of the story (verse 35) in your own words:

_____

_____

Forgiveness

The Old Testament book of Hosea describes God's forgiveness in the story of the prophet Hosea and his wife, Gomer. One Christian writer, Frederick Buechner, has re-told the story in modern language. Read his version and answer the questions that follow.

GOMER

She was always good company—a little heavy with the lipstick maybe, a little less than choosy about men and booze, a little loud, but great on a party and always good for a laugh. Then the prophet Hosea came along wearing a sandwich board that read "The End is at Hand" on one side and "Watch Out" on the other.

The first time he asked her to marry him, she thought he was kidding. The second time she knew he was serious but thought he was crazy. The third time she said yes. He wasn't exactly a swinger, but he had a kind face, and he was generous, and he wasn't all that crazier than everybody else. Besides, any fool could see he loved her.

Give or take a little, she even loved him back for a while, and they had three children whom Hosea named with queer names like Not-pitied-for-God-will-no-longer-pity-Israel-now-that-it's-gone-to-the-dogs so that every time the roll was called at school, Hosea would be scoring a prophetic bulls-eye in absentia. But everybody could see the marriage wasn't going to last, and it didn't.

While Hosea was off hitting the sawdust trail, Gomer took to hitting as many night spots as she could squeeze into a night, and any resemblance between her next batch of children and Hosea was purely coincidental. It almost killed him, of course. Every time he raised a hand to her, he burst into tears. Every time she raised one to him, he was the one who ended up apologizing.

He tried locking her out of the house a few times when she wasn't in by five in the morning, but he always opened the door when she finally showed up and helped get her to bed if she couldn't see straight enough to get there herself. Then one day she didn't show up at all.

He swore that this time he was through with her for keeps, but of course he wasn't. When he finally found her, she was lying passed out in a highly specialized establishment located above an adult bookstore, and he had to pay the management plenty to let her out of her contract. She'd lost her front teeth and picked up some scars you had to see to believe, but Hosea had her back again and that seemed to be all that mattered.

He changed his sandwich board to read "God is love" on one side and "There's no end to it" on the other, and when he stood on the street corner belting out

> How can I give you up, O Ephraim!
> How can I hand you over, O Israel!
> For I am God and no man,
> The Holy One in your midst.
> (Hosea 11:8-9)

nobody can say how many converts he made, but one thing that's for sure is that, including Gomer's, there was seldom a dry eye in the house. (Hosea 1-3, 11)

(Reprinted by permission from *Peculiar Treasures* by Frederick Buechner, copyright 1979 by Frederick Buechner, Harper & Row Publishers, San Francisco.)

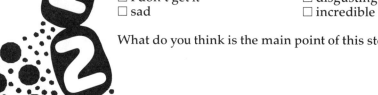

This story is, in my opinion:

☐ ridiculous   ☐ funny   ☐ impossible
☐ I don't get it   ☐ disgusting   ☐ heavy
☐ sad   ☐ incredible   ☐ touching

What do you think is the main point of this story?

Forgiveness

1 *What would you do?* Read the situations below and decide how you would most likely respond. (Be honest!) Write in the letter of your probable response:

a. Hold a grudge.
b. Get mad.
c. Get even.
d. Get depressed.
e. Avoid that person in the future.
f. Throw a tantrum.
g. Laugh.
h. Nothing.
i. Forgive and forget.
j. Talk to the person about it.
k. Pray.
l. Other: _____

_____ Someone starts a nasty rumor about you that is not true.

_____ Someone tells your folks about something bad you did.

_____ Someone cuts you down or calls you a derogatory name.

_____ Someone steals something from you.

_____ Someone copies your homework or test.

_____ Someone plays a practical joke on you that makes you look dumb.

_____ Someone spills ink on your best outfit.

_____ Someone borrows something from you and then damages it or doesn't return it.

_____ Someone goes out with your steady boyfriend or girlfriend.

_____ Someone lies to you.

_____ Someone physically hits or threatens you.

2 Which is most difficult for you:

☐ To forgive someone?
☐ To ask for their forgiveness?

3 *Read Matthew 5:9.* Now check the statement that best applies to you.

☐ I always do whatever I can to make peace with others.
☐ I sometimes try to make peace with others.
☐ I rarely try to make peace with others.
☐ I never try to make peace with others.

4 *Read Ephesians 4:31-32.* Is there a person you need to forgive? A person you need to ask for forgiveness? Write their initials here: _____

Servanthood

1 *Who is the Greatest?*

You are on the committee to decide who should receive the Nobel Prize for Greatness, an award given to someone who is a truly great person. Nominate someone you know (or have heard of) for this award and write your selection in the box below:

Why did you nominate this person?

_____

_____

2 Below are some actions which might be considered great. Which do you think are the greatest?

☐ Scoring the winning touchdown in the championship game.
☐ Being nice to someone who doesn't have any friends.
☐ Being the lead singer in a famous rock group.
☐ Volunteering to clean up after a youth group party.
☐ Having your picture on the cover of a glamour magazine.
☐ Helping plan a youth group activity.
☐ Getting straight A's on your report card.
☐ Having a really hot car.
☐ Giving some of your own money to support a youth-group mission project.
☐ Other: _____

3 *Read Mark 9:33-35 and Matthew 20:25-28.* How does Jesus define greatness?

_____

_____

What are some characteristics of a servant? (Circle those that you think Jesus was talking about.)

Helpful	Uneducated
Giving	Hard Working
Mistreated	Kind
Poor	Supportive
Humble	Bored
Underpaid	Humiliated

Servanthood

1 *Read John 13:1-9, 12-17*, then answer the questions below.

Why did Jesus wash the disciples' feet?

Why didn't Peter want Jesus to wash his feet?

What might be the equivalent to washing someone's feet today?

Can you think of a time when someone "washed your feet"?

2 *Read Philippians 2:1-11*. Verses 7 and 8 give us two keys to servanthood—*humility* and *sacrificial love*.

How do you define these two concepts? Read the statements below and check whether you agree or disagree.

A HUMBLE PERSON . . .	Agree	Disagree
Tries to "out-humble" everyone else		
Tries to follow the golden rule		
Always goes last in everything		
Never brags		
Has a low self-image		
Should not try to attain success		
Deliberately loses so the other person can win		
Puts others first, themselves second		
Has no rights to speak of		
Gets pushed around a lot		
Is motivated by love		
SACRIFICIAL LOVE IS . . .		
Not very practical nowadays		
Giving up something for someone else's good		
Painful and costly		
Having a martyr complex		
The highest form of love there is		
Usually unnecessary		
Awesome		
How all Christians should treat each other		
Self-denial		
Dying for somebody		
Doing whatever is required on behalf of someone else		

Servanthood

1 The Bible gives us a variety of ways to serve each other in the body of Christ. Listed below are a few examples. Next to each one, put a symbol to indicate your feelings:

☆ = I do pretty well with this one.
N = No, I never do this one.
↑ = I need God to help me with this one.
? = I don't understand this one.
♡ = Someone in this group has done this for me
S = This is our group's greatest strength
W = This is our group's greatest weakness

We are to . . .

_____ Pray for each other (Ephesians 6:18-19).

_____ Share our possessions with one another (Deuteronomy 15:7, Romans 12:13).

_____ Confess our sins to each other (James 5:16).

_____ Forgive each other (Colossians 3:12-13).

_____ Discipline each other (Galatians 6:1-2, Matthew 18:15, 2 Thessalonians 3:14-15).

_____ Bear each other's burdens (Galatians 6:2, Romans 15:1).

_____ Be kind to each other (Romans 14:19, 1 Thessalonians 5:11).

_____ Greet one another (Romans 16:16, 1 Corinthians 16:20, 2 Corinthians 13:12).

_____ Accept one another (Romans 15:7, 14:1).

_____ Show hospitality to each other (1 Peter 4:7-10).

_____ Teach one another (Colossians 3:16).

2 List three ways you could serve others in your church or youth group:

1.

2.

3.

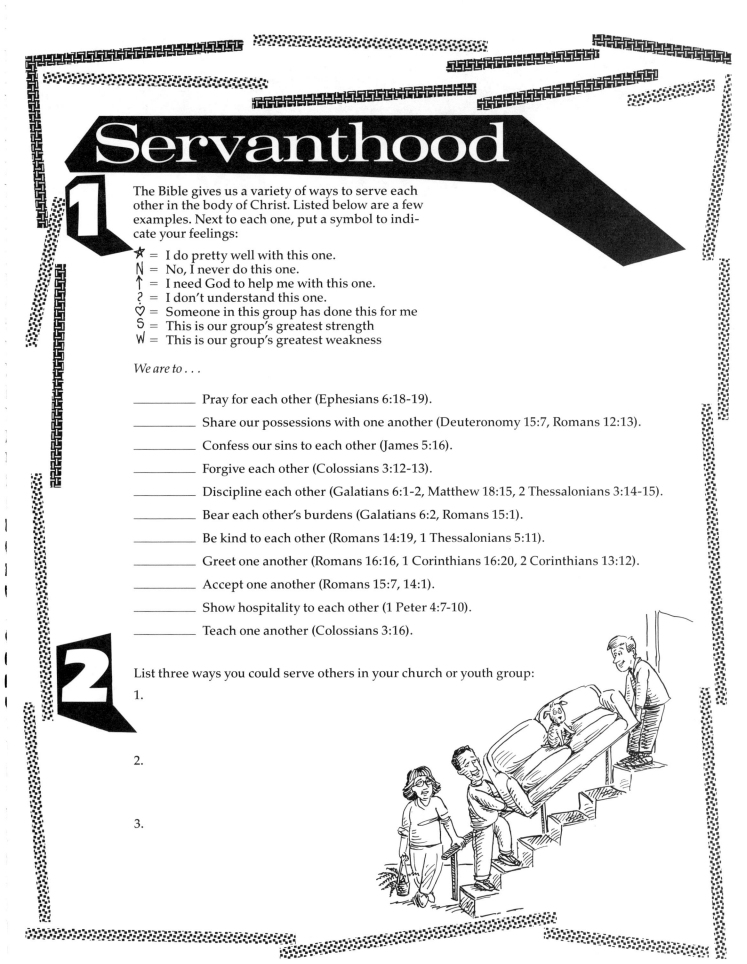

Servanthood

"WHAT IS REAL"
(from *The Velveteen Rabbit*
by Armand Eisen)

"What is REAL?" asked the Rabbit one day, when they were lying side by side near the nursery fender, before Nana came to tidy the room. "Does it mean having things that buzz inside you and a stick-out handle?"

"Real isn't how you are made," said the Skin Horse. "It's a thing that happens to you. When a child loves you for a long, long time, not just to play with, but REALLY loves you, then you become Real."

"Does it hurt?" asked the Rabbit.

"Sometimes," said the Skin Horse, for he was always truthful. "When you are Real you don't mind being hurt."

"Does it happen all at once, like being wound up," he asked, "or bit by bit?"

"It doesn't happen all at once," said the Skin Horse. "You become. It takes a long time. That's why it doesn't often happen to people who break easily, or have sharp edges, or who have to be carefully kept. Generally, by the time you are Real, most of your hair has been loved off, and your eyes drop out and you get loose in the joints and very shabby. But these things don't matter at all, because once you are Real you can't be ugly, except to people who don't understand."

1 Questions to think about:

How does this story make you feel? Why?

2 What do you think about "being real"? What does it mean?

3 When or how have you experienced "being real"?

4 Write out what you think is the moral of the story below.

My Self

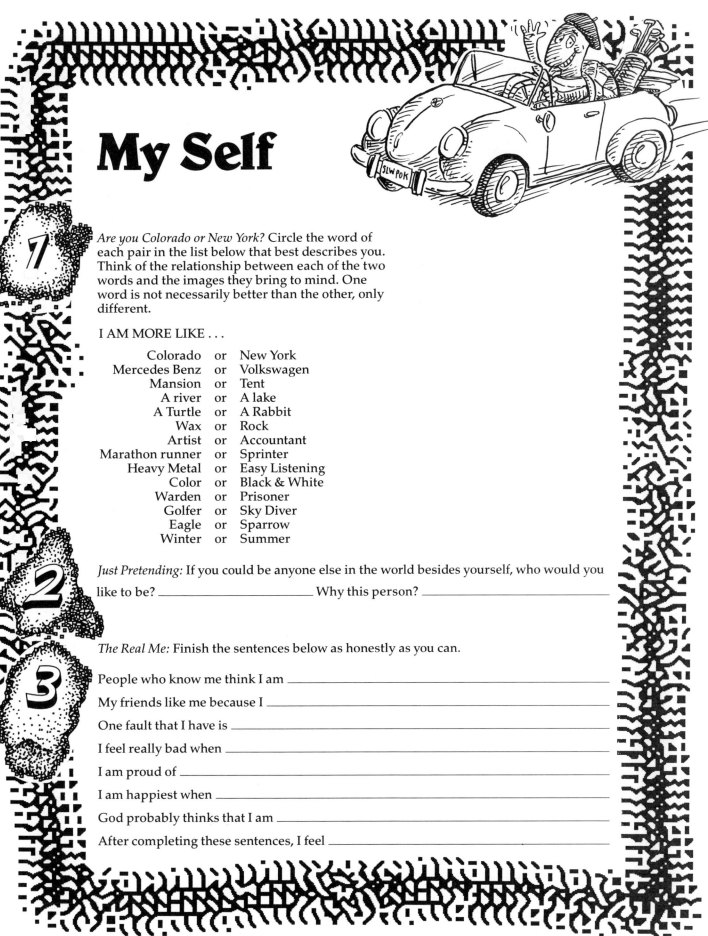

1 *Are you Colorado or New York?* Circle the word of each pair in the list below that best describes you. Think of the relationship between each of the two words and the images they bring to mind. One word is not necessarily better than the other, only different.

I AM MORE LIKE . . .

Colorado	or	New York
Mercedes Benz	or	Volkswagen
Mansion	or	Tent
A river	or	A lake
A Turtle	or	A Rabbit
Wax	or	Rock
Artist	or	Accountant
Marathon runner	or	Sprinter
Heavy Metal	or	Easy Listening
Color	or	Black & White
Warden	or	Prisoner
Golfer	or	Sky Diver
Eagle	or	Sparrow
Winter	or	Summer

2 *Just Pretending:* If you could be anyone else in the world besides yourself, who would you like to be? _____ Why this person? _____

3 *The Real Me:* Finish the sentences below as honestly as you can.

People who know me think I am _____

My friends like me because I _____

One fault that I have is _____

I feel really bad when _____

I am proud of _____

I am happiest when _____

God probably thinks that I am _____

After completing these sentences, I feel _____

My Self

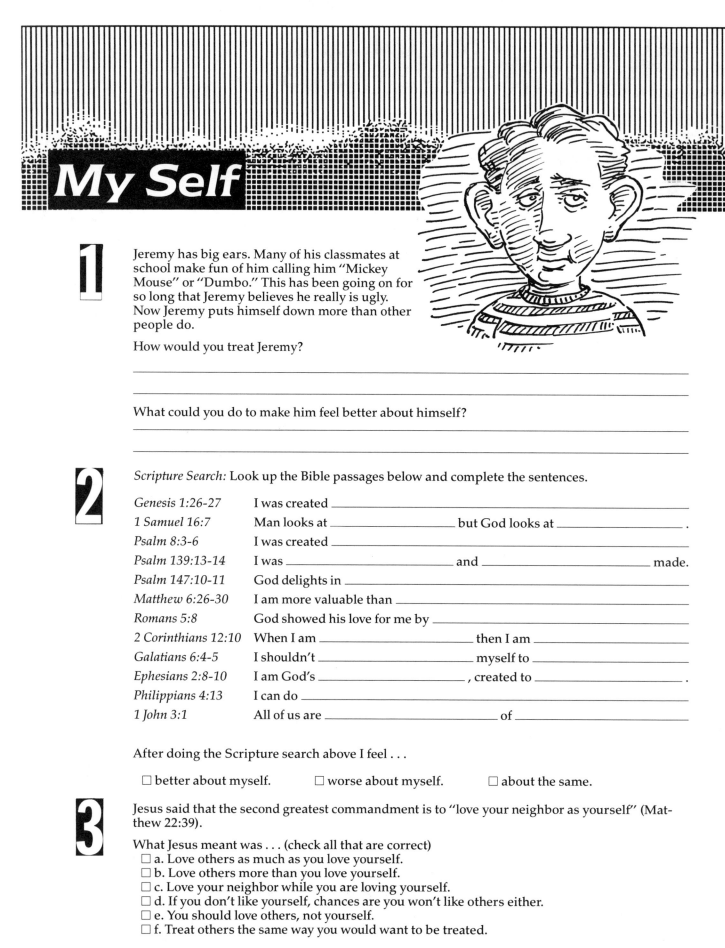

1 Jeremy has big ears. Many of his classmates at school make fun of him calling him "Mickey Mouse" or "Dumbo." This has been going on for so long that Jeremy believes he really is ugly. Now Jeremy puts himself down more than other people do.

How would you treat Jeremy?

_____

_____

What could you do to make him feel better about himself?

_____

_____

2 *Scripture Search:* Look up the Bible passages below and complete the sentences.

Genesis 1:26-27   I was created _____

1 Samuel 16:7   Man looks at _____ but God looks at _____ .

Psalm 8:3-6   I was created _____

Psalm 139:13-14   I was _____ and _____ made.

Psalm 147:10-11   God delights in _____

Matthew 6:26-30   I am more valuable than _____

Romans 5:8   God showed his love for me by _____

2 Corinthians 12:10 When I am _____ then I am _____

Galatians 6:4-5   I shouldn't _____ myself to _____

Ephesians 2:8-10   I am God's _____ , created to _____ .

Philippians 4:13   I can do _____

1 John 3:1   All of us are _____ of _____

After doing the Scripture search above I feel . . .

☐ better about myself.   ☐ worse about myself.   ☐ about the same.

3 Jesus said that the second greatest commandment is to "love your neighbor as yourself" (Matthew 22:39).

What Jesus meant was . . . (check all that are correct)
☐ a. Love others as much as you love yourself.
☐ b. Love others more than you love yourself.
☐ c. Love your neighbor while you are loving yourself.
☐ d. If you don't like yourself, chances are you won't like others either.
☐ e. You should love others, not yourself.
☐ f. Treat others the same way you would want to be treated.

My Self

HUMPTY DUMPTY REVISITED
by Vic Pentz
(Reprinted from *The Wittenburg Door*, June 1972)

Humpty Dumpty sat on the wall.
Humpty Dumpty had a great fall.
All the king's horses and all the king's men
Couldn't put Humpty back together again.

But soon the King himself heard of Humpty's fate. And he was deeply disturbed. So, setting aside his royal finery, disguised as a common peasant, the King slipped unnoticed through the majestic palace gates and into the rough and tumble street life of his kingdom.

The King meandered through the back streets and alleys in search of Humpty. After several days and nights the persistent King found him. Humpty's shattered body was scattered over a ten-foot circle amidst the broken glass and flattened beer cans of a back alley. Though weak from his recent journey, the King was overjoyed at the sight of Humpty. He ran to Humpty's side and cried, "Humpty! It is I—your King! I have powers greater than those of my horses and men who failed to put you together again. Be at peace, I am here to help!"

"Leave me alone. I've gotten used to this new way of life. I kind of like it now," Humpty's mouth retorted.

"But . . . " was all the King could get out before Humpty continued.

"I tell you I'm fine. I like it here. That trash can over there. The way the sun sparkles on the broken glass. This must be the garden spot of the world!"

"I assure you, my kingdom has much more to offer than this back alley. There are green mountains, rolling surf, exciting cities."

But Humpty would hear none of it. And the saddened King returned to the palace.

A week later one of Humpty's eyes rolled skyward only to see once again the concerned face of the King looking over his body.

"I've come to help," firmly stated the King.

"Look, leave me alone, will you?" said Humpty. "I've just seen my psychiatrist, and he assures me that I'm doing a fine job of coping with my environment as it is. You're a cop-out. A man has to deal with life as it comes. I'm a realist."

"But wouldn't you rather walk?" puzzled the King.

"Look," Humpty's mouth frowned, "once I get up and start walking I'll have to stay up and keep walking. At this point in my life I'm not ready to make a commitment like that. So if you'll excuse me, you're blocking my sun."

Reluctantly the King once again turned and walked through the streets of his kingdom back to the palace. It was over a year before the King ventured to return to Humpty's side.

But sure enough, one bright morning one of Humpty's ears perked up at the sure, steady strides of the King. This time he was ready. Humpty's eye turned toward the tall figure just as his mouth managed the words, "My King!"

Immediately the King fell to his knees among the broken glass. His strong, knowing hands gently began to piece together Humpty's fragments. After some time, his work completed, the King rose to full height, pulling up with him the figure of a strong young man.

The two walked hand in hand throughout the kingdom. Together they stood atop lush green mountains. They ran together along deserted beaches. They laughed and joked together as they strolled the gleaming cities of the King's kingdom. This went on forever. And to the depth, breadth, and height of their friendship there was no end.

Once while walking together down the sidewalk in one of the King's cities, Humpty overheard a remark that made his heart leap with both the joy of his new life with the King and the bitter memory of his former, shattered life in the back alley. Someone said, "Say, who are those two men?"

Another replied, "Why, the one on the left is old Humpty Dumpty. I don't know the one on the right, but they sure look like brothers!"

My Friends

1 *Buy a friend—Only a Quarter!* Here's your chance to buy the perfect friend. You have 25 cents to spend. How will you spend it?

Each of these qualities costs 6 cents:
— Has lots of money
— Very popular
— Very intelligent
— Strong Christian
— Kind and considerate

Each of these qualities costs 5 cents:
— Good looking
— Good conversationalist
— Outgoing personality
— Sense of humor
— High moral standards

Each of these qualities costs 4 cents:
— Has a car
— Has the right clothes
— Has a lot of time
— Extremely loyal
— Very dependable

Each of these qualities costs 3 cents:
— Likes the same things you do
— Honest
— Good listener
— Very generous

Each of these qualities costs 2 cents:
— Has a nice house
— Has sex appeal
— Has nice parents
— Same age as you

Each of these qualities costs 1 cent:
— Has athletic ability
— Lives close to your house
— Has no other friends
— Very talented

2 *What is a friend?* Write your definition of a good friend in the space below:

A good friend is someone who _____

_____

My Friends

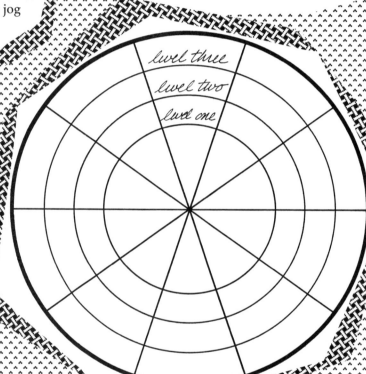

My Circle of Friends: **In the 10 pie-shaped pieces in the center of the circle below write the first names of your 10 best friends. Use the list below to jog your thinking.**

Friends you have in the youth group
Friends you have at school
Friends who live in your
   neighborhood
Adult friends
Girlfriends or
   boyfriends
Relatives, including
   parents
Friends who live
   out of town

Evaluate the level of each friendship according to the three possibilities below. Shade in the pie shapes for each person from the inside of the circle out. A completely shaded-in area would indicate a level three friendship.

LEVEL ONE: We are casual friends. I share little with this friend, and usually only when they initiate the conversation.
LEVEL TWO: We are close friends. We have a good relationship and talk about serious matters quite often.
LEVEL THREE: We are intimate friends. We share just about everything with each other, good or bad.

My Friends

1 *Good Friends:* Read about the Bible friendships below.

David and Jonathan   1 Samuel 18:1-4, 19:1-6
Jesus and Lazarus   John 11:11-14, 30-36

List as many qualities of friendship as you can find in those Scriptures:

_____   _____

_____   _____

_____   _____

_____   _____

_____

2 *Read Proverbs 18:24.* How do you "show yourself friendly?" In other words, what do you do to keep your friendships alive and well?

_____

_____

3 *Read Colossians 3:12-14.* Rate yourself on each of the eight characteristics of friendship described in Colossians by circling a number between one (low) and ten (high).

COMPASSION: I try to see things from my friends' point of view.
   1   2   3   4   5   6   7   8   9   10

KINDNESS: I take every opportunity to do nice things for my friends.
   1   2   3   4   5   6   7   8   9   10

HUMILITY: I try to build up and encourage my friends.
   1   2   3   4   5   6   7   8   9   10

GENTLENESS: I treat my friends as I would want to be treated. I avoid hurting them.
   1   2   3   4   5   6   7   8   9   10

PATIENCE: I am willing to go the second mile with my friends.
   1   2   3   4   5   6   7   8   9   10

BEARING: I try to help my friends whenever they need me.
   1   2   3   4   5   6   7   8   9   10

FORGIVING: I forgive rather than hold a grudge or get even.
   1   2   3   4   5   6   7   8   9   10

LOVING: I let my friends know that I really care a lot about them.
   1   2   3   4   5   6   7   8   9   10

My Community

1 *Complete this sentence:* The best thing about our youth group is

_____

_____

2 *Your Opinion Please:* Read the statements below and put a check next to all those you agree with. Cross out the ones you disagree with.

- I feel like I'm an important part of our youth group.
- The youth group is important to me.
- Our youth group is about the right size.
- I have a lot of good friends in our youth group.
- There are too many cliques in our youth group.
- I look forward to our youth group meetings and activities.
- I wouldn't come to this youth group if I had a choice.
- Our youth group has good leaders.
- I am doing my part to make our youth group better.
- I would be comfortable inviting my friends to our youth group.
- Our youth group has helped me become a better Christian.
- Our youth group is like a family to me.

3 *Scripture Search:* Read any four of the Scriptures below and answer the question that follows:

Psalm 68:6   2Corinthians 6:17   Ephesians 2:19
Ephesians 3:15   Galatians 6:10
Hebrews 2:11   Philippians 2:15   1Peter 4:17

How is the church like a family?

_____

_____

4 *Read 1 Thessalonians 2.* In this letter to the church at Thessalonica, Paul describes various relationships in the Christian community with words we use to talk about family. Study this chapter and answer the following questions:

1. Why would Paul call these Christians brothers?

2. What are some characteristics of motherly care as mentioned in verses 7-8?

3. What are some characteristics of fatherly guidance as mentioned in verses 10-12?

My Community

A FAMILY COAT-OF-ARMS

Many families have a coat-of-arms to symbolize their family's values and the history of their family name. Think of our youth group as a family and create a coat-of-arms to symbolize our values and history. There are six spaces on the coat-of-arms. Draw symbols or write words according to the instructions below:

1. Symbolize something our youth group has done for others in the past.
2. Symbolize the purpose of our youth group.
3. Draw what you think the most important activity of our youth group is.
4. Draw a picture to represent the quality of community in our group.
5. Symbolize what you feel is the greatest strength of our group.
6. Include three words that should be most important to our group as a family.

Communication

1 *The Good and Bad of Communication:* In the column at the left, write three words that describe or make for *good* communication. In the column at the right, write three words that describe or make for *bad* communication.

Good Communication	Bad Communication
_____	_____
_____	_____
_____	_____

2 *Good Communicator:* Think of a person who communicates well with you. This could be anyone—from your school, your family, your group of friends, your church.

Write that person's name here: _____ Relationship: _____

How does this person communicate well with you?

_____

How do you feel about this person?

_____

3 *Your Opinion:* How do you feel about the statements below? Write a 1, 2, or 3 beside each statement (1—That's Right! 2—Not Sure, 3—No Way!).

____ There is a lot of good communication in this youth group.
____ Honesty is always the best policy in communication.
____ If you don't have anything good to say, don't say it.
____ Only people who are good talkers can communicate well.
____ Sometimes it's better to just keep your mouth shut.
____ I am allowed to freely express my thoughts and feelings in this youth group.

____ There's a lot of gossip going around in this group.
____ I know that I can always speak my mind in this youth group without getting shot down.
____ Only a few people do all the talking in this youth group.
____ I have trouble expressing myself.
____ There is too much talking in this youth group.
____ Most of the communication in this youth group is healthy.
____ People are always putting each other down in this youth group.

4 *Scripture Search:* Read the passages below and apply them to yourself and your youth group in one sentence each:

Proverbs 18:8 _____

_____

Proverbs 15:1,4 _____

_____

James 4:11 _____

_____

Ephesians 4:25 _____

_____

Listening

1 *Who do you listen to? . . . I mean, really listen to? (In the list below, underline the people you listen to.)*

My mom	My dad	My brother	My sister
My best friend	My pastor		A teacher at school
A rock star	A relative		A DJ on the radio
My youth leader at church		God	A famous celebrity
The President of the U.S.			Nobody

Other: _____

2 Now circle the people above who listen—*really* listen—to *you*.

How do you feel when someone you are talking to isn't listening to you? (Check any of the following.)

☐ hurt ☐ understanding ☐ angry ☐ frustrated ☐ offended ☐ resentful
☐ happy ☐ disappointed ☐ puzzled ☐ fine ☐ grateful ☐ discouraged
☐ inferior ☐ insecure ☐ friendly ☐ rejected

3 *How well do you listen?* Write in the blanks below the letter of the statements that describe you, that describe how you are sometimes, that don't describe you at all.

That's me	That's sometimes me	That's not me
_____	_____	_____

When others are speaking to me—
a. I establish good eye contact with them.
b. I tune them out if I don't agree with what they're saying.
c. I restate things to make sure I'm hearing them correctly.
d. I jump to conclusions before the other person is finished talking.
e. I ask questions to get more information or to clarify what I heard them say.
f. I let my mind wander and don't hear everything they said.
g. I stop what I'm doing and give them my undivided attention.
h. I interrupt before they're finished talking.
i. I thank them for what they had to say.
j. I'm thinking about what I'm going to say while they are talking to me.

4 *Read James 1:19; Proverbs 18:2; 18:13.* Read these Scriptures and complete the sentences below:

One benefit of being a good listener is _____
_____

I think I can become a better listener by _____
_____

One person I need to listen to more is _____
_____

Session 11/LISTENING/TalkSheet #1

Resolving Conflict

1

Be honest! When you have a disagreement or a conflict with someone, what do you usually do? (Choose up to three answers that best describe what you do.)

☐ I try to get my way no matter what.
☐ I just give in and let the other side win.
☐ I try to reach a compromise with the other person so that both sides win.
☐ I get angry and take it out on someone.
☐ I get depressed.
☐ I try to get others to agree with me.
☐ I try to ignore the problem and hope it will go away.
☐ I cut off the other person and avoid being around them.
☐ I try to listen carefully to the other person's point of view.
☐ I pray about it.
☐ Other: _____

2

The Van versus the Ski Trip: Recently the youth group at First Church raised $500 by having a car wash. After the money was raised, the youth council decided to use the money to have the church van painted. But some group members were led to believe that the money would be used to help pay for a winter ski trip. If the money is used to paint the van, some kids won't be able to go on the ski trip. Now there is a lot of arguing and hard feelings in the group. How do think this conflict can best be resolved?

_____

_____

3

Scripture Search: Look up the passages below and restate the main idea of each one in your own words.

Matthew 5:38-42 _____

_____

Matthew 7:1-5 _____

_____

Matthew 18:15-17 _____

_____

1 Corinthians 1:10-13 _____

_____

Galatians 5:26 - 6:5 _____

_____

Ephesians 4:25-27 _____

Commitment to Community

UP CLOSE AND PERSONAL
FINAL EXAM

1   How would you define *Christian unity*?

2   What does it mean to be a part of the *body of Christ*?

3   What are *spiritual gifts* and why are they important?

4   How is *Christian love* different from other kinds of love?

5   Why do you think Christians should be *forgiving*?

6   How can Christian young people *serve* each other?

7   Why is having a positive *self-image* important?

8   Name one characteristic of a really good *friend*.

9   How is the Christian *community* like a family?

10   Give an example of *good communication*.

11   How can a person become a better *listener*?

12   When people are having *conflict* in the group, what are some steps that can be taken to resolve it?